Individualising Risk

"This timely and sobering book shows how the marketisation of social care can go wrong. Fiona Macdonald analyses how Australia's new National Disability Insurance Scheme works to shift risk and responsibility to individual support workers at the frontline, to the detriment of the quality of care and support for many people with a disability. Macdonald establishes that labour regulation – or the lack of it – is as critical as social care policy for shaping how care systems work, and who benefits and loses within them. She also shows how the growing presence of digital platforms in organising disability support work, and their promotion by public authorities, are undermining the conditions for decent work in social care. With important lessons for researchers, policy-makers and practitioners across the full range of social care services, the book raises challenging questions about how social care systems can balance the rights of people who need care and support with the rights of people whose job it is to help them."

—Gabrielle Meagher, *Professor Emerita, Macquarie University, Australia*

"Macdonald's top notch analysis decisively confirms that just when the world is in desperate need of consistent and high quality care, gig work and cash-forcare models are propelling Australia and other countries into a further crisis of substandard, low quality jobs and care. Presenting clear and compelling evidence, Macdonald shows that the marketization of social care results in precarity and further undermines this highly feminized and insecure sector."

—Donna Baines, *Director and Professor of Social Work, University of British Columbia*

"This detailed account of the marketisation of social care in Australia provides a sharp analysis of the way in which narratives of cost reduction and consumer choice have worked to stymie the development of decent work for the disability care workforce. Fiona Macdonald shows how the design and implementation of the Australian National Disability Insurance Scheme has failed to include adequate resources for the disability care workforce leaving them vulnerable to some of the lowest paid and insecure working conditions in Australia. The book locates the care workforce at the centre of analysis to provide a critical account of how the interface between care policy and employment regulation produces the conditions of individualised risk for social care workers. Macdonald concludes that a more collective approach to person-centred care based on organisation-based employment for care workers could ameliorate this risk, support high quality disability care support, gender equality, and a sustainable and equitable future of work."

—Elizabeth Hill, *Associate Professor, Department of Political Economy, The University of Sydney*

Fiona Macdonald

Individualising Risk

Paid Care Work in the New Gig Economy

palgrave
macmillan

Fiona Macdonald
RMIT University
Melbourne, VIC, Australia

ISBN 978-981-33-6365-6 ISBN 978-981-33-6366-3 (eBook)
https://doi.org/10.1007/978-981-33-6366-3

This Palgrave Macmillan imprint is published by the registered company Springer Nature Singapore Pte Ltd.
The registered company address is: 152 Beach Road, #21-01/04 Gateway East, Singapore 189721, Singapore

Acknowledgements

I acknowledge, with thanks, the support received from RMIT University through the award of a Vice-Chancellor's Senior Research Fellowship and the support from the Australian Research Council. This book was made possible by the contributions of many people. My deep thanks go to Eleanor Bentham whose insights, assistance and company throughout the research process were invaluable. Many thanks are also due to Jenny Malone, Danielle Miller, Mutsumi Karasaki, Karen Douglas, Andrew Nette and Ben Debney and the books reviewers. All helped make this a better book better through their contributions. I appreciate greatly the assistance and patience of the publishing team. My colleagues in the Work of Social Care group, the Centre for People, Organisation and Work and the School of Management at RMIT University have been supportive and encouraging. I am particularly grateful to Sara Charlesworth for her guidance and support. I am immensely grateful to everyone who participated in the research and especially to all the care and support workers who readily offered their time and their personal experiences. My final thanks go to Kevin Brown, who I thank for everything.

The research on which this book is based was funded by Australian Research Council Discovery Early Career Researcher Grant DE160100543.

Contents

CHAPTER 1

Social Care Work Matters

Introduction

In 2020 the global coronavirus pandemic turned a spotlight on social care workers providing long-term care as, along with healthcare workers, they faced new risks at the frontline of caring for vulnerable members of the community. A largely unnoticed and undervalued workforce, social care workers became the recipients of public expressions of gratitude arising in communities all over the world.

But real recognition of the social care workforce requires more than this. The highly feminised workforce who provide support and care to the aged and people with disability[1] are often low-paid workers in highly precarious employment. Social care workers above all else require fair treatment at work.

This book is about social care workers and how changing social care policies are shaping their work and employment, in interaction with ineffective labour regulation. Its focus is on those policies that personalise or individualise care and what they mean for the well-being, livelihoods and opportunities of the hundreds of thousands of mainly women who perform essential social care work. The book is motivated by my interest

[1] In Australia the term 'people with disability' is considered respectful and is widely adopted in preference to the term 'disabled people' that is preferred in some other parts of the world.

F. Macdonald, *Individualising Risk*,
https://doi.org/10.1007/978-981-33-6366-3_1

in prospects for decent work for paid care workers and my concern that, in individualised social care arrangements, the goal of decent work is becoming harder to reach.

The book presents a case study of the organisation and treatment of care work and frontline care and support workers in Australia's new National Disability Insurance Scheme (NDIS). As an individualised cash-for-care scheme for social care the NDIS re-frames care users as consumers and establishes a market for them to purchase their own care. Implemented from trials in 2013 to national coverage in 2020 the NDIS allocates funds to eligible people with 'permanent and significant disability' for them to purchase the supports they need to live 'an ordinary life' (National Disability Insurance Agency [NDIA] 2016, p. ii).

In international context the NDIS is not novel, as individualised funding schemes for social care have been operating since the 1990s. However, the Australian scheme is a wholesale and uncompromising shift to care individualisation; *all* public funding for care and support for people with disability is now allocated on an individual basis and, in a very short period of time, an entirely new, and largely unregulated, publicly-funded market has been created for people to purchase their care and support by the hour.

The new scheme is causing enormous disruption to the organisation of work and to employment arrangements as it moves social care work (and workers) out of more secure work in the public and not-for-profit sectors. Digital care platforms have entered the new care market and, along with other new market actors, are facilitating the treatment of social care workers as on-demand flexible services in a new gig economy of care. Care and care work are being re-shaped in ways that have implications for the sustainability of the workforce in the social care system and for the quality of care and support.

I refer to a *new* gig economy in the title of this book. This is not to emphasise the novelty or innovation of the digital platforms that have emerged in many service sectors in recent years (Aloisi 2016); rather, it is to emphasise that 'gig work' is an old phenomenon, used to refer to the organisation of highly precarious work where workers—usually in the arts sector—were engaged for one-off performances or for a limited season (Prassl 2018, p. 2). Indeed 'old' gig work has also been around for a long time in social care, often hidden in the privately-funded grey economy of nannying, care and domestic work (Poo 2017). In the new gig economy of care explored in this book *public social care policy and funding* are critical to the transformation of care work into gig work.

The book draws on documentary research and interviews with social care workers to understand the impacts Australia's new social care system is having on their work and employment. It details the findings of a three-year investigation of social care work and employment in the NDIS. The research sought to understand how the problems of low pay and poor quality of social care jobs are changed by individualised care policies and what the changes mean for decent work for social care workers. The research aims included: (i) to build knowledge about the organisation and dynamics of paid work in cash-for-care systems, (ii) to understand why labour regulation is or is not effective for progressing gender equality in work and protecting vulnerable workers and (iii) to consider how to achieve quality jobs and care in sustainable social care systems.

The idea of decent work adopted in this book is that outlined in the International Labour Organization's (ILO's) *Decent Work Agenda* (ILO 2020). Decent work encompasses respect for the physical and mental integrity of the worker and concerns the quality and dignity of work. It encompasses an inclusive workforce and satisfying jobs. Gender equality is a key aspect of decent work and an important focus for the research and this book.

The remainder of this chapter is in three parts. Below, I consider why care work matters before describing the research on which the book is based. The chapter ends with an overview of the structure and contents of chapters that follow.

I place social care work in broader context to show why this work matters—not just to the workers who perform the essential work, but to everyone. One part of this context concerns the importance of care work for gender equality Another concerns the importance of care work for the quality for care. I start with consideration of the importance of care work to the future of work.

Care Work Matters for the Future of Work

A common definition of care work is work comprising 'activities and relations involved in meeting the physical, psychological and emotional needs of adults and children, old and young, frail and able-bodied' (International Labour Organization [ILO] 2018, p. 6) This broad definition encompasses paid and unpaid care work and includes two overlapping activities: ***direct, face-to-face, personal care*** and ***indirect care***. Paid care workers engaged in direct care include teachers, nurses, doctors, childcare workers, therapists, health aides and personal care workers, all of whom work within care relationships with the people to whom they provide care. Indirect care activities involve household work, such as cleaning and cooking, that do not necessarily involve 'relational care' but, in practice, often overlap with it (ILO 2018, p. 6).

Globally, the paid care workforce is large and growing. Worldwide there are an estimated 249 million women and 132 million men employed in the care workforce, representing 11.5% of total global employment, 19.3% of global female employment and 6.6% of global male employment (ILO 2018, p. xxxviii). Women make up the overwhelming majority of the long-term care workforce, just over 90% on average across OECD countries (OECD 2020). Care employment is growing as a result of a combination of demographic, economic and social factors including ageing populations, changing social norms and care policies.

In Australia in 2018, the occupation of aged and disabled carers was among the 10 largest (of 300 occupations) in the country and more people were employed in aged and disabled care jobs than in any other health and community services occupation, except for nursing (Department of Jobs and Small Business 2019). Employment in social care work is growing much more strongly than in almost all other occupations, and this trend is expected to continue. In the five years to 2018, employment growth for all occupations combined was 10.4%, while for aged and disabled care workers it was 36.2%. New aged and disabled care jobs accounted for 15% of all new jobs over the period (Department of Jobs and Small Business 2018, 2019, p. 25). For the five years from 2018 to 2023, projected employment growth for care workers is four to five times that of the projected 7.1% growth for all occupations: for aged and disabled carers it is 39.3% (higher than for any other occupation), and for personal care workers it is 29.4% (Department of Jobs and Small Business 2018, p. 21, 2019, p. 45). While these estimates pre-date the major disruptions to employment occurring in 2020 due to COVID-19, it is likely these occupations will continue to grow in line with earlier projections (Xiao 2020).

The quality of employment in care jobs in Australia's new individualised disability care and support system is critical for the quality of Australian care jobs as growth in the NDIS workforce is a large contributor to current and anticipated employment growth in social care employment. Significant workforce growth has already taken place since the NDIS commenced in trial sites 2013 and there is a predicted doubling in size of the workforce between 2019 and 2023, from 100,000 to 190,000 workers. Over 70% of the newly created NDIS jobs are expected to be support worker roles (Robert 2019).

Assuming current trends, paid care work will continue to play an increasingly important role in employment in Australia and internationally. Significant losses in manufacturing jobs in many developed economies have occurred in recent decades, related to technological change and globalisation. Over the same period there has been an expansion of service jobs, including a large expansion of care jobs. In Australia, in the ten years to 2016, manufacturing jobs declined by about 270,000 while jobs in health care and social assistance increased by almost 400,000 (Cassells et al. 2018, p. 8). Forecasts of changes in work suggest care jobs will not be lost to automation (Balleister and Elsheikhi 2018, p. 16). Not only is there limited potential for replacing human care labour with technological solutions, as it involves social interactions and occurs in unpredictable environments, but automation of care work is 'a less attractive business proposition' as care work attracts relatively low wages (McKinsey Global Institute 2017, p. 6).

Care Work Matters for Gender Equality

> (S)pecialization in care is costly because it reduces both individual and collective bargaining power. That is, it puts individual caregivers at a disadvantage and makes it more difficult for women, as a group, to challenge gender bias and discrimination. In this context, 'disadvantage' does not connote lower happiness or subjective well-being, but rather less access to economic resources and less power to influence institutional change (Folbre 2018, p. 749).

Despite changes that have led to women's increased labour force participation, and large distributional shifts away from unpaid to paid work, care work remains as important for gender equality today as it was 40 years ago (ILO 2018). Most care is unpaid and provided by women in families, households and communities. Globally, women perform 76% of all unpaid care work, spending over three times more time on unpaid care than men (ILO 2018, xxix). While men's contribution to unpaid care has increased in some countries over the past 20 years, the pace of change continues to be very slow. The ILO estimates that at the current rate of change it will take 210 years for the gender gap in unpaid care work to be closed (ILO 2018, p. xxx).

The inequalities in, and the interactions and links between, unpaid care and paid care are at the heart of women's poorer opportunities for economic and social empowerment. Across the globe women continue to be excluded from market activities and are economically disadvantaged as a result of their disproportionate contribution to the unpaid work of caring for children and adults in their families and communities. Women's disadvantage arises from being economically dependent on men or the state, from having reduced opportunities for participation in education and training and from foregone wages, leading to life-long low-income levels and vulnerability to poverty (Orloff 2009, Razavi 2007).

Globally, in 2018, 606 million women, compared with 41 million men, were not actively participating in the labour market due to unpaid care work (ILO 2018, xxxi). This is, however, changing. Across the OECD, between 1906 and 2005, women's employment rate increased from 47% in 1960 to 62% (Wittenberg 2016, pp. 18–19, citing OECD Statistics 2008). Nonetheless, unpaid care work often means women are in part-time employment and locked out of access to better quality jobs. In many countries, women undertaking unpaid care work are more likely to be in self-employment or to work in the informal economy. In countries like Australia, where women's education participation is at least equal to men's, women's disadvantage and gender gaps in life-long incomes persist (Australian Bureau of Statistics 2020). Many women participate in the labour market, but on different terms from men. The fact that women are concentrated in part-time jobs often also means they are in jobs with poor employment conditions and in lower-paid industries and occupations (International Labour Organization 2016, p. 117, Joint Standing Committee on the National Disability Insurance Scheme 2017).

So, reducing women's economic disadvantage not only requires policies to reduce women's unpaid care work, but also increased support for decent paid work for women. Thus, low wages of paid care workers are a significant problem for the achievement of gender equality goals.

The idea of defamilialisation, developed in welfare state analysis, is helpful here as it encompasses both care aspects and gender relations of families as critical to gender equality goals for women. Defamilialisation refers to 'the degree to which individuals can uphold a socially acceptable standard of living independently of family relationships' (Lister 1994, p. 37). This perspective brings into focus, not only the problem of women's position as responsible for care, but also women's economic dependence on men. From a defamilialisation perspective, policies that facilitate the provision of care through care services outside the family are important for gender equality; they enable women's labour force participation by reducing the amount of time women devote to unpaid care work and enable increases in women's time in paid work. However, care services and increased labour market participation are not enough to secure women's independence. Policies that promote gender equality in the labour market and the family are equally important (Grimshaw et al. 2017, Orloff 2009, Razavi 2007). These must include policies that support the recognition of unpaid care, address gender gaps in labour market outcomes, increase sharing of unpaid care between men and women, and policies that ensure both women and men can gain work in decent jobs.

While addressing the quality of paid care jobs is essential for addressing gender gaps and improving labour market outcomes, large sectors of the expanding paid care workforce across the world, in both rich and poor countries, remain in poorly paid and highly insecure employment. As paid care work is highly feminised in most countries of the world, most of these workers are women. Women comprise 79% of all care workers and 89% of all domestic workers in Europe and Central Asia, for example, while in the Americas, women are 76% of care workers and 96% of domestic workers (ILO 2018, p. 172). In Australia, four out of five 'personal care workers' and 'aged and disabled carers' are women (Department of Jobs and Small Business 2018, p. 20, 2019, p. 48).

While not all care workers are poorly paid, some highly feminised segments of the care workforce experience low pay and poor working conditions. Along with gender inequality, inequalities of race and class are also evident in care work; this is an international phenomenon (Razavi 2007). Care workers in low-paid jobs include many vulnerable and disadvantaged workers, such as migrants who experience discrimination and may have insecure residency status, or lack full citizenship rights (ILO 2018; Michel and Peng 2017). In both rich and poor countries, the lowest paid care and domestic workers tend to come from population groups who face discrimination and inequality based on ethnicity, race and nationality. Globally, women migrate from poor to rich countries where they work in low-paid care jobs. In addition, while some groups of paid care users are likely to be wealthy—such as families in western nations who employ nannies in their homes to care for their children—many care users are also vulnerable and marginalised people. The low status or devaluing of people requiring care contributes to the low status of care work (Knijn and Verhagen 2007).

Lack of recognition of the skills involved in care work is another reason for care workers' low and inequitable remuneration. A care 'wage penalty' exists whereby paid care workers often earn less than workers in other occupations with similar education, skills and experience (England, Budig and Folbre 2002). Gendered undervaluation of ***paid*** care work arises from lack of recognition of the value of women's ***unpaid*** care work, as gender norms have care associated with 'natural' female inclinations rather than with any skill (Folbre and Nelson 2000). The relatively poor bargaining position of many care workers is another major contributing factor to low pay rates for care workers. As care work is intensive relational work in which emotional and moral engagement play a role it is very difficult for care workers to threaten to withdraw their labour. Close relational connections to the people they care for can also make care workers vulnerable to exploitation as they may work for less pay or for longer hours unpaid (Duffy et al. 2015).

A further contributing factor to low and inequitable remuneration is that the value of care workers' contribution is difficult to measure. Care workers cannot personally claim all the value of the outcomes of care because care outcomes often depend on others, including the recipients of care themselves. Nevertheless, care work remains a public good that has a value greater than that charged by service providers and paid by consumers, due to the benefits care work generates for society. Economic models of supply and demand rely on consumers making a rational choice about the value of the services they purchase. As some of the benefits of care work accrue to others, consumers of care undervalue care work, and the market wage-setting mechanism is distorted. Low pay for care workers is the result (England et al. 2002, Folbre 2018).

The neo-classical economic theory of compensating wage differentials claims that people choosing care work are adequately compensated in their jobs because the emotional and relational benefits of their work provide their primary motivation, not monetary reward. In other words, 'altruism is its own reward' (England et al. 2002, p. 458)—or, as Julie Nelson (1999, p. 44) has put it, workers 'simply choose to take a portion of their pay in warm feelings instead of cash'. From this point of view, low pay doesn't matter much, as workers will be satisfied with their jobs despite it. Feminist economists acknowledge that altruism can be a part of the motivation for caring labour and a factor in low pay (England et al. 2002). However, they point out that every job self-selects for workers who have some interest in the work, most jobs are intrinsically rewarding to some workers, and the pay penalty in care work cannot be explained by preferences. Further, the theory of compensating wage differentials ignores the gendered power relations that socialise women to believe in the value of altruism in providing care (England et al. 2002, Nelson 1999).

In Australia, home care workers report that low pay and poor working conditions are the causes of dissatisfaction and stress in their jobs (Evesson and Oxenbridge 2017). Disability support workers responding to a large-scale survey expressed similar levels of satisfaction with most aspects of their work to the rest of the female workforce in Australia, except for their pay. These workers had markedly lower satisfaction with their pay than other workers (Martin and Healy 2010). In 2017, the majority of employers responding to a national survey reported the main reason for disability support workers leaving their jobs was to gain better pay and conditions elsewhere, often in other industries (Department of Jobs & Small Business 2018, p. 18). Disability support and aged care workers in Australia and in many other developed and wealthy countries are not only in low-paid and undervalued jobs; they are often in highly precarious employment; employment characterised by income and working-time insecurity, and without access to paid leave and other employment benefits (ILO 2018).

Understanding how the cash-for-care model of social care affects gendered undervaluation, low pay and poor quality of jobs in social care was a key motivation for the research that is the subject of this book. Another was to learn more about how to build quality jobs in high-quality flexible care systems. An important underpinning assumption is that the quality of care work matters for the quality of care as explained briefly below.

Care Work Matters for the Quality of Care

Care is a social process in which the labour of care workers is central. In adult social care, care workers' labour is the main cost of care, the workforce is dispersed in the community, and there is little management oversight of the work. This combination of factors means that care workers are one of the main determinants of care quality (Meagher and Cortis 2008, Rubery and Urwin 2011). The link between care workers and care quality is recognised in care policies, although often the policy focus may be restricted to workers' availability, motivation and skill development (Atkinson et al. 2018, Rubery and Urwin 2011).

Ideas about what constitutes good quality care vary. Measures of quality at the policy level may focus on service inputs, governance, responsiveness or delivery processes, or they may focus on 'technical' measures or user perceptions of outcomes. With policy shifts to consumer-directed care, the notion of quality has become more closely associated with individual care recipients' ability to exercise choice and control over their services and with their satisfaction with care services (Glasby and Littlechild 2016).

Evidence suggests that the well-being of workers and/or the quality of their jobs is strongly connected to the quality of care people receive. Studies of home care services—home-based care services for the aged and people with disability—have found service users' positive perceptions of care and care quality to be associated with better organisation of workers, more training, longer employment tenure and stability of working time (Defourny et al. 2010, Netten et al. 2007, Whitfield 2015). Social care recipients commonly name consistency of care as important for quality of care; yet, this is exactly what is undermined where poor working conditions and low pay lead to high turnover of care workers. As discussed in Chapter 2, such problems are endemic in many social care workforces.

Some analysts have argued that good quality care should take account of the views and experiences of care workers in addition to the perspective of care recipients. For example, Daly (2001, pp. 47–48) expands the idea of good quality care by taking it to be 'the "good" for policy purposes in relation to care'. She argues that, from the point of view of the caregiver, 'the opportunity to provide high-quality care', the choice to provide care and the conditions under which it is provided are important—the latter including working conditions, pay, hours and security. This approach, which I adopt in this book, also brings into focus other questions about the distribution of social advantage and disadvantage under marketisation strategies, given that social policy's key purposes are to reduce inequality and poverty (Meagher and Goodwin 2015).

About the Research

The introduction of a new national individualised funding scheme for disability care and support (the NDIS) in Australia presents a unique opportunity to build new knowledge about the organisation and dynamics of paid work in cash-for-care and to contribute to a better understanding of how care labour markets are regulated. This book is based on a case study of care work and workers in Australia's disability care and support system during a period of transformation to a new individualised care market. The research has tracked developments as they occurred—from the expression of ideas and goals for the scheme to their translation into policy and regulation and implementation in practice.

The NDIS is a radical reform; it establishes a national system in which public funding for care and support for people with disabilities is allocated to individuals for them to purchase their supports in the market. It is a highly unregulated system, has universal (i.e. non means-tested) application and mandatory individualisation of disability support. The new services market is open to unregulated service providers and to private for-profit businesses. The NDIS replaces funded services and programmes mostly run by not-for-profit service providers under contracts to Australia's state and territory governments. Under the NDIS people have the choice to manage their support funds themselves and directly employ their own support workers.

A study of paid work in Australia's new disability support and care system has value in its own right, due to the significance and rapidity of the policy and system changes in the Australian context. It also has value in the international context as a 'critical' case (Flyvberg 2006, p. 230), with strategic importance to questions about *how* work in quasi or managed markets is shaped by social care policy, *how* employment regulation intersects with care policy to shape work and what *social care work might look like in the future*, including as new business models enabled by digital technologies emerge.

Some of the key questions motivating the research included: What institutions regulate care work in individualised funding systems and how do they interact to construct different employment arrangements and outcomes for workers? What patterns of work relationships and employment arrangements are present in individualised care systems and in what ways these associated with outcomes for 'decent work'? What regulatory arrangements are likely to produce the best outcomes for decent work and gender equality in paid care workers in cash-for-care schemes that provide flexible, quality care?

I took a multi-disciplinary approach to the research and adopted different methods to answer different questions. The main components of the empirical research were: (i) analysis of dozens of policy-related and operational documents relating to the design, development, management and operations of the NDIS individualised care scheme and market; (ii) one-to-one in-depth interviews with 62 disability care and support workers and focus groups with another 32 workers; (iii) individual or group interviews with service providers, digital care platform operators, bureaucrats, consumer and carer advocates and other policy actors and stakeholders in Australia (22) and England (15). Over a period of several years I undertook periodic scans of the labour market for disability support work and I was an active participant in industry and policy forums.

The purpose of the documentary analysis was to explore the ideas and values shaping the individualised care policy to understand the normative frameworks and tensions contained therein. Through identifying narratives contained in the documents my intention was to make sense of the policy strategies and their contradictions. This is a similar approach to that taken by Needham and Dickinson (2018) to compare UK personalisation and Australia NDIS narratives and adopted by Miller and Hayward (2017) for their analysis of the ideas underlying the NDIS.

Interviews with disability support workers were conducted from 2015 to 2019, in three Australian states and in regional and metropolitan, but not remote, communities. The focus of interviews varied with workers' situations. Situations ranged from providing support to people with complex needs who require assistance with basic tasks of daily living to supporting people to develop independent living skills or participate in the community. One job might involve working in a community setting in a team on a 24-hour seven-day roster, another could involve travelling between multiple short home visits spread throughout the day and another meeting a person in their workplace to assist them with a meal. Most support workers participating in the research worked only part-time hours. Their employment situations were diverse: some were permanent or casual employees of not-for-profit NDIS-registered disability service providers; some were casual labour hire or 'agency' employees who moved between workplaces; others were directly employed or contracted workers whose employers or clients were the individuals they supported; and others were workers whose work relationships were mediated or brokered by third parties including digital platforms. Many workers held multiple jobs and were employed in different arrangements in different jobs.

The purpose of interviews with service providers, policy stakeholders, industry representatives and others was, in some instances, to hear perspectives on policy processes. In others, it was primarily to understand policy impacts, learn about business models or about aspirations for the individualised system. I undertook ethnographic research in four service provider organisations. This involved observation of business and work processes in organisations identified by informants as having innovative approaches that supported decent working conditions for care workers including two cooperatives. Interviews in England provided insight into international developments and policy debates and a point of reference for developing my research into care and support work in the new Australian system.

Organisation of the Book

Together Chapters 2 and 3 locate Australia's NDIS in the international landscape of marketised and individualised care. Chapter 2 provides historical and comparative context for this development and introduces some key ideas and debates about care marketisation and individualisation policies. Human rights concerns underpin many individualised care systems; individualisation is a response to the historical patronising treatment of people with disability and aims to empower people through enabling them to choose and purchase their own care services, including to directly employ their own care workers. However, another common driver is belief in market-based competition for efficiency and service responsiveness and cost containment. Chapter 2 also presents the framework used to guide exploration of the main institutional structures and processes that have been found to shape care work in individualised care systems: the care and employment 'regimes' (Williams 2012). Drawing on insights from feminist socio-economics, comparative institutionalist approaches and labour market segmentation theory, this framework is consistent with a 'new labour market segmentation approach' (Grimshaw et al. 2017). The chapter finishes with a consideration of the evidence concerning how care workers fare in individualised systems.

Chapter 3 explores ideas about individualisation in social care and their significance in social policy reform agendas. My focus is on debates conducted in the United Kingdom (UK) about social care individualisation, or 'personalisation' as it is known there, and on evidence from the English social care system. That system has had some provision for individualised care—including direct payments to individuals—for over two decades. The designers of Australia's new scheme drew heavily on the English experience and on ideas that have been debated in the UK over the last 15–20 years or so. The English experience provides a reference point for understanding the Australian policy rationale and system design and it provides some pointers to the ways in which individualisation might re-shape care work and employment when implemented in a more radical transformation process as in the Australian case. In this chapter I also review evidence relating to how individualised social care impacts on frontline care workers. This review of research suggests policymakers and researchers have paid little attention to frontline direct care workers in what are the *most* individualised care employment relationships, that is, where workers are employed directly by care users. Direct engagement or employment is a phenomenon that has grown significantly in England only recently and it is an arrangement that is supported and promoted heavily in Australia's new publicly-funded system, with its emergence on a large-scale facilitated by digital care platforms.

Many of the ideas underpinning the NDIS are those central to individualised care funding implemented in the United Kingdom (UK) under the banner of personalisation. The designers of Australia's NDIS drew heavily on both the ideas and the implementation of individualised funding in adult social care in England (Productivity Commission 2011, van Toorn 2018).

The case study of the individualised NDIS commences in Chapter 4. Drawing on analysis of NDIS legislation, policy and operations documents and related documents (such as submissions) I make the argument the vision for an NDIS workforce is at odds with the existing workforce, including in relation to their skills and employment arrangements. NDIS policy envisages the new workforce as highly informalised; an idea at odds with existing employment standards. There is limited accountability for the workforce in policy and there is an assumption that consumer choice and greater efficiency will lead to good outcomes for workers as well as service users. In policy and in management of the social care market consumer choice and efficiency are both linked to lean models of service provision and to a large deregulated market sector. In tension with this, the NDIS establishes strong expectations for good quality and safe support built on worker capabilities.

Employment and care regimes fundamentally shape and structure the nature and experience of care work and employment. Chapter 5 is concerned with labour regulation as a key structural pillar of the employment regime. In international comparison Australia has a comprehensive safety net of industry/occupation specific standards and minimum wages. However, there are gaps and deficiencies in Australia's system of labour market regulation and many of these reflect and reinforce historically strong gendered norms around a male breadwinner model. The regulation of part-time and casual employment, in which women predominate, provides less protection for workers from risks and insecurities and fewer benefits than for equivalent full-time employment. Gendered undervaluation in regard to both pay and conditions has been a long-standing problem in feminised social care including for disability support workers. Further, labour laws and other labour market regulations affecting workers' rights leave significant space for the feminised care and support workforce to be refashioned as an independent sole-trader service provider workforce and/or an informalised workforce performing 'private' work partly governed by domestic and familial relations. As in many other countries, Australia's labour market regulation does not effectively protect workers in these types of arrangements. Yet, in the new Australian publicly-funded and managed long-term care system, NDIS policymakers and market managers promote such arrangements for a growing proportion of the frontline care and support workforce.

In Chapter 6, I explore the make-up of the supply side of the new NDIS market. In the lightly regulated market there is a growing number of for-profit firms, many acting as intermediaries in care and/or employment relationships as brokers of care and support labour. These third parties—including digital care platforms—exert some control over workers' access to employment, their pay and conditions of work, their autonomy at work and their opportunity to collectively bargain. The chapter shows how it is in the intersections of care policy and employment regulation that employers and other market actors shape disability support work and employment and direct the future character and form of the workforce and labour market.

Chapters 7 and 8 draw on interviews with disability support workers employed in different employment arrangements to investigate how the developing market arrangements impact on workers, their employment and the quality of their jobs. The idea of ***individualised risk*** is employed to describe different risks for workers associated with structural changes in the organisation of care and work under individualisation. The chapters explore how individualised risk plays out at the micro-level of care and support work relationships: in the labour process and social relations of work, in working time arrangements, and in rewards and protections attached to employment. The focus of Chapter 7 is on how the individualised care system introduces new risks of ***reinforcing the gendered undervaluation of care and support work.*** It shows how individualised care heightens risks of gendered undervaluation in two ways: by removing workers' access to many of the mechanisms and avenues that might be used to tackle undervaluation of the work and by reversing past gains made towards recognition and valuing of the work.

The exploration of frontline workers' experiences continues in Chapter 8, focusing on the individualised risks of ***isolating and individualising workers***, and ***fragmenting work, working time and working lives***. Risks of isolating and individualising workers include risks arising from the transfer of responsibility and decision-making to people with disability and to individual workers. There is a large imbalance between, on the one hand, the responsibility and associated risks devolved to frontline workers and, on the other hand, the absence of recognition and reward for workers. The risks of fragmenting work, working time and life are perhaps the most conspicuous of the individualised risks. These risks are highly problematic for individual workers and for the prospects for a skilled and sustainable workforce. They impact on workers' ability to earn a living, enjoy time away from work and participate in work and employment in ways that support skills development.

In the final chapter, focusing on government as the key actor responsible for the outcomes of the public social care system, I put forward some suggestions for strategies to address the problems identified in this study. I argue that governments must act to ensure genuine valuing of care and care work; to build opportunity for collective effort, responsibility and voice; and to re-fashion care jobs as sustainable and secure work. Based on the evidence presented in this book it is clear there is an urgent need for changes to both the care system and employment regulation.

References

Aloisi, A. (2016). Commoditized workers: Case study research on labor law issues arising from a set of on-demand/gig economy platforms. *Comparative Labor Law and Policy Journal*, *37*(3), 653–690. https://heinonline.org/HOL/LandingPage?handle=hein.journals/cllpj37&div=40&id=&page=.

Atkinson, C., Crozier, S., & Lucas, R. (2018). Workforce policy and care quality in english long-term elder care. *Public Performance & Management Review*, *41*(4), 859–884. https://doi.org/10.1080/15309576.2018.1473784.

Australian Bureau of Statistics. (2020). *Gender indicators*. Cat no. 4125.0. Canberra: Australian Bureau of Statistics.

Balleister, T., & Elsheikhi, A. (2018). The future of work: a literature review. *ILO Research Department Working Paper no. 29*. Geneva: International Labour Office.

Cassells, R., Duncan, A., Mavisakalyan, A., Phillimore, J., Seymour, R., & Tarverdi, Y. (2018). Future of work in Australia: preparing for tomorrow's world. *Focus on the States* Series, No 6/18. Perth, WA: Bankwest Curtin Economics Centre.

Daly, M. (2001). *Care work: The quest for security*. Geneva: International Labour Office.

Department of Jobs and Small Business. (2018). *The labour market for personal care workers in aged and disability care, Australia 2017*. Canberra: Commonwealth of Australia.

Department of Jobs and Small Business (2019). Australian jobs 2019. Department of Jobs and Small Business. Canberra: Commonwealth of Australia.

Defourny, J., Henry, A., Nassaut, S., & Nyssens, M. (2010). Does the mission of providers matter on a quasi-market? The case of the Belgian 'service voucher' scheme. *Annals of Public and Cooperative Economics, 81*(4), 583–610. http://doi.org/10.1111/j.1467-8292.2010.00423.x.

Duffy, M., Armenia, A., & Stacey, C. L. (2015). On the clock, off the radar: paid care work in the United States. In M. Duffy, A. Armenia, & C. L. Stacey (Eds.), *Caring on the clock: Complexities and contradictions of paid care work* (pp. 3–13). New Brunswick, New Jersey and London: Rutgers University Press.

England, P., Budig, M., & Folbre, N. (2002). Wages of virtue: The relative pay of care work. *Social Problems, 49*(4), 455–473. http://doi.org/10.1525/sp.2002.49.4.455.

Evesson, J., & Oxenbridge, S. (2017). *The psychosocial health and safety of Australian home care workers: risks and solutions* (p. 147). Sydney: Centre for Applied Disability Research.

Flyvbjerg, B. (2006). Five misunderstandings about case-study research. *Qualitative Inquiry, 12*(2), 219–245. https://doi.org/10.1177/1077800405284363.

Folbre, N. (2018). The care penalty and gender inequality In S. Averett, L. M. Argy, & S. D. Hoffman (Eds.), *The Oxford handbook of women and the economy* (pp. 749–766). New York: Oxford University Press.

Folbre, N., & Nelson, J. (2000). For love or money—or both? *The Journal of Economic Perspectives, 14*(4), 123–140. http://doi.org/10.1257/jep.14.4.123.

Glasby, J., & Littlechild, R. (2016). *Direct payments and personal budgets: putting personalisation into practice*. Bristol: The Policy Press.

Grimshaw, D., Fagan, C., Hebson, G., & Tavora, I. (2017). A new labour market segmentation approach for analysing inequalities: Introduction and overview. In D. Grimshaw, C. Fagan, G. Hebson, & I. Tavora (Eds.), *Making work more equal: A new labour market segmentation approach* (pp. 1–32). Manchester, England: Manchester University Press.

International Labour Organization (ILO). (2016). *Non-standard employment around the world: Understanding challenges, shaping prospects*. Geneva: International Labour Office.

International Labour Organization (ILO). (2018). *Care work and care jobs: for the future of decent work*. Geneva: International Labour Office.

International Labour Organization (ILO). (2020). Decent Work. ILO. https://www.ilo.org/global/topics/decent-work/lang–en/index.htm. Accessed 22 June 2020.

Joint Standing Committee on the National Disability Insurance Scheme (2017). *Progress report*. Parliament of Australia. Canberra: Commonwealth of Australia.

Knijn, T., & Verhagen, S. (2007). Contested professionalism payments for care and the quality of home care. *Administration & Society, 39*(4), 451–475. https://doi-org.ezproxy.lib.rmit.edu.au/10.1177/0095399707300520.

Lister, R. (1994). She has other duties—women, citizenship and social security. In S. Baldwin, & Falkingham, J. (Eds.), *Social security and social change: New challenges to the Beveridge model* (pp. 31–44.). Hemel Hempstead: Harvester Wheatsheaf.

Martin, B., & Healy, J. (2010). *Who works in community services? A profile of Australian workforces in child protection, juvenile justice, disability services and general community services*. Adelaide: National Institute of Labour Studies, Flinders University.

McKinsey Global Institute (2017). Jobs lost, jobs gained: workforce transitions in a time of automation. McKinsey & Company. https://www.mckinsey.com/featured-insights/future-of-work/jobs-lost-jobs-gained-what-the-future-of-work-will-mean-for-jobs-skills-and-wages. Accessed 22 February 2020.

Meagher, G., & Cortis, N. (2008). The political economy of for-profit paid care: Theory and evidence. In D. King & G. Meagher (Eds.), *Paid care in*

Australia: profits, purpose, practices (pp. 13–42). Sydney: Sydney University Press.

Meagher, G., & Goodwin, S. (2015). Introduction: Capturing marketisation in Australian social policy. In G. Meagher & S. Goodwin (Eds.), *Markets, rights and power in Australian social policy* (pp. 1–27). Sydney: Sydney University Press.

Miller, P., & Hayward, D. (2017). Social policy 'generosity' at a time of fiscal austerity: The strange case of Australia's National Disability Insurance Scheme. *Critical Social Policy, 37*(1), 128–147. https://doi.org/10.1177/0261018316664463.

Michel, S., & Peng, I. (2017). *Gender, migration, and the work of care. A multi-scalar approach to the Pacific Rim.* New York: Palgrave MacMillan.

National Disability Insurance Agency (NDIA) (2016). Towards an ordinary life. Annual Report 2015–2016. NDIA. https://www.ndis.gov.au/about-us/publications/annual-report/annual-report-2015-16. Accessed 8 April 2020.

Needham, C., & Dickinson, H. (2018). 'Any one of us could be among that number': Comparing the policy narratives for individualized disability funding in Australia and England. *Social Policy & Administration, 52*(3), 731–749. https://doi.org/10.1111/spol.12320.

Nelson, J. A. (1999). Of markets and martyrs: is it ok to pay well for care? *Feminist Economics, 5*(3), 43–59, http://doi.org/10.1080/135457099337806.

Netten, A., Jones, K., & Sandhu, S. (2007). Provider and care workforce influences on quality of home-care services in England. *Journal of Aging & Social Policy, 19*(3), 81–97. http://doi.org/10.1300/J031v19n03_06.

Organisation for Economic Co-operation and Development (OECD). (2020). *Who cares? Attracting and retaining care workers for the elderly*. Paris: OECD Health Policy Studies, OECD.

Orloff, A. S. (2009). Gendering the comparative analysis of welfare states: An unfinished agenda. *Sociological Theory, 27*(3), 317–343. http://doi.org/10.1111/j.1467-9558.2009.01350.x.

Poo, A-J. (2017). Out from the shadows: Domestic workers speak in the United States. Open Democracy. 16 June. https://www.opendemocracy.net/en/beyond-trafficking-and-slavery/out-from-shadows-domestic-workers-speak-in-united-states/. Accessed 2 November 2020.

Prassl, J. (2018). *Humans as service: The promise and perils of work in the gig economy*. Oxford: Oxford University Press.

Razavi, S. (2007). The political and social economy of care in a development context. Conceptual issues, research questions and policy options. *Gender and Development Programme Paper* (pp. 50). Geneva: United Nations Research Institute for Social Development.

Robert, S. (The Hon.). (2019). The NDIS Plan. *Speech delivered to the National Press Club,* Canberra, 14 November. Canberra. Ministers for the Department of Social Services. https://ministers.dss.gov.au/speeches/5266. Accessed 14 May 2020.

Rubery, J., & Urwin, P. (2011). Bringing the employer back in: Why social care needs a standard employment relationship. *Human Resource Management Journal, 21*(2), 122–137. http://doi.org/10.1111/j.1748-8583.2010.00138.x.

Whitfield, D. (2015). *The new health and social care economy.* Bootle, UK: European Services Strategy Unit.

Williams, F., & Brennan, D. (2012). Care, markets and migration in a globalising world: Introduction to the Special Issue. *Journal of European Social Policy, 22*(4), 355–362. https://doi.org/10.1177/0958928712449777.

Wittenberg, R. (2016). Demand for long-term care and support for older people. In C. Gori, J.-L. Fernandez, & R. Wittenberg (Eds.), *Long-term care reforms in OECD countries* (pp. 9–24). Bristol: Policy Press.

Xiao, A. (2020) Healthcare and social services could be key for future job security post-coronavirus. *ABC News*. 18 July. https://www.abc.net.au/news/2020-07-18/healthcare-social-services-stable-jobs-after-coronavirus/12462670. Accessed 22 August 2020.

CHAPTER 2

Marketisation and Cash-for-Care

Introduction

Markets are now central to the provision of publicly-funded care in many OECD countries, with governments increasingly adopting market mechanisms in public care from the 1980s onwards. Marketisation processes have involved the privatisation of public care services in the pursuit of savings, often founded on a belief that competition will produce the best outcomes most efficiently. While governments remain the architects, regulators, managers and often primary funders of care systems and have significant control over their outcomes, there has been increased involvement of private capital in care markets.

Cash-for-care involves marketising care at the level of the individual care recipient or care 'consumer'. Cash-for-care schemes vary in their design and operation, but a key element of many schemes is the substitution of care services with a cash allocation or direct payment made to the individual citizen for them to purchase their own care in the market. Cash-for-care or individualised funding schemes are also referred to as consumer-directed care or self-directed support, reflecting the underlying idea that this type of scheme can empower service users by placing them in control of the services and supports they need for day-to-day living.

In this Chapter 1 explore some key ideas and touch on contemporary debates about marketised and individualised care to provide a context for the study of Australia's new National Disability Insurance

F. Macdonald, *Individualising Risk*,
https://doi.org/10.1007/978-981-33-6366-3_2

Scheme (NDIS). I draw on international research that has examined what cash-for-care schemes mean for the often low-paid frontline workers who provide personal support and care. Drawing also on contemporary employment and industrial relations scholarship I identify a framework for the investigation of how individualised care shapes care employment.

Care Goes to Market

Drawn from ideas from comparative welfare state analyses, Razavi's (2007) notion of a four-pointed 'care diamond' is helpful in conceptualising the broad institutional architecture through which care is provided. Each of the points on the care diamond represents one of the four main institutions responsible for care provision, with these being (i) the state, (ii) the market, (iii) the family/household and (iv) the not-for-profit sector (including voluntary and community provision). The simple care diamond typology does not account for all possible configurations of care. However, it does direct our attention to the institutional sites of care provision critical in determining who gets care, who pays for care, who provides care and the circumstances and structural conditions of their labour.

Commencing in the 1980s, the role of markets in long-term care has continually expanded to the point where they are now central to care provision in many countries (Brennan et al. 2012, Marczak and Wistow 2016). In some cases, this has occurred as care provision has moved from the family to the market; however, it has also occurred as a result of care provision moving from the public service and not-for-profit charitable or voluntary sector to the market. Australia's new individualised funding scheme for support and care for people with disability reallocates responsibility for the provision of this social care from the public and not-for-profit sectors to the market. The NDIS also expands public funding for disability care and support, providing funds to some people who had not previously had access to government-funded support, and in doing so, potentially reallocates some care provision from the family to the market.

The term 'marketisation' has been broadly used as interchangeable with 'commodification' to describe the processes by which 'care as unpaid labor and as a "use value" has been gradually turned into a commodity following market rules' (Farris and Marchetti 2017, p. 110). A more specific use of the term describes marketisation as *actions taken by governments* to expand the role of markets in care provision. Adopting the latter approach, I take marketisation to refer to the introduction of 'government measures that authorise, support or enforce the introduction of markets, the creation of relationships between buyers and sellers and the use of market mechanisms to allocate care' (Brennan et al. 2012, p. 379). This includes 'processes through which policymakers shift ownership, provision, financing and/or regulation' from the public to the private (for-profit or not-for-profit) sector (Meagher & Goodwin 2015, p. 4).

As implied by this definition, the role of government is critical in locating and shaping care provision, as it is governments that make many of the decisions about their own and other institutions' roles and responsibilities. Governments design welfare and other social policies—including policies that shape unpaid care—they establish regulatory frameworks, and they are usually the main funder of paid care (Colombo et al. 2011). They create, fund and regulate 'public service markets' (also referred to as managed markets and quasi-markets) to fulfil a public purpose such as providing care (Carey et al. 2018).

Markets have been promoted as a solution to the problems of meeting growing needs for care and other social services since the 1970s, a time when capitalist welfare states also began looking for ways to reduce public expenditure (Le Grand 1991). The marketisation of care is also a part of broader liberalisation and globalisation policies (Fine and Davidson 2018, Gingrich 2011). However, care marketisation has taken different forms in different countries and, within countries, it has taken different forms in different care contexts (e.g. childcare compared to disability support or elder care).

Often, care and other public services are marketised via the introduction of market mechanisms and ideas *within* the public sector, termed 'new public management' (Hood 1991). In addition, public services can be marketised by outsourcing and contracting care provision to private for profit and/or not-for-profit service providers. Marketised individualised care entails direct payments from the state to individuals for them to purchase their care directly in a market. In each of these situations, it is possible to have different mixes of public and private funding. For example, individual care users may pay fees to access public care services or may purchase care with a combination of their own money and public funds, and not-for-profit service providers may use privately-raised funds to supplement publicly-funded services (Marczak and Wistow 2016; Meagher and Goodwin 2015).

Marketisation of social care services for people with disability and the aged has taken a variety of forms. Historically, in most countries where there has been welfare state provision of social care for people with disability and older people, care has been provided through in-kind services delivered by public agencies, or by the not-for-profit sector. However, since the 1990s, there has been growing use of individualised funding or cash-for-care schemes (Colombo et al. 2011). Marketised approaches to care have been adopted by countries usually considered to be quite different from each other in their degree of market orientation, including schemes involving cash payments or vouchers—the most individualised forms of marketised care (Arksey and Kemp 2008).

Market mechanisms are used for the provision of care to both children and adults, and widespread marketisation of childcare has taken place, especially in the liberal welfare regimes of Australia, Canada, New Zealand, the UK and the USA (Gallagher 2018, see also Brennan et al. 2012). Pressures for marketisation of childcare are apparent in other countries as well, including in the Nordic states, where, for example, both Finland and Sweden have introduced market reforms (Mahon et al. 2012).

The ideas and ideologies behind marketisation are complex and, across care systems, diverse policy objectives and rationales drive marketisation strategies. Nevertheless, some common discourses underpin the marketisation of care and other public services in many countries (Anttonen and Meagher 2013; Brennan et al. 2012; Martinelli et al. 2017). Inspiring most marketisation policies is a neoliberal conviction in market-based competition between service providers as the best means to enhance efficiency, service responsiveness and quality. According to this logic, under the discipline of the market, competition drives costs down to the benefit of service users, efficient and effective service providers are rewarded with profit, and inefficient and low-quality service providers fail and leave the market. This reasoning has it that reduced (or no) provision by the state is necessary to gain the full benefits of the market, and it is often underpinned by a critique of government paternalism (Brennan et al. 2012, Le Grand 1991).

Observers and analysts critical of market-based approaches to care and other publicly-funded social services have argued that they promote individualism over community collective action; bolster private interests while undermining public ownership, space and capacity; weaken public accountability and privatise citizenship (Fine and Davidson 2018,

Needham 2003, Whitfield 2015, Yu and Oliver 2015). Evidence exists that markets can cement inequities, with disadvantaged groups having poor outcomes (O'Sullivan and Considine 2015). In care markets, poor quality care and market failures have been linked to the dominance of for-profit providers (Cabin et al. 2014, Meagher and Cortis 2008, Meagher and Szebehely 2013, Sumsion 2012). However, Meagher and Cortis (2008, p.11) note there is some evidence pointing to the character of contracts and regulation as possibly more important influences on the organisational behaviour of care providers than whether the organisation is for-profit or not-for-profit. Overall, the literature highlights the importance of taking account of structure, politics, implementation and management of marketised care systems, along with other aspects of the welfare states within which care systems exist, to understand how particular outcomes are produced.

Individualised Funding, Care Consumers and Cost Containment

Associated with a belief in market mechanisms as the best way to provide care and other social services is an ideology of consumerism. From this perspective the exercise of choice by individuals—as consumers—is seen as an intrinsic good (Glendinning 2008). Policies offer choice by using market mechanisms that are intended to personalise or individualise services to meet the unique needs and circumstances of individual care users, with these needs and circumstances reframed as the unique demands of individual service *consumers* (Clarke 2006, Le Grand 1991). Some advocates of consumerism in public (or publicly funded) services see it as offering a pathway to active citizenship through enabling people to become 'co-producers' of services. Co-production is also assumed to result in effective services because people are involved in producing 'the public goods they value' (Leadbeater 2004, p. 7). Individualised funding has been promoted as a market-based approach that provides the means for a more person-centred approach, entailing choice and control over care and support.

People with disability have been strong advocates of individualised funding for care and support. Across Europe and North America many individualised funding programmes have their roots in the independent living movement originating in the 1960s in the USA in California and led by people with physical disability (Glasby and Littlechild 2016, Morris

1993, see also Boris and Klein 2012, pp. 97–104), as well as being linked to other campaigns for social inclusion for people with intellectual disability (Needham 2011, p. 67). Choice and control over supports has been seen as central to citizenship, social inclusion and human rights (Morris 1993, 2006); these claims have been recognised internationally in the 2007 United Nations Convention on the Rights of Persons with Disabilities (Power 2014). Thus, there is a convergence in policy themes around discourses of choice and control linked to inclusion and empowerment, and discourses of the market and consumerism.

Individualised funding has been viewed as a way for governments to contain care costs, with this achieved partly through reducing institutional care. In the context of increased demand for care, arising from ageing populations, women's increased labour force participation and increasing care costs, a shift from residential institutions to home-based care for aged people (those aged 65 years and over) has been a common aspect of long-term social care reforms in many countries (Gori et al. 2016). For governments, individualised funding also reduces the transaction costs associated with care provision as a result of reduced bureaucracy and labour overheads. Related to this, cost minimisation may also be achieved by paying individuals less than the full costs of care, including where it is assumed that family carers will provide care for less than the cost of care in the market (Arksey and Kemp 2008).

Some cash-for-care schemes have been established where there has previously been little or no state provision or support for care. In these cases, rationales for individualised funding can include recognising and supporting informal carers (Ungerson and Yeandle 2007). While some schemes can reduce women's unpaid care work and facilitate their participation in paid work outside the home, others reinforce familial care through paying family carers (Da Roit and Le Bihan 2010, Pavolini and Ranci 2008).

Among wealthy nations moves to use cash transfers for care began in the 1980s, with the introduction of individualised funding, with policies providing for personalisation or self-directed support emerging in the 1990s. Some funding programmes that fall under the 'cash-for-care' banner were designed primarily as income support schemes for unpaid family carers. The present study is primarily concerned with cash-for-care as personalised or self-directed support schemes. These schemes direct individualised funding to people with disability and other care users to enable them to purchase their own supports as an alternative to service provision by the state (Alakeson 2016). While these schemes have been in place for some time now there is a very limited knowledge of their implications (Carey and Dickinson 2017).

Cash-for-care schemes for long-term care and support for people with disability and/or older people (social care) have been implemented in many OECD countries including Austria, Belgium, Canada, France, Finland, Germany, the Netherlands, Italy, New Zealand, Sweden, the United Kingdom (UK) and the United States (USA) (Alakeson 2016, Dickinson 2017, Fleming et al. 2019). Considerable variation exists in individualised funding arrangements, even though schemes often have similar aims to empower consumers and achieve some degree of cost containment. Alakeson (2016) distinguishes between two types of individualised funding models, the first where cash payments are made to individuals for their care with few or no rules around how the money can be spent and the second—more common today—where the individual payment is linked to a personalised plan that specifies or limits the supports and services which can be purchased.

This distinction is included in a longer list of key variations in individualised funding models summarised by Cortis et al. (2013, pp. 10–11), as follows:

> Models have differed significantly in terms of their aims and structure, and the context in which they were introduced. Models have different rules about who is eligible; who can hold and manage the funds; the forms of support that funding can be used for; how providers are regulated; whether and under what conditions recipients can directly employ staff; whether they can purchase services from family members; and the role of intermediary organisations in managing funds and/or giving support and advice to users (Council of Australian Governments [COAG] 2011; Fisher et al. 2010). Models also differ in terms of the existence and extent of workforce planning and development in the broader policy framework (and) the adequacy of individualised payments the extent to which the size of payments enable recipients to fully meet their needs.

The differences in models can lead to distinct differences in how schemes operate, making comparison and evaluation of individualised funding arrangements difficult. As Dickinson (2017) observes, a further challenge for assessing the efficacy of individualised funding schemes is that multiple, often conflicting, ideas exist about what they should deliver. However, there are some common claims for the schemes, which are that they save money and improve 'customer satisfaction and outcomes' (Dickinson 2017, p. 6). Assessing the international experience against the common claims, Dickinson (2017) finds there is a lack of good quality evidence for both the efficacy and effectiveness of individualised funding schemes. Other recent reviews of the international experience generally share this conclusion (Alakeson 2016, Fleming et al. 2019, Webber et al. 2014). Echoing an earlier observation made by Needham (2011) in regard to personalisation (i.e. individualised funding) in the UK, Dickinson (2017, p. 3) has noted there are some problems with the quality of the international evidence, including 'because the majority of the literature concerning individual funding systems has an intrinsically positive hue'.

In relation to equity and broader social impacts of individualised funding schemes, conclusions from a recent meta-review of the evidence on these schemes and inequality included that 'there is good reason to suspect that personalisation schemes are entrenching social inequity' (Carey et al. 2019, p. 180). Drawing on earlier evidence from a five-country study, Ungerson and Yeandle (2007) identified several issues for the sustainability of individualised funding schemes for long-term care. Concerns related to quality of care, payment of relatives, the employment of undocumented migrant workers and that cost containment objectives are achieved through keeping the costs of care labour very low.

The international evidence pertaining to how social care workers fare in individualised schemes is sparse but growing. Before turning to consider that body of work, in the next section I develop a broad conceptual framework for my investigation of social care work in the new disability support system in Australia. Drawing in particular on the work of Williams (2012) I identify the specific institutional factors that are likely to shape paid care work in cash-for-care schemes.

Intersecting Regimes, Segmented Labour Markets and Individualised Care

While the care diamond mentioned above locates care according to the four main institutions that can be involved in its provision, more detailed analyses at different levels and across a broader range of institutional structures and processes are necessary to understand how care work and employment are shaped in marketised care systems and in individualised funding schemes.

Scholarship has drawn on multiple theoretical traditions to understand how paid care work is influenced by, and located within, societal structures of inequality. In the discussion of why social care work matters in Chapter 1, I drew on scholarship from feminist socioeconomics to show how the connections between unpaid work and paid work are critical to the quality of paid care jobs, including through gendered undervaluation of care work. Comparative institutional approaches have also informed scholarship on care work (Brennan et al. 2012, Michel and Peng 2017, Williams 2012). These approaches are based on an understanding of labour markets as socially constructed—unlike neoclassical economic—approaches to work and employment—and a key strength is that they bring a broad range of institutions and actors into the analysis. For example, a comparative institutionalist approach brings into focus the connections and interactions between social policy and care regulation on the one hand, and employment and labour market policy and regulation on the other, to understand how care work and employment are shaped and located in relation to the production of inequalities through work. I draw on insights from both feminist socioeconomics and comparative institutionalist theoretical traditions in this book as well as on a third theoretical approach; labour market segmentation theory.

Neo-classical economics depicted the labour market as a single competitive market with divisions based on human capital availability or productivity differences; labour market segmentation theory was developed over the 1970s and 1980s as a refutation of this approach (Doeringer and Piore 1971, Gordon et al. 1982). Contemporary formulations of labour market segmentation theory (Grimshaw et al. 2017, Rubery 2007) see labour market divisions and inequalities as the result of multiple institutional and social forces, with labour markets understood to be socially regulated by diverse forms of regulation ranging from formal labour laws to informal work norms (Peck 1996). An important and key feature of a labour market segmentation approach is a focus on power relations and employer choices in the shaping of employment outcomes. As Grimshaw et al. (2017, p. 3) explain, according to this approach:

> Inequalities are not fostered only on the supply side through exogenous societal or cultural rules and conventions but also, and perhaps predominantly, through formal and informal institutionalised policies and practices in labour markets and workplaces.

Drawing on insights from the three theoretical traditions of feminist socio-economics, comparative institutionalist approaches and labour segmentation theory, the approach I take to the investigation of care and support work in this book broadly aligns with what Grimshaw and colleagues (2017) refer to as a 'new labour market segmentation approach'. This is a multi-dimensional approach to understanding inequalities in work and employment that recognises the important roles and interactions of a broad range of policy reforms and employer strategies and practices in creating and addressing inequalities, precarious work, gendered wage gaps and labour market exclusions. It is particularly suited to my project of building knowledge of how social policy interacts with labour market and employment regulation and employer choices and actions to shape employment in a new individualised care market.

My approach draws on the work of Fiona Williams on intersecting care, migration and employment regimes. In the context of undertaking international comparative research on migrant care work and attempting to develop links between different levels of analysis, Williams (2012) adopted the idea of regimes to analyse the meso-level of societal or national institutional factors that shape the micro-level of day-to-day care relationships. Her analysis also included a macro-level of processes that contribute to the transnational political economy of care. Based on findings from comparative empirical studies of migrant care work, Williams proposed that migrant care work and employment are shaped at the intersections of three regimes of care, employment and migration that exist at the meso-level within a country. A regime is conceptualised as including 'the political, cultural, ideational and relational' and is comprised of 'clusters of policies, practices, legacies, discourses, social relations and forms of contestation' (Williams 2012, p. 371).

From her empirical studies, Williams identified indicators, or the specific aspects of the three types of regimes important for showing how it is at the intersections of the regimes that practices and actions are shaped and variations in care work and migration emerge across countries. I draw from Williams' regime indicators to develop an adapted set of indicators to guide my analysis of paid care work in the Australian labour market and individualised funding scheme. My approach does not include a focus on the transnational macro-level nor does it highlight the migration regime. Australia's migration regime has been growing in significance for care work, with growth in temporary non-resident migration visas for students and working holiday makers and others who fill low-paid jobs over the last decade (Brennan et al. 2017). Proposals have also been put forward for temporary migration schemes for people from Pacific Island states to undertake care work (Curtain et al. 2016). However, to date, in the implementation of the NDIS, there is no evidence to indicate the migration regime has played a strongly defining role in shaping care work in the disability support sector.

My main adaptation of Williams' list of indicators is to incorporate insights identified by Grimshaw et al. (2017) as underpinning their new labour market segmentation approach. Much overlap can be found between the two approaches, but the latter brings into the meso-level analysis a stronger focus on market actors' business and employment strategies and practices. Institutional factors, such as pricing of care by the care authority, influence the shape of the market, and the strategies of market actors, and thus influence the nature of employment arrangements. Business and employment strategies and practices and labour process conditions are not, however, pre-determined by these factors.

Market actors can, in addition, respond to shape market conditions (Grimshaw et al. 2018). This possibility may be particularly important in a new market such as Australia's NDIS care and support market. The new publicly-funded market has attracted new service provider organisations and other new market actors, including 'gig economy' digital care labour platforms, and other labour and care brokers. The adapted set of indicators I use as my guide for the exploration of meso-level institutional influences on care work and employment in the new Australian individualised care scheme is set out here:

The Care Regime

- The regulation of care provision.
- The regulation of care work
- The sectors from which commodified care is provided (public, private, voluntary/not-for-profit).
- The level and forms of individualised funding and conditions for receipt and use of funding.
- Occupational sex segregation (including feminised part-time work) and the gendered and racialised basis of the care workforce, its hierarchies of skills and the relationship of these to remuneration (including gendered undervaluation).

- The history of care policies and the gendered relational practices of care/domestic work in the home.
- Political negotiation and struggle at national and local policy-making levels involving, for example, trade unions, disability and carers' movements.

The Employment (and Migration) Regimes, Market Structures and Organisation and Employer Strategies and Practices

- Existing labour market divisions and their exclusions and hierarchies (i.e. by gender, ethnicity, migration and nationality).
- The impact of (de)regulation in shaping precarious employment in the care labour market.
- How far forms of social protection are extended to care workers.
- The forms of worker political mobilisation. Relevant immigration policies and practices and historical treatment of migrant labour.
- Employers' employment and pay strategies and their strategies in relation to workers' collective representation (including divide and rule strategies). Employers' investment in skill and technologies.
- Labour market intermediaries and their strategies in relation to workers.

*Adapted from Williams (*2012*, p. 327), drawing on Grimshaw* et al. *2017 (Table 1.1, pp. 5–7) and Ungerson (*2004*, p. 191).*

Two aspects of the care regime and one aspect of the employment regime appear to be particularly important in producing variations in outcomes for frontline social workers in cash-for-care schemes. In the discussion below I draw on the growing body of international research into cash-for-care schemes to identify, in the care regime: (i) the level and forms of individualised funding and conditions for receipt and use of funding; and (ii) the extent to which cost containment underpins the individualised scheme; and, in the employment regime: (iii) the regulation of care work, as critical.

How Do Workers Fare in Cash-for-Care?

In the 1990s, as individualised funding schemes were being adopted in various countries, Ungerson (1997, 1999) observed that these schemes attached cash to formerly unpaid care in a way that was leading to the development of hybrid forms of 'work' and 'care'. Ungerson described a breakdown of the boundaries between unpaid care and paid care work in individualised funding schemes whereby 'the cash nexus enters the care relationship in the domestic domain and the nexus of affect enters and permeates the work relationship' (Ungerson 2004, p. 189).

Ungerson mapped the different ways care work was organised in the individualised care schemes of five European countries she studied. She found that outcomes for care workers, and for informal/family carers, varied with two major aspects of individualised funding arrangements: *regulation* and *the type of care relationship*. Here, regulation refers to the regulation of care delivery and the extent to which care work is construed and regulated as 'work' within the care scheme. The type of care relationship refers to the extent that care work in an individualised funding scheme can be organised like informal care, in which the care relationship is 'based on kinship and affect rather than contract' (including with family members providing the care) or, alternatively, care is organised in paid work relationships based on contract (Ungerson 2004, p. 192).

According to Ungerson (2004), individualised funding schemes produced very different outcomes for both paid care workers and family care givers, depending on the extent of care regulation and whether the care relationship is constructed and treated as care or work. The *labour market* was an additional crucial determinant of who cares and the conditions under which they care. For example, in a care system in which the care work is treated and regulated as 'work', it was likely that care workers (i) were recruited from the labour market (as opposed to being recruited from informal networks), (ii) were employed in formal employment arrangements with contracts and regular working time (as opposed to being in relationships based on family obligation and being available 24/7) and (iii) that their employment was subject to the same rights and protections as other employees.

In such systems, care delivery was regulated, for example, through occupational standards and qualifications requirements and registration of service providers (Ungerson 2004, pp. 192–193). Conversely, where care work was not construed and regulated like other paid work, and care workers were recruited through informal networks, their employment was likely to be outside the boundaries of regulated employment. Aspects of the migration regime were also important, as the presence of insecure migrant workers was a contributing factor where unregulated care work was undertaken as low-paid work in an informal economy by vulnerable workers, rather than as 'care' by carers in individuals' informal networks.

The significance of Ungerson's work is that it brings into sharp focus two key aspects of individualised funding schemes that differentiate them from most other kinds of publicly-funded care schemes. These two key aspects also differentiate individualised funding schemes from each other in the outcomes they can produce for care workers. These aspects of schemes are: first, *the extent to which care work is constructed and treated as work*, and second, *the extent to which the work is undertaken within the domain of family and friends' networks* (i.e. the type of care relationships).

Subsequent cross-national research into individualised funding systems has produced consistent findings and identified a third factor: *the extent to which cost containment underpins the individualised scheme*, as an interacting aspect of individualised care systems that is also very important for shaping outcomes for paid care workers (Da Roit and Le Bihan 2010, Rummery 2009, Ungerson and Yeandle 2007). A growing body of international evidence attests to the fact that the three aspects of individualised care systems can be decisive in shaping work and employment for care workers, including in affecting how these workers are positioned in relation to formal systems of employment regulation, and how they are able to benefit from them. Systems of direct payments to individuals to purchase their care push care work and workers out of the public sector and out of formal employment arrangements. Where family members can be paid to provide care, the work becomes harder to distinguish from unpaid care in families and recognition and treatment of it as skilled work is undermined (Knijn and Verhagen 2007). These informalising pressures of direct payments overlay long-standing problems of lack of recognition of care work where this work is located in private homes.

This examination of the international literature provides a broad basis for investigating the new Australian individualised care and support system, the NDIS. My examination of individualised social care in England and the debates about individualisation in the UK in the next chapter provide for a more in-depth look at individualised funding in theory and in practice. It also provides an opportunity for a closer examination of what is known about what this social care policy means for social care workers. Many of the ideas underpinning Australia's NDIS are those central to individualised care funding implemented in the UK under the banner of personalisation. The designers of the NDIS drew heavily on both the ideas and the experience of individualised funding in adult social care in England (Productivity Commission 2011, van Toorn 2018), in what they have claimed was a strong evidence-based policy process (Banks 2018).

References

Alakeson, V. (2016). Self-direction in long-term services and supports: International differences and current challenges. *Public Policy & Aging Report, 26*(4), 143–148. https://doi.org/10.1093/ppar/prw018.

Anttonen, A., & Meagher, G. (2013). Mapping marketisation: Concepts and goals. In G. Meagher, & M. Szebehely (Eds.), *Reforms in long-term care policies in Europe: Investigating institutional change and social impacts* (pp. 13–22). https://doi.org/10.1007/978-1-4614-4502-9_3.

Arksey, H., & Kemp, P. A. (2008). Dimensions of choice: a narrative review of cash-for-care schemes [Working Paper]. York: Citeseer. http://www.york.ac.uk/inst/spru/research/pdf/CashReview.pdf. Accessed 18 February 2020.

Banks, G. (2018, November 30). Whatever happened to 'evidence-based policymaking'? *The Mandarin*. https://www.themandarin.com.au/102083-whatever-happened-to-evidence-based-policymaking/. Accessed 1 November 2019.

Boris, E., & Klein, J. (2012). *Caring for America. Home health workers in the shadow of the welfare state*. New York: Oxford University Press.

Brennan, D., Cass, B., Himmelweit, S., & Szebehely, M. (2012). The marketisation of care: rationales and consequences in Nordic and liberal care regimes. *Journal of European Social Policy, 22*(4), 377–391. https://doi.org/10.1177/0958928712449772.

Brennan, D., Charlesworth, S., Adamson, E., & Cortis, N. (2017). Out of kilter: Changing care, migration and employment regimes in Australia. In S. Michel, & I. Peng (Eds.), *Gender, migration, and the work of care. A multi-scalar approach to the Pacific rim* (pp. 143–165). New York: Palgrave Macmillan.

Cabin, W., Himmelstein, D. U., Siman, M. L., & Woolhandler, S. (2014). For-profit medicare home health agencies' costs appear higher and quality appears lower compared to nonprofit agencies. *Health Affairs*, 13. https://doi.org/10.1377/hlthaff.2014.0307.

Carey, G., Dickinson, H., Malbon, E., & Reeders, D. (2018). The vexed question of market stewardship in the public sector: examining equity and the social contract through the Australian National Disability Insurance Scheme. *Social Policy & Administration, 52*(1), 387–407. https://doi.org/10.1111/spol.12321.

Carey, G., Crammond, B., & Malbon, E. (2019). Personalisation schemes in social care and inequality: Review of the evidence and early theorising. *International Journal for Equity in Health, 18*(1), 170–180. https://doi.org/10.1186/s12939-019-1075-2.

Clarke, J. (2006). Consumers, clients or citizens? Politics, policy and practice in the reform of social care. *European Societies, 8*(3), 423–442. https://doi.org/10.1080/14616690600821966.

Colombo, F., Ana, L., Jérôme, M., & Frits, T. (2011). *Help wanted? Providing and paying for long-term care*. Paris: OECD Publishing.

Cortis, N., Meagher, G., Chan, S., Davidson, B., & Fattore, T. (2013). Building an industry of choice: Service quality, workforce capacity and consumer-centred funding in disability care. *Social Policy Research Centre Report Series*. Social Policy Research Centre, University of New South Wales.

Council of Australian Governments. (2011). *National Disability Strategy 2010–2020*. Canberra: Commonwealth of Australia.

Curtain, R., Dornan, M., Doyle, J., & Howes, S. (2016). *Pacific Possible. Labour mobility: the ten billion dollar prize*. Canberra: Australian National University and the World Bank.

Da Roit, B., & Le Bihan, B. (2010). Similar and yet so different: cash-for-care in six European countries' long-term care policies. *Milbank Quarterly, 88*(3), 286–309. https://doi.org/10.1111/j.1468-0009.2010.00601.x.

Dickinson, H. (2017). Individual funding systems: What works? *Evidence Base, 3*(3), 1–18. https://doi.org/10.21307/eb-2017-003.

Doeringer, P. B., & Piore, M. J. (1971). *Internal labor markets and manpower analysis*. Lexington, Mass.: Heath.

Farris, S. R., & Marchetti, S. (2017). From the commodification to the corporatization of care: European perspectives and debates. *Social Politics: International Studies in Gender, State & Society, 24*(2), 109–131. https://doi.org/10.1093/sp/jxx003.

Fine, M., & Davidson, B. (2018). The marketization of care: Global challenges and national responses in Australia. *Current Sociology, 66*(4), 503–516. https://doi.org/10.1177/0011392118765281.

Fisher, K. R., Edwards, R., Gleeson, R., Purcal, C., Sitek, T., Dinning, B., et al. (2010). Effectiveness of individual funding approaches for disability support. Research and Analysis Branch: Australian Government Department of Families, Housing, Community Services and Indigenous Affairs Occasional Paper no. 29. Canberra: Commonwealth of Australia.

Fleming, P., McGilloway, S., Hernon, M., Furlong, M., O'Doherty, S., Keogh, F., et al. (2019). Individualised funding interventions to improve health and social care outcomes for people with a disability: a mixed-methods systematic review. *A Campbell Systematic Review 2019:3*. Oslo: Campbell Collaboration.

Gallagher, A. (2018). The business of care: Marketization and the new geographies of childcare. *Progress in Human Geography, 42*(5), 706–722. https://doi.org/10.1177/0309132517702970.

Gingrich, J. (2011). *Making Markets in the Welfare State*. Cambridge: Cambridge University Press.

Glasby, J., & Littlechild, R. (2016). *Direct payments and personal budgets: putting personalisation into practice*. Bristol: The Policy Press.

Glendinning, C. (2008). Increasing choice and control for older and disabled people: A critical review of new developments in England. *Social Policy & Administration, 42*(5), 451–469. https://doi.org/10.1111/j.1467-9515.2008.00617.x.

Gordon, D. M., Edwards, R. C., & Reich, M. (1982). *Segmented work, divided workers: The historical transformation of labor in the United States*. Cambridge: Cambridge University Press.

Gori, C., Fernandez, J.-L., & Wittenberg, R. (2016). *Long-term care reforms in OECD countries*. Policy Press.

Grimshaw, D., Fagan, C., Hebson, G., & Tavora, I. (2017a). A new labour market segmentation approach for analysing inequalities: Introduction and overview. In D. Grimshaw, C. Fagan, G. Hebson, & I. Tavora (Eds.), *Making work more equal: A new labour market segmentation approach* (pp. 1–32). Manchester, England: Manchester University Press.

Grimshaw, D., Fagan, C., Hebson, G., Tavora, I., & Rubery, J. (2017b). *Making work more equal: A new labour market segmentation approach*. Manchester, England: Manchester University Press.

Grimshaw, D., Cartwright, J., Keizer, A., & Rubery, J. (2018). Market exposure and the labour process: The contradictory dynamics in managing subcontracted services work. *Work, Employment & Society, 33*(1), 76–95. https://doi.org/10.1177/0950017018759206.

Hood, C. (1991). A public management for all seasons? *Public Administration, 69*(1), 3–19. https://doi.org/10.1111/j.1467-9299.1991.tb00779.x.

Knijn, T., & Verhagen, S. (2007). Contested professionalism: Payments for care and the quality of home care. *Administration & Society, 39*(4), 451–475. https://doi.org/10.1177/0095399707300520.

Leadbeater, C. (2004). *Personalisation through participation: A new script for public services*. London: Demos.

Le Grand, J. (1991). Quasi-markets and social policy. *The Economic Journal, 101*(408), 1256–1267.

Mahon, R., Anttonen, A., Bergqvist, C., Brennan, D., & Hobson, B. (2012). Convergent care regimes? Childcare arrangements in Australia, Canada, Finland and Sweden. *Journal of European Social Policy, 22*(4), 419–431. https://doi.org/10.1177/0958928712449776.

Marczak, J., & Wistow, G. (2016). Commissioning long-term care services. In C. Gori, J.-L. Fernandez, & R. Wittenberg (Eds.), *Long-term care reforms in OECD countries* (pp. 117–142). Bristol: Policy Press.

Martinelli, F., Anttonen, A., & Mätzke, M. (2017). *Social services disrupted: Changes, challenges and policy implications for Europe in times of austerity*. Northampton, MA: Edward Elgar Publishing.

Meagher, G., & Cortis, N. (2008). The political economy of for-profit paid care: Theory and evidence. In D. King & G. Meagher (Eds.), *Paid care in Australia: Profits, purpose, practices* (pp. 13–42). Sydney: Sydney University Press.

Meagher, G., & Goodwin, S. (2015). Introduction: Capturing marketisation in Australian social policy. In G. Meagher & S. Goodwin (Eds.), *Markets, rights and power in Australian social policy* (pp. 1–27). Sydney: Sydney University Press.

Meagher, G., & Szebehely, M. (Eds.). (2013). *Marketisation in Nordic eldercare: A research report on legislation, oversight, extent and consequences*. Sweden: Department of Social Work, Stockholm University.

Michel, S., & Peng, I. (2017). *Gender, migration, and the work of care. A multi-scalar approach to the Pacific Rim*. New York: Palgrave Macmillan.

Morris, J. (1993). *Independent lives? Community care and disabled people*. Basingstoke: Macmillan.

Morris, J. (2006). Independent living: The role of the disability movement in the development of government policy. In C. Glendinning & P. A. Kemp (Eds.), *Cash and Care: Policy Challenges in the Welfare State* (pp. 235–248). Bristol: The Policy Press.

Needham, C. (2003). *Citizen-consumers: New labour's marketplace democracy*. London: Catalyst.

Needham, C. (2011). Personalization: From story-line to practice. *Social Policy & Administration, 45*(1), 54–68. https://doi.org/10.1111/j.1467-9515.2010.00753.x.

O'Sullivan, S., & Considine, M. (2015). *Contracting-out welfare services: Comparing national policy designs for unemployment assistance*. London: Wiley-Blackwell.

Pavolini, E., & Ranci, C. (2008). Restructuring the welfare state: Reforms in long-term care in Western European countries. *Journal of European Social Policy, 18*(3), 246–259. https://doi.org/10.1177/0958928708091058.

Peck, J. (1996). *Work-place: The social regulation of labor markets*. New York: Guilford Press.

Power, A. (2014). Personalisation and austerity in the crosshairs: Government perspectives on the remaking of adult social care. *Journal of Social Policy, 43*(4), 829–846. https://doi.org/10.1017/S0047279414000373.

Productivity Commission Report no. 54 (2011). Disability Care and Support. 31 July 2011. Canberra: Productivity Commission. https://www.pc.gov.au/inquiries/completed/disability-support/report/disability-support-volume1.pdf. Accessed: 21 Nov 2019.

Razavi, S. (2007) The political and social economy of care in a development context. Conceptual issues, research questions and policy options. *Gender and Development Programme Paper*. Geneva: United Nations Research Institute for Social Development.

Rubery, J. (2007). Developing segmentation theory: A thirty year perspective. *Économies et Sociétés, 28*(6), 941–964.

Rummery, K. (2009). A comparative discussion of the gendered implications of cash-for-care schemes: Markets, independence and social citizenship in crisis? *Social Policy & Administration, 43*(6), 634–648. http://doi.org/10.1111/j.1467-9515.2009.00685.x.

Sumsion, J. (2012). ABC Learning and Australian early education and care: A retrospective ethical audit of a radical experiment. In E. Lloyd & H. Penn (Eds.), *Childcare markets: Can they deliver an equitable service?* (pp. 209–223). Bristol: The Policy Press.

Ungerson, C. (1997). Social politics and the commodification of care. *Social politics, 4*(3), 362–381. https://doi.org/10.1093/sp/4.3.362.

Ungerson, C. (1999). Personal assistants and disabled people: An examination of a hybrid form of work and care. *Work, Employment & Society, 13*(4), 583–600. https://doi.org/10.1177/09500179922118132.

Ungerson, C. (2004). Whose empowerment and independence? A cross-national perspective on cash for care schemes. *Ageing & Society, 24*(2), 189–212. https://doi.org/10.1017/S0144686X03001508.

Ungerson, C., & Yeandle, S. (2007). *Cash for care in developed welfare states*. Gordonsville, USA: Palgrave Macmillan.

Van Toorn, G. (2018). *The new political economy of disability: Transnational networks and individualised funding in the age of neoliberalism.* Doctoral dissertation, University of New South Wales and University of Glasgow.

Webber, M., Treacy, S., Carr, S., Clark, M., & Parker, G. (2014). The effectiveness of personal budgets for people with mental health problems: A systematic review. *Journal of Mental Health, 23*(3), 146–155. https://doi.org/10.3109/09638237.2014.910642.

Whitfield, D. (2015) The new health and social care economy. Bootle, UK: European Services Strategy Unit. https://www.european-services-strategy.org.uk/publications/public-bodies/health-and-social-care/the-new-health-and-social-care-economy-dexte. Accessed 12 June 2020.

Williams, F. (2012). Converging variations in migrant care work in Europe. *Journal of European Social Policy, 22*(4), 363–376. https://doi.org/10.1177/0958928712449771.

Yu, S., & Oliver, D. (2015). *The capture of public wealth by the for-profit VET sector*. Sydney: Workplace Research Centre, University of Sydney.

CHAPTER 3

Perspectives on Personalisation and the English Social Care Experience

Introduction

England's social care system has provided for individualised care and support funding, including through direct payments to individuals, for some twenty years. Over this period the job insecurity, poor working conditions and low pay of the frontline care and support workforce have received increasing attention. Historically, problems for frontline care workers have mostly been linked to ongoing austerity funding (Pearson and Ridley 2017). However, in debates about *the idea* of social care individualisation—known as personalisation in the UK—and the *design* of personalised social care, impacts on workers do receive some attention. These debates highlight tensions and ambiguities in the rationales for individualised funding policies that are highly germane to Australia's new individualised care and support system. Along with knowledge gained from experience of individualised social care in England, critiques and debates about personalisation provide strong reference points for embarking on an appraisal of Australia's new cash-for-care approach. They highlight some of the problems and ambiguities underlying the individualised approach. The English experience highlights some limitations of the evidence base relating to outcomes of cash-for-care systems while providing some indications of the potential of contemporary systems for re-shaping care work and employment.

F. Macdonald, *Individualising Risk*,
https://doi.org/10.1007/978-981-33-6366-3_3

Personalisation and Individualised Social Care in England

In 1996, the UK Government passed the *Community Care (Direct Payments) Act 1996* introducing direct payments for eligible people with a disability, allowing people to purchase their own services or directly employ a personal support worker (referred to in the UK as a personal assistant). Trials of direct payments for working-age adults were initiated, including an influential pilot of personal budgets by the In Control network. In Control was an important player in the early development of personalisation policies in the UK; their model of individualised funding is seen to be the basis for the personal funding allocations, or 'personal budgets', adopted as policy in England in the mid-2000s (Glasby and Littlechild 2016, pp. 71–73; Needham 2011a, p. 31). Van Toorn (2018) identifies advocacy by an offshoot of the group—In Control Australia—as key in driving policy thinking and the adoption of individualised funding in Australia.

In 2000 direct payments were extended to older people receiving home-based care services, although eligibility and take-up among the elderly has been very limited until recently. The *Health and Social Care Act 2001* made it compulsory for local authorities to offer people eligible for community care services the option of direct payments (Glasby and Littlechild 2016, p. 35). In 2007, New Labour's major policy paper *Putting People First*, heralded the 'transformation of adult social care' and set out the framework for the Government's 'commitment to independent living for all adults' (UK Government 2007, p. 1).

Putting People First introduced a 'personalised' system of social care. In this system individual 'personal budgets' were the primary mechanisms for enabling eligible people to obtain services tailored to their needs (Manthorpe et al. 2011). The full roll out of personal budgets occurred in 2010 and, a few years later, the *Care Act 2014* mandated that all eligible users of social care services should be offered a personal budget. The *Care Act 2014* had as a central aim to provide people with more choice and control over the services and supports necessary for their well-being. Other changes included extension of rights to family/unpaid carers, including the right to a personal budget of their own, and new duties placed on local authorities, including a duty to shape local care markets (Needham et al. 2018).

When introduced in the mid-2000s, the government promoted personalisation as:

> the process by which services are tailored to the needs and preferences of citizens. The overall vision is that the state should empower citizens to shape their own lives and services they receive (Cabinet Office 2007, cited by Ettelt et al. 2017).

However, in relation to social care, the meaning of personalisation has often been narrowed to the idea of individuals gaining choice and control over services through personal budgets, and especially through direct payments. While personal budgets were only one aspect of the various changes to social care, they became 'synonymous with personalisation for many commentators' (Needham and Glasby 2014b, p. 12).

In England, under the *Care Act 2014*, all people eligible for government-funded social care in the community received a personal funding allocation or personal budget which could be taken and managed in one of several ways: (i) as a direct cash payment to the individual for them to employ staff and/or purchase services; (ii) as a budget managed by the local government authority, with that authority contracting service providers; or (iii) as an 'individual service fund' managed by a service provider under contract to the local authority (Tomlinson and Livesey 2013, pp. 8–9). Similar systems of 'self-directed support', with some differences, were established elsewhere in the UK, including in Scotland under the *Social Care (Self-directed Support) (Scotland) Act 2013* (Manthorpe et al. 2015, Pearson and Ridley 2017).

Personalisation policies—along with outsourcing of social care services that had occurred in England over a longer period—were about marketising care, as well as empowering people. Implicit in the policies, and in the New Public Management initiatives that preceded them, was the idea that the market is the best and most efficient mechanism for providing care services that meet people's needs and preferences. Reflecting this, over a couple of decades, social care reforms have massively reduced public service provision of care (Needham and Glasby 2014b). In the 1980s, the public service provided most social care in England. Now, outsourced social care is mostly provided by private for-profit and not-for-profit services through a 'managed' or 'quasi' market in which the state is the market regulator (through the Care Quality Commission) and main funder. Under this regime, local government authorities have monopsony power as the major purchasers of services in their localities (Needham et al. 2018). As an indication of the extent to which social care has been marketised, in 2019 across England, there were 9,400 registered home care services (also referred to as domiciliary care services) with an estimated total workforce of 520,000. Only 19,000 (just under 3%) members of this workforce were employed by local government authorities, with the vast majority employed in the 'independent' sector (Skills for Care 2019a).

Across the UK, public policy expressions of the aims of personalisation have always included cost-efficiency as a strong theme (Pearson and Ridley 2017). When individual funding allocations for social care were implemented in the mid-2000s it was with an expectation of cost-neutrality. Personal budgets were to provide better value for money through providing better outcomes, rather than through increasing government outlays. Since then, government austerity programmes to reduce budget deficits have had severe impacts on the funding of personalised social care, especially in England (Pearson and Ridley 2017; see also Manthorpe et al. 2015).

Analysts and observers link the problems of insecurity, low pay and poor working conditions of frontline social care workers to ongoing austerity funding (Pearson & Ridley 2017). Beyond the dominant focus on the constraints of poor funding, there has been less attention paid to how personalisation *itself* might be affecting social care workers and the nature and quality of social care employment.

Personalisation Debates

> A good life is built from combining our connections, our capacities, our community resources and our personal control … We might say that this is the **essence of personalisation** – helping people to achieve everyday citizenship, helping people to use and develop their own real wealth and often working to overcome the obstacles created by a welfare system that frustrates these goals. (Duffy, 2011, p. 8)

The personalisation agenda pursued by UK governments from the mid-2000s is much broader than social care, with personalisation of public services proposed across areas including education, employment services, criminal justice, housing, children's services and health. Within this broad personalisation agenda, social care has been the key site of change. Ideas from social care have led innovations for achieving the government's vision (Barnes 2011). Yet, while it may have been 'the big new idea for public service reform' (Barnes 2011, p. 154), personalisation itself is ambiguous, including in the sphere of social care.

Simon Duffy, founder of In Control, describes personalisation as 'a banner term' for practical reforms, 'whose primary purpose is to increase the power and dignity of people using social care' (Duffy 2010, p. 202). Others suggest that, in social care discourses, personalisation is 'short-hand' for 'choice and control over aspects of daily life' (Needham et al. 2018, p. 48). Needham (2011a, p. 7) maintains that, rather than being a coherent idea or framing of policies, personalisation is best understood as a narrative of 'transformation based on the failure of older or alternative approaches'. She has put forward a cogent argument that 'ambiguity is a key element of what has made personalisation such a potent narrative for change' (Needham 2011a, p. 6).

The ambiguity of personalisation is evident in the considerable debates among UK-based academics, policymakers and stakeholders on the topic (Needham and Glasby 2014a). At the heart of some of these debates are perceived tensions between social justice and neoliberal aims of personalisation policy and approaches. A strong criticism of personalisation has been that it has acted as 'a mechanism for individualising, privatising and consumerising the welfare state' (Needham 2011a, p. 8). A related argument is that the social justice aims of providing for individual autonomy and empowerment have been subordinated to neoliberal aims (Beresford, 2011; Ferguson, 2012; Mladenov et al. 2015; Needham 2011b).

One aspect of these criticisms is that personalisation is part of a broader restructuring of the welfare state, involving a decline in collective responsibility and collective services provision. It has also been suggested that there is compatibility between the emancipatory and neoliberal aims of personalisation policies. As one observer has put it:

> (E)fforts for emancipation from patronising relationships and top-down expertise have been in tune with the neoliberal project of undermining an allegedly omnipotent state through market mechanisms. (Mladenov 2015, p. 452)

As implied in this observation, the broad aim of shifting power away from the state to the individual in a market entails a shift in power from service providers to the people who use the services. Personalisation promises a democratisation of choice and decision-making as it challenges ideas of professional expertise. This also has the effect of challenging the control of professionals over people with disability, and others who have been treated as passive recipients of care (Mladenov et al. 2015, p. 309; see also Beresford 2008, Spandler 2004). This has been another tension in personalisation, evident in discussions about the role of social workers as social care professionals (Glasby and Littlechild 2016).

While individual funding in the UK has varied origins, early experiments in Britain were not prompted by groups with pro-market motivations; rather, they were led by the disabled people's movement with a commitment to collectivist action. Individual funding was only one element of a model of user-led services, based on principles of peer support (van Toorn 2018). Arguably, the contemporary system of personalisation is far removed from these origins. Under-funded services are now outsourced to the private (not-for-profit and for-profit) sectors and empowerment of individual fund holders is as consumers. As suggested by one analyst:

> From [direct payments] as a means to empowerment, we have moved to what is essentially an under-funded voucher system. From a replacement for a traditional and inadequate set of services, we have moved to an exchange relationship, which casts the service user as a consumer, not a citizen with rights – to a model that is market based and market driven rather than liberatory in intent. (Beresford 2011, p. 40)

While much criticism of personalisation has been directed to the dominance of personalisation policy's neoliberal aims, arguably, the policy is in place *because* it has appealed to diverse groups and is able to be understood in different ways (Glasby and Littlechild 2016; Needham 2011a). This suggests it may not be possible to separate the idea of personalisation from the implementation and practice of personalisation, as Simon Duffy, founder of In Control, has noted. The ambiguity of the concept, and its dual aims, allow for multiple meanings in practice:

> It is, of course, possible to argue that the personalisation itself is fine—it is just being misused or misinterpreted by the system. But this is naive. Any tool or system will be defined by those who use it. Personalisation has allowed a whole range of such shifts in meaning … (Duffy, 2014, p. 180)

Among the shifts in meaning Duffy identifies are that resource allocation systems 'designed to create robust and meaningful entitlements ... (are) now used to rationalise unfair and unreasonable cuts'. Individual budgets 'designed to give people more control ... (are) now used to pretend that people have control when they do not' (Duffy 2014, p. 180). Thus, Duffy connects the ideas of personalisation and individual payments to their application in practice at the system level. Much of the UK academic literature evaluating personalisation does not do this. However, there are academics who have argued that personalisation should be assessed in relation to its broader impacts on social justice, as outlined below.

Research accounts and evaluations of personalisation tend to focus on the experiences of individuals of the mechanisms of personalised care. They rely on self-reporting of individual experiences of personal budgets and direct payments, often without reference to the broader effectiveness of the care system. Yet, there can be very different answers to the question 'how successful has personalisation been?' depending on whether the reference point is confined to the micro-level of individual experiences of people with personal budgets and direct payments or broadened to encompass the functioning of the social care system as a whole. Success at either level may not be matched by success at the other.

How Successful Has Personalisation Been?

The absence of a good evidence base is one of the main barriers to evaluating the effectiveness of England's social care personalisation mechanisms—personal budgets and direct payments—for producing positive outcomes for people receiving personalised care and support. However, when it comes to assessing the outcomes of the public personalised social care system *overall*, there is no shortage of evidence indicating that the system is failing, with many people not having their care and support needs met. Here, I consider the literature evaluating outcomes for individuals of personal budgets and direct payments before turning to consider how successful the personalised care *system* has been.

Personalisation and Individual Outcomes

Since the early days of individualised funding trials in UK social care, various small-scale studies have reported benefits from individualised approaches. However, the wider implementation of personalised budgets was not based on much evidence (Pearson and Ridley 2017). Needham has argued that a powerful narrative in support of personalisation gained acceptance on the basis of individual testimonies and an 'it works' storyline 'supported by claims to self-evidence and common sense' rather than any strong evidence (Needham 2011a, p. 49). This narrative is highly resistant to criticism, as it relies on assumptions that personalisation will work *because* it is person-centred and thus based on individual preferences and strengths (Needham 2011b).

In this field, the evaluation of published research findings is problematic. One issue is that in academic and policy literature—including reports of empirical research—a clear distinction between personalisation and its main mechanisms (direct payments and personal budgets) is often lacking. This means there can be confusion and/or conflation of concepts (Manthorpe et al. 2011). Additionally, some of the studies policymakers have relied on most heavily as key sources of evidence of positive outcomes (van Toorn 2018, p. 135) are conducted by individualised funding advocates, In Control, with Lancaster University and, more recently, are published by Think Local Act Personal [TLAP], a body funded by government to progress the take-up of personal budgets and individual payments. These studies are the POET (Personal Budgets Outcome Evaluation Tool) surveys of personal budget users (Hatton and Waters 2011, 2013), In Control et al. 2017, Poll and Duffy 2008, Poll et al. 2006, Waters and Hutton 2014).

Multiple criticisms have been levelled at the methodology and interpretations of findings of some of these influential surveys (Slasberg and Beresford 2015, 2016; Slasberg et al. 2012a, 2015). However, in some key literature on personalisation, others refer to the surveys unproblematically (e.g. Glasby and Littlechild 2016, pp. 94–95). The surveys continue to be relied on as the source of 'the most comprehensive data about the link between personal budgets and care outcomes' (Needham et al. 2018, p. 46).

Another large study of outcomes is the 2008 individual budgets (ISBEN) evaluation (Glendinning et al. 2008). This is one of the most rigorous studies to date; it found mixed results for recipients. In their review of the early literature, Manthorpe et al. (2015) concluded that, overall, a critical knowledge gap exists when it comes to understanding effects of personalisation on users of services. A 2016 UK parliamentary inquiry (House of Commons Committee of Public Accounts 2016) and a National Audit Office review of 'personalised commissioning' (NAO

2016) both concluded there was little good quality research to back up the claimed benefits of personal budgets and individualised funding, or to explain the underlying reasons for outcomes (see also reviews by Bentham 2018, Manthorpe et al. 2010).

Within the limited evidence base there are some consistent findings of improved outcomes for users of care services where ***direct payments***, rather than personal budgets more generally, are in place (Slasberg and Beresford 2016). Personalisation advocates see direct payments as the form of funding that provides for the greatest autonomy and independence. Therefore, the take-up of direct payments in a care system may be understood to be critical to the goals of an individualised care system. Direct payments are also the mechanism through which individuals can directly employ or engage their own workers. So, direct payments are critical to the nature of care work and employment in the individualised system.

Opinions differ as to the probable reasons why direct payments might contribute to improved outcomes. Glasby and Littlechild (2016) argue that the positive impacts of direct payments for recipients are due to providing opportunity—through the exercise of choice in the market—for people to have more control over their lives. Slasberg and Beresford (2015) disagree, arguing that advocates of marketised systems that construct service users as consumers have misconstrued the exercise of consumer choice as the grounds for preferencing benefits of direct payments over traditional service provision. Drawing on the early experience of the disabled people's movement, these authors identify the success of direct payments as arising from three factors: 'support plans built from accurate assessment of needs, sufficiency of resources and flexibility of provision' (Slasberg and Beresford 2015, p. 480).

In relation to resources, these analysts claim that direct payment recipients have received higher levels of funding than other personal budget recipients (Slasberg et al. 2012a). Regarding flexibility of provision, where there are adequate resources and direct payments' recipients employ their own care workers, referred to in England as 'personal assistants' (Skills for Care 2019c, p. 36), improved outcomes have been found (Rodrigues and Glendinning 2015; Slasberg and Beresford 2016, Stainton and Boyce, 2004).

Overall, while most studies usually identify more positives than negatives, the findings on outcomes of direct payments for individuals are mixed (Glasby and Littlechild 2016, Leece 2010; Manthorpe and Hindes 2010). Evaluations and data also show that context matters and that, in some circumstances, direct payments have had negative outcomes for some groups. Again, funding levels appear to be an important factor, with better outcomes occurring where better funding is available, while age, aspects of disability, family resources and quality of care and support are also factors (Bentham 2018; Slasberg et al. 2012b, Glendinning et al. 2008). More generally, these findings raise questions about the achievement of social justice aims of personalisation, as there are groups of consumers who lack market power or information, or otherwise cannot meaningfully benefit from the purchasing power provided by personalised funding (Benoot et al. 2020, Ferguson 2012, Slasberg and Beresford 2014).

Findings of several studies suggest that some people receiving direct payments have difficulties managing their direct payments, including managing their roles and responsibilities as employers (Glendinning et al. 2000, Graham 2015, McGuigan et al. 2016). These studies highlight risks for individuals as direct employers of personal assistants; some also consider risks for workers. However, often where there is focus on direct employment in research and in policy and practice guidance, there can be limited attention to—and sometimes even dismissal of—risks for care workers (see, e.g., Glasby and Littlechild 2016, pp. 157–160).

How Successful Is England's Social Care System?

Dominated by small studies and largely reliant on self-reported outcomes of small numbers of people (Manthorpe et al. 2015), the body of research on the effectiveness for individuals of direct payments is limited as an evidence base for assessing overall outcomes of English personalised social care. At least until 2013, most people with local government authority 'managed budgets' received fairly standardised services (Slasberg et al. 2013). At that time relatively small numbers of eligible people had taken up direct payments, although the numbers increased considerably between 2014 and 2017 (Skills for Care 2020).

More generally, England's social care system has been under enormous pressure over the past decade from ongoing and large expenditure cuts. Local government authorities have responded to this austerity by limiting eligibility for publicly-funded care and limiting the amount of care provided to people who are eligible. A 2019 parliamentary inquiry into social care funding found provisions to be £700 million less than in 2010/2011 in real terms, despite continuing increases in the numbers of people who need care (House of Lords 2019). Concerns around the quality of care—particularly care provided by some large for-profit companies—are such that social care is widely recognised as being in 'crisis' in England and in other parts of the UK (e.g. Age UK 2019, House of Lords 2019). Given this, the significance of some of the above research findings that compare individual care outcomes is unclear.

What is clear is that the quality of social care commissioned by local authorities has declined as councils have refocused their care commissioning to reduce costs (Needham et al. 2018). Many services are commissioned on a 'time and task' basis to reduce care worker visit times, with this affecting quality and continuity of care, including as a result of increased staff turnover, poor retention and lack of training of workers (Atkinsonet al. 2016; Lewis and West 2014). As Needham et al. (2018, p. 35) point out, social care commissioning that focuses on getting basic tasks done 'runs counter to the Care Act and the articulation of personalised care and support in the Care and Support Statutory Guidance'.

In 2019, in their annual report on the sector, the UK Care Quality Commission (CQC) stated 'the stability of the adult social care market remains a particular concern'. The CQC pointed to two instances where local authorities had to be notified 'that there was a credible risk of service disruption because of providers' businesses failing' noting also that the provider in one of these instances was 'one of the largest domiciliary care providers in England'. The CQC concluded that such notifications were 'pointing to increasing fragility in the market' (CQC 2019, p. 20).

The development and functioning of the personalised social care market in the UK have been shaped crucially by this context of increasingly constrained funding and questions around the benefits of the market-based model. The vision for personalisation relies on the idea of a market in which innovation flourishes, a diversity of service offerings are available that meet individual needs and preferences, and user-led service organisations have equal opportunity to participate in the market (Needham 2011a). Experience to date suggests significant problems with achieving this vision. In the poorly-funded market, growth has been mainly in large care providers, and these organisations have been in the spotlight for providing poor quality care (CQC 2017) while they also pay workers less (Cominetti et al. 2020), suggesting fundamental problems with reliance on a market model.

The majority of social care providers are small operators with limited capacity for innovation as their time is taken up with 'meeting regulatory requirements and managing day-to-day business' (Needham et al. 2018, p. 39 citing IPC 2014). In my research fieldwork in England in 2015 and 2018, I followed leads I had been given for innovative service providers; I came across several small organisations whose attempts to do things differently to provide personalised services (and decent work for care and support workers) had been stymied by difficulties they had just managing day-to-day business under tight funding constraints. As Beresford (2014) has pointed out, the market does not offer a level playing field to small user-led, community-based and ethnic minority organisations.

Workforce supply and retention are major challenges for social care providers and for the social care market. Low pay, lack of investment in training and poor working conditions of care workers underpin problems of recruitment and retention and they underpin problems of care quality. In many areas, the social care workforce has become highly reliant on migrant workers (Skills for Care 2019b, Bottery and Babalola 2020). In England, the vacancy rate for care workers in September 2019 was 9.0%, and for directly employed care workers or personal assistants it was 8.2%, while the average job vacancy rate across all industries was 2.8%. The turnover rate for workers providing home-based care and assistance—home care workers—was 43.7%, with pay being one of several key factors in this (Skills for Care 2019b, p. 46; 2019c, p. 107).

While care workers' pay has increased in recent years thanks to national living wage legislation, it has increased more slowly than for workers in other sectors. Adult social care workers' wages remain uncompetitive (Bottery and Babalola 2020). High turnover directly impacts on quality of care, with consistency of care as important a factor for care users as control over funding (Needham et al 2018). Common factors identified in research on what makes good quality care in home-based care for the aged and people with disability in the UK include communication, continuity of care, building relationships, and staff development and training (Bennett et al. 2018)—all of which are undermined by high turnover.

Personalisation and the Invisible Frontline Social Care Worker

There is no question that, overall, frontline care workers in England have fared poorly in marketised social care over the past two decades. Despite clear evidence of this, the low-paid care workforce and their employment conditions have rated barely a passing mention in some policy discussions of the problems besetting social care in England (Economic Affairs Committee 2019, Humphries et al. 2016). Nevertheless, over the past decade public attention has increasingly been drawn to the growing body of evidence concerning undervaluation, low wages and poor working conditions of adult social care workers—home care workers and the directly-employed personal assistants—who provide care and support to aged people and people with disability living in their own homes.

While about a quarter (24%) of England's social care workforce is employed on zero-hours contracts, this is the case for 43% of the domiciliary care services workforce, and for 58% of the frontline home care workers in this workforce (Skills for Care 2019c pp. 36 & 39). Prior to the establishment of the UK National Living Wage in 2016, adult social care workers were at greater risk than other workers of not receiving the lower National Minimum Wage (NMW) (Low Pay Commission, 2016: xxvii). Researchers have estimated that between 10% (Hussein 2018) and 60% (Bessa et al. 2013, pp. 27–28) of home care workers are effectively paid less than the NMW.

Low pay and underpayment are underpinned by the common practice of paying home care workers for only the time they are directly providing face-to-face care, leading to high levels of unpaid work (Hayes 2017, Rubery et al. 2015). Further, some home visits to provide care are extremely short. According to Freedom of Information data obtained by one of the main trade unions covering England's social care workers (UNISON 2016), over half of social care workers experienced being asked to provide care to someone they had never met before in a 15-minute visit. A recent detailed ethnographic study (Hayes 2017) has illustrated the poor quality—including low pay, undervaluation and economic precarity—of home care work in England. Hayes who combines her ethnography with evaluation of care policy and employment regulation refers to the situation of home care workers as 'institutionalised humiliation', defined as:

> a failure of respect afforded by the state to homecare workers as a collective group; homecare workers' own recognition of being treated unjustly as a group; and the lived reality of economic and social detriment. (2017, p. 4)

An important question for the present study concerns how care workers in England have fared where they are directly employed by—or engaged as contractors to—social care users who receive their personal budgets as direct payments. As with the broader literature on the personalised social care system, relatively little has been written about social care workers and individual direct payments.

Even where academic and policy literature does focus on the role of the social care workforce in making personalisation work for people with direct payments, *direct care workers* are largely absent from discussions. References to 'frontline' social care workers are almost invariably references to social workers, not to home care workers or 'personal assistants' as they are referred to in the UK. The engagement of social workers in the personalisation project is critical to the successful transition from a social care system based on professional expertise and control to one based on individual empowerment. For consumers to determine their own needs and choose how to meet these needs via a social care market requires a transfer of power away from social work professionals to consumers (Glasby and Littlechild 2016). Social workers are often portrayed as presenting barriers to personalisation due to a perception, and some evidence, that they may be reluctant or unable to adapt their professional practices to recognise the rights and capacity of people who use services to also take control of these services (Beresford 2014, Glasby and Littlechild 2016).

However, the central role played by social workers in shifting to co-production of services alone fails to explain the absence of attention to the direct care workers who provide the bulk of care and support on a daily basis in face-to-face relationships, including as direct employees of the people they support. It may be testament to the lack of power wielded by these *other* frontline social care workers that they have been barely visible in much of the literature on personalisation until very recently. Their invisibility can also be explained in part by the fact that the personal assistant workforce was quite small until a few years ago. However, growth in numbers of direct payments recipients since 2014—to around 28% of all eligible budget holders—has led to growth in the directly employed and self-employed care workforce. This growth, along with a growing interest by healthcare budget holders in the role of direct employment of care workers (Bottery & Babalola 2020), may explain the recent increase in interest in these workers.

According to Skills for Care (2020), in 2013 an estimated 35,000 people were receiving social care direct payments and directly employing their own care staff/personal assistants. Between 2014 and 2017, growth in direct payments saw the number of people employing their own care workers double. However, no growth in direct payments has been seen since 2017. In 2019, of an estimated 230,000 people receiving direct payments, 70,000 directly employed their own staff. These individual employers directly employed an average of just under two staff each, with the total number of directly-employed care worker jobs estimated to be 135,000 in 2019 (Skills for Care 2020, p. 4).[1]

An important difference between the directly employed care workforce and the larger social care workforce in England that is sometimes overlooked or not reported in empirical studies is that a large proportion of the former are family members or friends of their employer; in 2019 the proportion was 53% of all directly employed care workers (Skills for Care 2019c, 2020, p. 14).[2] This is arguably a significant factor when comparing individual outcomes and levels of job satisfaction in direct employment and other care arrangements. At the system level, it potentially increases the likelihood that norms of gendered family relations and unpaid care operate to devalue and informalise care work (Ungerson 2004). Possibly it also contributes to the relative lack of attention paid to this workforce, if they are invisibilised as female family workers who are not generally a matter of interest to regulators and others concerned with employment and labour regulation (Delaney and Macdonald 2018, Fudge 2014).

There is virtually no regulatory oversight of directly employed and engaged care workers (personal assistants), whereas home care provider organisations are audited and inspected by the Care Quality Commission (CQC 2017). Some local government authorities do promote standards for care through services they provide to assist people who directly employ care workers, but it is not known how widespread this is (Woolham et al. 2019a). Self-employed workers are included in counts of 'directly

[1] Some people in the UK also employ care workers/personal assistants using their own funds or other funding such as personal health budgets, but there is no data available on the number of workers employed in these arrangements (Skills for Care 2020, p. 9).

[2] There are restrictions on employment of family members, as employment is not permitted where a family member is resident in the household of the person being supported.

employed' care workers in Skills for Care industry surveys. In 2019, they made up 9% of this workforce (Skills for Care 2020, p. 15). Little information exists on this group, although one of the few large studies of personal assistants (Woolham et al. 2019a) found this group had highly informal employment arrangements.

A scan of academic literature for references to direct employment of care workers in England shows that the main sources relied on for knowledge about workers in this type of employment are a handful of studies undertaken some years ago. The largest of these is a survey of direct employers by IFF Research (2008); this included a short questionnaire completed by 486 workers, and a longer follow up telephone survey of 100 directly employed workers. The workers in this study had poorer job security, less training and worked more unsocial hours than other care workers. However, they had higher job satisfaction (IFF Research 2008). Other studies are much smaller and there are other shortcomings with the evidence base. An observation made some years ago by Cortis et al. (2013, p. 23) that the empirical evidence about workforce issues is 'limited to studies focused primarily on the experiences of service users and their families, or which capture issues for workers from the perspectives of service managers or policy officials' is still relevant.

Despite these shortcomings, the research literature does suggest some significant problems and risks for the directly employed workforce. These include low pay compared to other low-paid social care workers, poor support, vulnerability to health and safety risks and exploitation through casual and highly informal employment arrangements (Christensen and Manthorpe 2016, Hayes 2017, Land and Himmelweit 2010, Leece 2010, Manthorpe et al. 2011). Labelling directly employed workers as personal assistants adds to the characterisation of their work as low-skilled and most have little or no access to training and professional development (Glendinning 2012). They are less likely than other social care workers to have engaged in care training (Skills for Care 2018, p. 95).

A recent study collecting data from directly employed workers through telephone interviews (Woolham et al. 2019a) appears to be the first large study that has not relied entirely on employers to access this workforce for research. This study found the directly employed personal assistants generally had high job satisfaction. While concluding there was possibly less turnover among this group of workers than the general social care workforce, the researchers reported that some workers did not see the job as a long-term option due to the low pay. The study found some workers' employment conditions were not in compliance with laws; it concluded that directly employed workers shared the labour market vulnerabilities and lack of social protection of other social care workers but that, for them, 'risks are exacerbated by the lack of oversight of their employer or regulatory interest in their work. These may have implications for the sustainability of care and its quality' (Woolham et al. 2019b, p. 297). These findings are highly relevant to the present study as they suggest some serious risks of direct engagement, an option that potentially will be taken up much more widely in the new Australian individualised system than it has been in England to date.

Conclusion

While the research base is small, the developing picture is one that raises many questions about the use of direct employment arrangements in publicly-funded individualised care. Direct employment relationships have grown slowly in England's personalised social care system, with their take-up limited by a variety of factors. In contrast, the new Australian individualised disability support system, from the outset, mandates individualised funding, places self-management of funds at the forefront of its goals and removes the possibility for local collective commissioning of services. The designers of Australia's new system drew heavily on the English experience. However, while they appear to have embraced the narratives of personalisation described earlier in this chapter, they have been less concerned about the risks of individualised funding for the publicly-funded care workforce. I turn to this issue in the next chapter.

References

Age UK. (2019). Care in crisis, Age UK. https://www.ageuk.org.uk/our-impact/campaigning/care-in-crisis/. Accessed 20 February 2020.

Atkinson, C., Crozier, S., & Lewis, L. (2016). *Factors that affect the recruitment and retention of domiciliary care workers and the extent to which these factors impact upon the quality of domiciliary care*. Cardiff: Welsh Government.

Barnes, M. (2011). Abandoning care? A critical perspective on personalisation from an ethic of care. *Ethics and Social Welfare, 5*(2), 153–167. https://doi.org/10.1080/17496535.2010.484265.

Bennett, L., Honeyman, M., & Bottery, S. (2018). *New models of home care*. London: The King's Fund.

Benoot, T., Dursin, W., Verschuere, B., Roose, R. J. D., & Society (2020). Lessons from Ricoeur's 'capable human being' for practices of personalisation in three European countries. *Disability and Society*, 1–23. https://doi.org/10.1080/09687599.2020.1769561.

Bentham, E. (2018). Personalisation in the UK: Personal budgets, direct payments, and PAs. *CPOW working paper* (pp. 25). Melbourne: Centre for People, Organisation and Work, RMIT University.

Beresford, P. (2008). What future for care? *Viewpoint: Informing debate* (pp. 16 pages): Joseph Rowntree Foundation.

Beresford, P. (2011). Are personal budgets necessarily empowering for service users? If not, what's it all about. *Research, Policy and Planning, 29*(1), 37–43.

Beresford, P. (2014). Advancing the positives of personalisation/person-centred support: A multi-perspective view. In C. Needham & J. Glasby (Eds.), *Debates in personalisation* (pp. 153–166). Bristol: Polity Press.

Bessa, I., Forde, C., Moore, S., & Stuart, M. (2013). *The national minimum wage, earnings and hours in the domiciliary care sector*. London: University of Leeds and Low Pay Commission.

Bottery, S., & Babalola, G. (2020). Social care 360. https://www.kingsfund.org.uk/publications/social-care-360#a-fragile-sector. Accessed 20 April 2020. Accessed 12 August 2020.

Care Quality Commission (2017). The state of health care and adult social care in England 2016/17. https://www.cqc.org.uk/sites/default/files/20171123_stateofcare1617_report.pdf. Accessed 19 June 2020.

Care Quality Commission. (2019). The state of health care and adult social care in England 2018/19. https://www.cqc.org.uk/sites/default/files/20191015b_stateofcare1819_fullreport.pdf. Accessed 20 April 2020.

Christensen, K., & Manthorpe, J. (2016). Personalised risk: New risk encounters facing migrant care workers. *Health, Risk & Society, 18*(3–4), 137–152. https://doi.org/10.1080/13698575.2016.1182628.

Cominetti, N., Gardiner, L., & Kelly, G. (2020) What happens after the clapping finishes? The pay, terms and conditions we choose for our care workers *Spotlight*. Resolution Foundation.

Cortis, N., Meagher, G., Chan, S., Davidson, B., & Fattore, T. (2013). *Building an industry of choice: Service quality, workforce capacity and consumer-centred funding in disability care*. Social Policy Research Centre Report Series. Social Policy Research Centre, University of New South Wales.

Delaney, A., & Macdonald, F. (2018). Thinking about informality: Gender (in)equality (in) decent work across geographic and economic boundaries. *Labour & Industry, 28*(2), 99–114. https://doi.org/10.1080/10301763.2018.1475024.

Duffy, S. (2010). The citizenship theory of social justice: Exploring the meaning of personalisation for social workers. *Journal of Social Work Practice, 24*(3), 253–267. https://doi.org/10.1080/02650533.2010.500118.

Duffy, S. (2011). *A fair society and the limits of personalisation* (p. 27). Sheffield: The Centre for Welfare Reform.

Duffy, S. (2014). After personalisation. In C. Needham & J. Glasby (Eds.), *Debates in personalisation* (pp. 167–184). Bristol: The Policy Press.

Economic Affairs Committee. (2019). *Social care funding: Time to end a national scandal*. UK Parliament: House of Lords.

Ettelt, S., Wittenberg, R., Williams, L., Damant, J., Lombard, D., Perkins, M. (2017). Evaluation of direct payments in residential care trailblazers, final report. London: Policy Innovation Research Unit.

Ferguson, I. (2012). Personalisation, social justice and social work: A reply to Simon Duffy. *Journal of Social Work Practice, 26*(1), 55–73. https://doi.org/10.1080/02650533.2011.623771.

Fudge, J. (2014). Feminist reflections on the scope of labour law: Domestic work, social reproduction, and jurisdiction. *Feminist Legal Studies*, *22*(1), 1–23. https://link.springer.com/article/10.1007/s10691-014-9256-2.

Glasby, J., & Littlechild, R. (2016). *Direct payments and personal budgets: Putting personalisation into practice* (3rd ed.). Bristol: The Policy Press.

Glendinning, C. (2012). Home care in England: Markets in the context of underfunding. *Health and Social Care in the Community, 20*(3), 292–299. https://doi.org/10.1111/j.1365-2524.2012.01059.x.

Glendinning, C., Halliwell, S., Jacobs, S., Rummery, K., & Tyrer, J. (2000). New kinds of care, new kinds of relationships: how purchasing services affects relationships in giving and receiving personal assistance. *Health and Social Care in the Community*, 8(3), 201–211. https://doi.org/10.1046/j.1365-2524.2000.00242.x.

Glendinning, C., Challis, D., Fernandez, J., Jacobs, S., Jones, K., Knapp, M., et al. (2008). *Evaluation of the individual budgets pilot programme: Final report*. York: Individual Budgets Evaluation Network (IBSEN).

Graham, K. (2015). Cash payments in context: (self)regulation in the new social relations of assistance. *Disability & Society, 30*(4), 597–613. https://doi.org/10.1080/09687599.2015.1037951.

Hatton, C., & Waters, J. (2011). *The national personal budget survey*. London: In Control.

Hatton, C., & Waters, J. (2013). *Second National Personal Budget Survey (POET)*. Think Local Act Personal. London: In Control Publications.

Hayes, L. J. (2017). *Stories of care: A labour of law: Gender and class at work*. London: Springer.

House of Commons Committee of Public Accounts (UK Parliament) (2016). Personal budgets in social care: Second report of Session 2016–2017. Report, together with formal minutes relating to the report. In House of Commons (Ed.), (pp. 67). London, UK: Her Majesty's Stationery Office (HMSO).

House of Lords (2019). Social care funding: Time to end a national scandal. *House of Lords Paper 392.*

Humphries, R., Thorlby, R., Holder, H., Hall, P., & Charles, A. (2016). *Social care for older people: Home truths*. London: The King's Fund and Nuffield Trust.

Hussein, S. (2018). The English social care workforce: The vexed question of low wages and stress In K. Christensen, & D. Pilling (Eds.), *The Routledge handbook of social care work around the world* (pp. 74–87). Oxon: Routledge.

IFF Research (2008). Employment aspects and workforce implications of direct payments. *Skills for care* (pp. 253). London: IFF Research.

In Control, TLAP, & Lancaster University. (2017). *Personal outcomes evaluation tool for adults in receipt of social care support*. London: In Control.

Land, H., & Himmelweit, S. (2010). *Who cares: Who pays? A report on personalisation in social care*. London: Unison.

Leece, J. (2010). Paying the piper and calling the tune: Power and the direct payment relationship. *British Journal of Social Work, 40*(1), 188–206. https://doi.org/10.1093/bjsw/bcn085.

Lewis, J., & West, A. (2014). Re-shaping social care services for older people in England: Policy development and the problem of achieving 'good care'. *Journal of Social Policy, 43*(01), 1–18. https://doi.org/10.1017/s0047279413000561.

Low Pay Commission (2016). National minimum wage: Low Pay Commission report, Spring 2016.

Manthorpe, J., & Hindes, J. (2010). *Employing direct care workers through public and private funding: A scoping review of the literature*. London: King's College.

Manthorpe, J., Martineau, S., Moriarty, J., Hussein, S., & Stevens, M. (2010). Support workers in social care in England: A scoping study. *Health and Social Care in the Community, 18*(3), 316–324. https://doi.org/10.1111/j.1365-2524.2010.00910.x.

Manthorpe, J., Hindes, J., Martineau, S., Cornes, M., Ridley, J., Spandler, H., et al. (2011). *Self-directed support: A review of the barriers and facilitators*. Edinburgh: Scottish Government Social Research, Edinburgh.

Manthorpe, J., Martineau, S., Ridley, J., Cornes, M., Rosengard, A., & Hunter, S. (2015). Embarking on self-directed support in Scotland: A focused scoping review of the literature. *European Journal of Social Work, 18*(1), 36–50. https://doi.org/10.1080/13691457.2014.885883.

McGuigan, K., McDermott, L., Magowan, C., McCorkell, G., Witherow, A., & Coates, V. (2016). The impact of direct payments on service users requiring care and support at home. *Practice, 28*(1), 37–54. https://doi.org/10.1080/09503153.2015.1039973.

Mladenov, T. (2015). Neoliberalism, postsocialism, disability. *Disability & Society, 30*(3), 445–459. https://doi.org/10.1080/09687599.2015.1021758.

Mladenov, T., Owens, J., & Cribb, A. (2015). Personalisation in disability services and healthcare: A critical comparative analysis. *Critical Social Policy, 35*(3), 307–326. https://doi.org/10.1177/2F0261018315587071.

National Audit Office (NAO). (2016). *Personalised commissioning in social care*. London: HMSO.

Needham, C. (2011a). *Personalising public services: Understanding the personalisation narrative*. Bristol, UK: The Policy Press.

Needham, C. (2011b). Personalization: from story-line to practice. *Social Policy & Administration, 45*(1), 54–68. https://doi.org/10.1111/j.1467-9515.2010.00753.x.

Needham, C., & Glasby, J. (Eds.). (2014a). *Debates in personalisation*. Bristol: The Policy Press.

Needham, C., & Glasby, J. (2014b). Taking stock of personalisation. In C. Needham & J. Glasby (Eds.), *Debates in personalisation* (pp. 11–24). Bristol: The Policy Press.

Needham, C., Hall, K., Allen, K., Burn, E., Mangan, C., & Henwood, M. (2018). *Market shaping and personalisation in social care: A realist synthesis of the literature*. Birmingham: Health Services Management Centre, University of Birmingham.

Pearson, C., & Ridley, J. (2017). Is personalization the right plan at the wrong time? Re-thinking cash-for-care in an age of austerity. *Social Policy and Administration, 51*(7), 1042–1059. https://doi.org/10.1111/spol.12216.

Poll, C., & Duffy, S. (2008). *A report on In Control's second phase: Evaluation and learning*. London: In Control Publications.

Poll, C., Duffy, S., Hatton, C., Sanderson, H., & Routledge, M. (2006). *A report on In Control's first phase 2003–2005*. London: In Control.

Rodrigues, R., & Glendinning, C. (2015). Choice, competition and care—developments in English social care and the impacts on providers and older users of home care services. *Social Policy & Administration, 49*(5), 649–664. https://doi.org/10.1111/spol.12099.

Rubery, J., Grimshaw, D., Hebson, G., & Ugarte, S. M. (2015). "It's all about time": Time as contested terrain in the management and experience of domiciliary care work in England. *Human Resource Management, 54*(5), 753–772. https://doi.org/10.1002/hrm.21685.

Skills for Care. (2018). The state of the adult social care sector and workforce in England, September 2019. *Workforce intelligence publication*. Leeds: Skills for Care.

Skills for Care. (2019a). *Domiciliary care services in the adult social care sector*. Leeds: Skills for Care.

Skills for Care. (2019b). The size and structure of the adult social care sector and workforce in England, 2019. *Workforce intelligence publication*. Leeds: Skills for Care.

Skills for Care. (2019c). The state of the adult social care sector and workforce in England, September 2019. *Workforce intelligence publication*. Leeds: Skills for Care.

Skills for Care. (2020). *Individual employers and the personal assistant workforce report, 2020*. Leeds: Skills for Care.

Slasberg, C., & Beresford, P. (2015). Building on the original strengths of direct payments to create a better future for social care. *Disability & Society, 30*(3), 479–483. https://doi.org/10.1080/09687599.2015.1007672.

Slasberg, C., & Beresford, P. (2016). The false narrative about personal budgets in England: Smoke and mirrors? *Disability & Society, 31*(8), 1132–1137. https://doi.org/10.1080/09687599.2016.1235309.

Slasberg, C., Beresford, P., & Schofield, P. (2012a). How self-directed support is failing to deliver personal budgets and personalisation. *Research, Policy and Planning, 29*(3), 161–177.

Slasberg, C., Beresford, P., & Schofield, P. (2012b). Can personal budgets really deliver better outcome for all at no cost? Reviewing the evidence, costs and quality. *Disability & Society, 27*(7), 1029–1034. https://doi.org/10.1080/09687599.2012.736671.

Slasberg, C., Beresford, P., & Schofield, P. (2013). The increasing evidence of how self directed support is failing to deliver personal budgets and personalisation. *Research, Policy and Planning, 30*(2), 91–105.

Slasberg, C., Beresford, P., & Schofield, P. (2015). Further lessons from the continuing failure of the national strategy to deliver personal budgets and personalisation. *Research, Policy and Planning, 31*(1), 43–53.

Spandler, H. (2004). Friend or foe? *Towards a Critical Assessment of Direct Payments, Critical Social Policy, 24*(2), 187–209. https://doi.org/10.1177/2F0261018304041950.

Stainton, T., & Boyce, S. (2004). 'I have got my life back': users' experience of direct payments. *Disability & Society, 19*(5), 443–454. https://doi.org/10.1080/0968759042000235299.

Tomlinson, C., & Livesey, M. (2013). *Individual service funds for homecare*. In Control: Wythall.

Ungerson, C. (2004). Whose empowerment and independence? A cross-national perspective on cash for care schemes. *Ageing & Society, 24*(2), 189–212. https://doi.org/10.1017/S0144686X03001508.

UNISON (2016) Suffering alone at home. A UNISON report on the lack of time in our homecare system. London: UNISON.

UK Government. (2007). *Putting people first: A shared vision and commitment to the transformation of adult social care*. Department of Health. https://webarchive.nationalarchives.gov.uk/20130104175839/http://www.dh.gov.uk/en/Publicationsandstatistics/Publications/PublicationsPolicyAndGuidance/DH_081118/. Accessed 10 February 2020.

Van Toorn, G. (2018). *The new political economy of disability: Transnational networks and individualised funding in the age of neoliberalism*. Doctoral dissertation, University of New South Wales and University of Glasgow.

Waters, J., & Hatton, C. (2014). *Third national personal budget survey*. Think Local Act Personal. London: In Control Publications.

Woolham, J., Norrie, C., Samsi, K., & Manthorpe, J. (2019a). Roles, responsibilities, and relationships: Hearing the voices of personal assistants and directly employed care workers. (pp. 152). London: NIHR Policy Research Unit in Health and Social Care Workforce, The Policy Institute, King's College London.

Woolham, J., Norrie, C., Samsi, K., & Manthorpe, J. (2019b). The employment conditions of social care personal assistants in England. *The Journal of Adult Protection, 21*(6), 296–306. https://doi.org/10.1108/JAP-06-2019-0017.

CHAPTER 4

Imagining, Making and Managing Cash for Care in Australia

Introduction

This chapter begins my analysis of the new Australian individualised social care regime with an overview of the NDIS, locating it in the historical institutional structure of Australian social care provision and in comparative context with the English system of personalisation. This highlights that the foundational infrastructure for social care provision for people with disability was a severely under-funded not-for-profit sector. It provides a grounding for understanding the significance of the changes introduced by the new cash-for-care scheme including the potential for the development of a large unregulated social care sector. First, I draw on the text of a key report by Australia's Productivity Commission (2011) that is regarded as providing the blueprint for the NDIS to consider how evidence-based the Productivity Commission's policy design process was, and to explore the considerations given to the social care workforce in this process.

My analysis of NDIS design and operational documents shows how the government and the managing authority, the National Disability Insurance Agency (NDIA) have adopted strongly market-led approaches to the NDIS development. I show how both bodies have placed a high priority on keeping unit costs down while taking little or no responsibility for the workforce or the nature of jobs in the publicly-funded social care market. The documentary analysis also reveals some of the ideas and values

F. Macdonald, *Individualising Risk*,
https://doi.org/10.1007/978-981-33-6366-3_4

embedded in NDIS design and policies and points to some of their implications for frontline NDIS disability support workers and for prospects for decent work for this growing social care workforce. Narratives of consumer choice and cost reduction underpin pricing arrangements and funding levels that promote lean service provider organisations; that is, organisations that can devolve the risks and costs of service provision and employment to individual service users and social care workers. Consumers are encouraged to determine what makes a quality service. Workers are characterised as unskilled.

At the same time, analysis of NDIS quality and safeguarding policy documents reveals expectations for high-quality services that require frontline workers to be trained, skilled and supervised and that give workers responsibility for quality and safe practice. The analysis in this chapter reveals some inherent tensions and apparent contradictions in the NDIS design, market approach and system aspirations for quality and safety through good practice based on worker capabilities. In turn these tensions and contradictions suggest risks for the ongoing sustainability of the workforce, for workers as well as for people being supported. Two strong themes are identified as key to the character of the design, management and regulation of the new individualised social care scheme as it concerns frontline social care workers. These themes are *consumer choice and control* and *the market as the basis for fair pay and conditions*.

Australia's 'Most Fundamental Social Reform' Since the 1970s

Australia's NDIS was heralded as 'the most fundamental social reform' since the introduction of a universal healthcare system in the 1970s (Gillard 2013). The policy established a new national system for support for people with significant and permanent disability to replace a poorly-funded, fragmented and inadequate system of programmes and services that varied across Australian states and territories. Eligibility for support in the new system was to be based on need, the available funding doubled and a patchwork system of 'miserly, bureaucratised and often unpredictable services' replaced by a national social investment approach (Miller and Hayward 2017, p. 134).

The transformation of Australia's system of support for people with disability has been rapid. After commencing regional trials in 2013, the national NDIS roll out occurred from 2016 to 2020. While implementation problems have contributed to the slow entry into the system of eligible people with disability, in early 2020 there were 370,000 of an expected final 460,000 NDIS 'participants' receiving individualised funding (NDIA 2020a, p. 14).

The NDIS transforms long-standing publicly-funded programmes and services into a single fully consumer-directed individualised and market-based social care system. The *National Disability Insurance Scheme Act 2013* (NDIS Act) gives effect to Australia's obligations under the international Convention on the Rights of Persons with Disabilities. The objects of the NDIS Act include to 'enable people with disability to exercise choice and control in the pursuit of their goals and the planning and delivery of their supports', and to support their 'independence and social and economic participation'. The NDIS provides funding for people with 'significant and permanent disability' for the purchase of 'reasonable and necessary supports' (NDIS Act 2013, Section 3(1)(e)). An uncapped scheme, under the NDIS the amount of funding for a person's support is based on an individual support plan developed in collaboration with the National Disability Insurance Agency (NDIA), an independent statutory authority established to run the scheme. The NDIA uses actuarial principles to estimate costs and benefits of the scheme over a lifetime (Buckmaster and Clarke 2018).

The NDIS did not herald the initiation of marketisation of disability support services. As with other social care services in Australia, aspects of marketisation have occurred unevenly over several decades prior to the NDIS. Previously most publicly-funded disability services were provided by not-for-profit organisations, including faith-based charities and other voluntary organisations, with many of the latter being small organisations that were originally established by families and others as self-help groups to support adults and/or children with particular types of disabilities (Green and Mears 2014). Historically, the not-for-profit sector has been a key provider of disability support and other government-funded care, social support and welfare services, known collectively in Australia as *social and community services*. Provision of social and community services by for-profit businesses has grown as various Australian federal and state governments have adopted marketisation strategies (Meagher and Goodwin 2015).

As the public sector had never been the main provider of disability support services marketisation has not been simply a matter of increasing privatisation. Rather, it has been a process of gradually increasing competition principles in funding arrangements. Providers of publicly-funded disability support services have generally been contracted by governments to provide broadly specified services and programmes to particular population groups under what are known as 'block-funded' contracts of months' or years' duration.

Social care and other social and community services provision has been routinely under-funded by governments. Not-for-profit service providers have managed to get by through cross-subsidising across programmes and services and relying on other funding sources such as philanthropic donations and monies raised from social enterprises. In 2010, the Productivity Commission estimated that social and community services were under-funded by 30% of the full cost of the service delivery specified in contracts (Productivity Commission 2010, p. 281). Under-funding has had major consequences for the undervaluation of work in the highly feminised social and community services sector, an issue I return to in Chapter 5.

Prior to the NDIS, state and territory governments had primary responsibility for disability services, under agreements with the Commonwealth (i.e. Australian federal) government. Public sector agencies were direct providers of some disability support services. Local government authorities provided some social care services for people with disability through home and community care programmes. Support and care services for people with disability provided under all arrangements included supported accommodation, home and community support, community access, respite, employment and advocacy. Criteria for determination of eligibility varied by locality and access to services was patchy (Productivity Commission 2011).

In comparison with personalised adult social care in England—which encompasses aged care as well as disability care and support (see Chapter 3)—the social care system for people with disability established under Australia's NDIS represents a more radical marketisation and individualisation. The NDIS is radical for its rapid and wholesale transformation to a new market-based and for its very lightly regulated, individualised system. The NDIS establishes a market for supports for people with a disability that is fully open to businesses from the private for-profit sector for the first time. All funding is individualised and, unlike the English system, there is no role for local authorities to act as commissioning bodies. Market management or 'stewardship' falls to a national agency, the NDIA, and to the Australian Government.

The Australian system has arguably provided much greater opportunity for unregistered service providers and social care labour brokers than the English system. Individual 'self-management' and 'plan-management' of NDIS funding—arrangements that do not require the use of NDIS-registered care and support service providers—are the aspiration for as many people as possible in the NDIS. Everyone with NDIS funding has a new support plan and has gone through the process of choosing their providers. The NDIA, the central agency that develops and approves individual support plans for people with NDIS funding, has heavily promoted and facilitated the adoption of self- and plan-managed arrangements that entail minimal quality and safeguarding obligations (Independent Advisory Council to the NDIS 2017; NDIA 2018e). Another difference from the English system of adult social care is that, people entering the NDIS are not the aged. In England this is a group who have been much less likely than younger people with disabilities to take-up direct payments/self-management (Bottery and Babalola 2020). In terms of size, the NDIS is expected to fund supports for about 460,000 people, about half the number of people who receive publicly-funded long-term care in the English social care system.

Individual Funding, Pricing and Service Provision in the NDIS

The design of the NDIS provides for relatively light touch regulation of the use of individual funds, although funds *are* tied to specified goals in an individual's 'support plan'. The main category of funding is for 'core supports' and people have considerable flexibility in how they can spend their core supports funds. The four categories of core supports are: 'assistance with daily living', 'assistance with social and community participation', 'consumables' (e.g. continence products or low-cost assistive technologies) and 'transport' (NDIA 2020b). Generally, people are permitted to spend their core supports funding flexibly across any of the first three categories. So, a person might choose to use their core support funds to employ someone to assist with household cleaning or, instead, they could use the money to enrol in a gym class. Thus, the NDIS establishes a market in which there is limited oversight of how public funding is spent on care and support.

Prices for supports are regulated to the extent that *registered* service providers can only charge for NDIS-funded supports up to a level determined by the NDIA as the price cap. The amount of government funding for supports is the same as the capped price. There are no caps on prices that *unregistered* service providers can charge for support services (NDIA 2019e). The NDIA has proposed that in future all pricing under the NDIS will be deregulated. The current NDIS price caps (and government funding) for personal care and support services are calculated using a formula based on the minimum regulated wages for workers in the social and community services industry plus overheads and a small margin (NDIA 2019c). There have been major concerns that the NDIS fixed price for personal support and care is too low, including that it is too low for many traditional not-for-profit services that have established permanent and skilled workforces to remain viable (Cortis et al. 2017; Carey et al. 2020; Naufal 2020). Low pricing is a key driver of changes in frontline care and support work and employment.

People with an NDIS support plans can have their funds managed in one of three ways: by the NDIA, by a registered 'plan manager' (a financial intermediary such as an accountant or bookkeeper) or they can 'self-manage' funds (NDIA 2018e). As already noted, where the NDIA manages a person's support funds, services must be purchased from registered service providers (NDIA 2019a). Under the other two options there is no requirement for individuals to purchases their services from registered providers (NDIA 2020a, p. 46).[1] So, a person self-managing or plan-managing their funds can use their NDIS funding to purchase care and support services from providers of their choice including directly employing their care and support workers or engaging workers as self-employed contractors.

In 2018, a system for regulating quality and safety of NDIS care and support provision began to be put in place with the establishment of the NDIS Quality and Safeguards Commission. Now, NDIS-registered service providers, but not unregistered providers, must meet NDIS Practice Standards and pass a quality audit, and they must conduct basic screening checks on their employees. The regulator also oversees an NDIS

[1] There are three types of supports which can only be provided by an NDIS-registered provider. These are specialist disability accommodation; specialist behaviour support services; and supports where the provider may need to use a restricted practice (NDIA 2018e).

Code of Conduct; this applies to all organisations and workers providing NDIS-funded services and supports, whether they are registered service providers or not (NDIS Quality and Safeguards Commission 2020a).

Since the commencement of the NDIS, a gradual shift has taken place away from people having their individual support funds managed by the NDIA (requiring use of registered service providers) to self-management and plan-management of funds. The NDIA considers self-management of funding to be a key indicator of choice and control (NDIA 2018a, p. 66) and increasing self-management is an explicit goal for the NDIS (NDIA 2018d, p. 10). Between 2017 and early 2020 the proportion of people with NDIS support plans with funding managed by the NDIA declined from 71 to 32% (NDIA 2020a, Appendix E, p. 116, Figure E.17). By early 2020 almost one in three people fully (19%) or partly (12%) self-managed their funding and another 38% used a plan manager.

This means 68% of people who receive NDIS support funding can purchase some or all of their support services from unregistered service providers (NDIA 2020a, Appendix E, p. 116, Figure E.17). This does not mean that there is no system-regulation of the bulk of care and support currently funded under the NDIS as, in early 2020, 61% of NDIS plan *budgets* were still NDIA-managed; however, agency management of funds is declining (NDIA 2020a, Appendix E, p. 118, Table E.53).

Selling 'Cash for Care' and a Rosy Future for the Workforce

In the making of Australia's new scheme for disability support, very little public debate occurred about its design as a cash-for-care scheme. Australia's Productivity Commission (2011) made a recommendation for an individualised funding scheme in the report of their public inquiry and investigation into the feasibility of new approaches for funding and delivery of disability care and support. The inquiry and study were undertaken at the request of the Australian Government.

The dominant NDIS 'narrative' in much public discussion and in the Productivity Commission's report was one of universality, of a national insurance scheme that would benefit all Australians into the future (Miller and Hayward 2017; Needham and Dickinson 2018). It was claimed reform was needed to fix a broken system, provide better supports and enable Australia to meet it international obligations. The NDIS was also said to be about establishing a universal entitlement and it was described as a social investment that would reap returns through increased economic and social participation while also preventing spiralling costs (Productivity Commission 2011). Personalisation and self-directed support were not at the forefront of public arguments about the need for change. Nevertheless, several Australian states were already experimenting with limited individualised funding trials. As Van Toorn (2018) has documented in detail, a great deal of advocacy by individualised funding advocates—including the UK-affiliated In Control Australia—had taken place behind-the-scenes in government policy circles in the years leading up to, and during, the development of the NDIS.

The Productivity Commission (2011) presented the individualised funding design of Australia's proposed new system of disability support and care as the outcome of evidence-based policy development in a report of almost 1,000 pages plus appendices. However, there was surprisingly limited canvassing of the extensive international experience of cash-for-care schemes—other than for the English and USA cases—and only limited engagement with UK debates about personalisation in the report. What does run through the report of the 'pro-market pro-privatisation' Productivity Commission (Miller and Hayward 2017, p. 33) is the expression of strong faith in a market-based approach and empowerment for people through consumer choice. The Productivity Commission considered an individualised funding scheme to offer the 'most evolved form of consumer choice' (Productivity Commission 2011, p. 344). Echoing some of the UK personalisation narratives discussed in Chapter 3, in arguing for individualised funding, the Commission appealed to a self-evident truth of the benefits of consumer choice and markets, as illustrated by this extract from their report:

> There are strong rationales for a consumer choice approach, since people know their needs better than others, it can increase pressures on suppliers to perform, and people value choice in its own right. (Productivity Commission 2011, p. 343)

In advancing the argument for a fully individualised funding scheme with direct payments (i.e. self-management of funds), the Productivity Commission relied heavily on some English studies. Based on their assessment of this evidence, and in support of their recommendation for an individualised scheme, the Productivity Commission (2011, p. 31) asserted '(t)here is *widespread and compelling evidence* (my emphasis) that [individualised funding] leads to good outcomes … and potentially all at lower cost'. The 'compelling' evidence referred to by the Productivity Commission is from findings of the individualised funding studies in England: The Individual Budgets Pilot study (Glendinning et al. 2008), the early POET surveys (Duffy and Waters 2008) and the IFF Research (2008) (Productivity Commission 2011, Appendix E, pp. E1–E2). Yet, as noted in my discussion of the English experience in Chapter 3, these studies show mixed results and some have attracted considerable criticism. Recent reviews of this and other evidence for positive outcomes of individualised funding social care schemes in England and elsewhere in Europe and North America suggest the case is less than compelling (Alakeson 2016; Dickinson 2017; Fleming et al. 2019; Webber et al. 2014).

The Productivity Commission's conclusions give every appearance of reflecting a determined enthusiasm for a market-based individualised scheme seemingly regardless of the evidence. This seems evident in their evaluation of evidence and conclusions regarding opportunities and risks for the care and support workforce. The Productivity Commission's assessment was that the future fortunes of the workforce in an Australian individualised funding scheme would be very positive, which they summed up as follows:

> The new system will translate to greater pay, more jobs, better working conditions, the capacity for innovative practice, enough resources to do the job properly, recognition of the critical role of workers, more choice of employers, and greater satisfaction from working in a system that achieves better outcomes for the people they support. (Productivity Commission 2011, p. 50)

This seems a highly optimistic assessment, considered in the light of the international evidence I have discussed in Chapters 2 and 3, and especially when considering the evidence the Productivity Commission themselves cite in their report (see also Macdonald and Charlesworth 2016). A close reading of the report suggests their upbeat assessment of the likely outcomes for workers is based firstly, and mainly, on their assertion that strong demand for labour in a competitive market will lead to better pay and conditions. Secondly, it is based on a view that, even if pay is low, this may not be of any real consequence for workers, as they enjoy their work (Productivity Commission 2011, p. 393, pp. E.24–E.29).

With the NDIS now in place, similarly optimistic views to those of the Productivity Commission concerning the feminised frontline care and support workforce prevail among the managers of the NDIS quasi-market. However, as discussed below, overall there is not much evidence of *any* concern or accountability for workers by the NDIA or those in the Australian government responsible for the publicly-funded care scheme.

Who's Managing the Market and Where Are the Workers?

> This individually commissioned market for disability services harnesses the power of the market to achieve better outcomes for people with disability. (NDIA 2016, p. 6)

> While individualised funding was supported by many, some shortcomings have been identified: … (including that) governments tend to abrogate their responsibility for individual support and service development once payments are devolved. (Senate Standing Committee on Community Affairs 2007, p. 126)

To enable the creation of the NDIS, most responsibility for disability support was transferred to the Commonwealth Government from the states and territories with management and governance responsibilities being shared by a number of public bodies. The NDIA was established as a statutory authority to take responsibility for the delivery of the scheme, including for approving individual support plans. High-level policy responsibility for the NDIS sits with an intergovernmental body, the Council of Australian Governments (COAG), that has representation from federal and state and territory governments (Buckmaster and Clarke 2018). The federal minister for the NDIS is responsible for making the NDIS Rules and, taking advice from the COAG Ministerial Council on Disability Reform, for directing the NDIA. The Department of Social Services (DSS) is the Commonwealth government agency providing policy guidance and with high-level responsibility for oversight of the performance of the NDIS, including the NDIS care and support market.

As noted above, in 2018, the NDIS Quality and Safeguards Commission was set up as care regulator and it gained national coverage in 2020 (NDIA 2016; NDIS Quality and Safeguards Commission 2020b).

From the outset, the market and a market logic have been dominant in policy and rhetoric about how the NDIS will work. Georgia van Toorn, in her detailed analysis of the politics of the NDIS design, argues the Australian Government is committed to a 'hyper-marketised model' of individualised funding (van Toorn 2018, p. 155). Gemma Carey, a public policy analyst who, with colleagues, has followed the NDIS development and operations closely, refers to 'free market fanaticism' in the implementation of the scheme. Carey argues that the 'rhetoric of a hands-off, free-market approach to the NDIS' has been far stronger in the rollout than it was in the design, as it had been anticipated in the design that there could be a need for some collective service arrangements (Carey 2019, n.p.; see also Carey et al. 2018a). Her assessment is that:

> Fairly early on in implementation, block-funding and commissioning became thought of as a sign of failure by scheme implementers in Commonwealth. A move away from the pure market vision of the NDIS, which never actually existed at its outset. (Carey 2019, n.p.)

The NDIA has adopted the idea of market stewardship to describe the organisation's role in overseeing the NDIS market (NDIA 2016, 2018c). Market stewardship is not a term used widely in public policy literature but, according to Gash et al. (2013, p. 35), it describes a 'government's overall role in relation to public services where market mechanisms play a central role … (and the government) does not directly control the way services are delivered'. Market stewardship is 'an approach (that) focuses on ensuring long-term outcomes and value for money'. It involves policymakers engaging closely with all stakeholders, setting the 'rules of the game', constantly monitoring market development and adjusting the rules to 'steer the system' to achieve high-level policy aims (Gash et al. 2013, p. 6). The term stewardship serves nicely to emphasise that the government's responsibility is understood as to steer only, not to row. The key role for a market steward is to adjust levers to achieve effective choice and competition, which, in turn, are assumed to deliver high-level outcomes (Gash et al. 2013, p. 19, Fig. 3).

The potential market interventions the NDIA suggest they might make as market steward include 'improv(ing) the market' by influencing demand through setting prices, and taking indirect actions to support market functioning, including providing information and developing systems to support transactions. While the NDIA could directly commission services (NDIA 2016, p. 5), they make it clear that their intention is to commit—wherever possible—to an absolute reliance on market solutions for all people eligible for supports in all circumstances. Thus, their 'Market Approach' strategy states that the agency 'will have a starting point, with respect to market interventions, of as minimal interference as possible in the market' (NDIA 2016, p. 20). The long-term project is a strong, contestable marketplace for disability supports.

While various government bodies have some responsibility for oversight of the NDIS and its market, there has been considerable lack of clarity about who is taking responsibility for what. Notably, several years into the implementation of the scheme, the parliamentary Joint Standing Committee on the National Disability Insurance Scheme (2018, p. 10) recommended 'the DSS and the NDIA urgently develop a strategy document that clearly articulates the roles, responsibilities and activities of all those responsible for market stewardship'. This recommendation came two years after the Australian National Audit Office (ANAO) observed that it 'would be useful for DSS and the NDIA to publish statements defining their respective "market oversight" and "market stewardship" roles, to improve transparency and support accountability for these responsibilities' (ANAO 2016, p. 9). The Productivity Commission (2017) made similar recommendations in the report of a 2017 inquiry into NDIS costs. The strong parallels with concerns raised about stewardship of the individualised care system in England (Needham et al. 2018) are suggestive of some fundamental problems with a light-touch free-market approach. In England in 2016, in a report on personal budgets in social care, the British House of Commons Committee of Public Accounts (2016, p. 14) remarked:

> … it struck us that the 'steward' role is poorly defined, and it is not clear who is accountable for failures in local care markets, nor whether the Department (of Health) has effective levers to change local care markets. The Department told us it is pulling together a workforce strategy and a national market position statement, which we look forward to reading.

Ambiguity and absence of accountability for *the care and support workforce* is very evident in the texts of NDIS market and workforce policies—and in the management of the NDIS. This has been remarked on by academic analysts, regulatory bodies and others (ANAO 2016; Carey et al. 2018b; Dickinson et al 2014; Joint Standing Committee on the National Disability Insurance Scheme 2018; Malbon et al. 2019; Nevile et al. 2019). In 2017, in a report on NDIS costs, the Productivity Commission (2017, p. 319) pointed to the need for 'a clearer delineation of roles and responsibilities for developing workforce policy for a more coordinated response' and also remarked on the need for an 'evidence base on the number of workers in the sector, and their conditions and working arrangements'. At the time of writing in 2020 there was still no reliable source of data on the NDIS-funded care and support workforce.

The ANAO (2016) noted the absence of accountability for the social care workforce and workers in their assessment of the NDIS 'Integrated Market, Sector and Workforce Strategy' (Senior Officials Working Group for the Disability Reform Council 2015). The NDIS document, developed by the Department of Social Services (DSS), at a cost of $56 million, was considered by the ANAO as 'not providing a clear basis for coordinated actions, as it does not commit jurisdictions to specific deliverables, with agreed timeframes, accountabilities and milestones' by the ANAO (2016, p. 32). The strategy document barely mentions workers.

While the responsible government ministers have repeatedly lauded the NDIS as 'one of the largest job-creation opportunities in Australia's history' (Fletcher and Henderson 2018, p. 1; Robert 2019, p. 1) the nature and quality of the publicly-funded care and support jobs are barely visible as a concern for the managers of the NDIS market. However, workers are not *invisible* in NDIS policy. How policymakers view the future of the NDIS and their ideas and strategies for progress to a 'mature' NDIS market (DSS 2019, p. 1) entail ideas and assumptions about workers, their roles and the future shape and prospects of the growing care and support, as described below.

Workers as Efficient Services in the Managed Market

Two distinct sets of NDIS policy, regulatory and operational documents exist in which workers are centrally implicated. One set comprises market-related documents produced by the NDIA, the DSS, the Productivity

Commission and associated bodies and consultants. These documents relate to the pricing and funding of NDIS supports and to the growth, development and regulation of the NDIS market, including workforce growth. Workers are often not explicitly mentioned in these documents. However, references to services or to supports often contain implicit assumptions about workers and their jobs and have significant implications for the nature and quality of care and support employment. A second set of documents is concerned with regulating care and support practice to ensure quality services and safeguarding of NDIS service users. In this section I examine the market-related texts before turning to those concerned with regulating care and support provision in the section that follows.

Analysis of the texts of the market-related documents reveals two strong narratives concerning workers. The first is a *cost reduction narrative*, a central aspect of which relates to the need to reduce inefficiencies in service provision. The second is a *consumer choice narrative* that defines good social care services (and workers) as being the social care services (and workers) that customers want and that will result from a competitive market.

The Cost Reduction Narrative: Less Inefficiency and More Value for Money

> Organisations wanting to win a share of this new marketplace will need to be competitive and efficient, but more importantly they will need to attract and retain consumers and demonstrate a clearly articulated value proposition to the participant as a priority including consideration of value for money for the participant. (NDIA 2016, p. 9)

In NDIS policy a cost reduction narrative largely establishes the limits of possible actions that might be taken to increase labour supply under the expanded disability support system. So, although it is recognised that low wages could be a problem for workers, as well as a problem for labour supply (DSS 2019; Productivity Commission 2017), the option of increasing NDIS regulated price caps and funding for individual supports to improve wages and conditions is rarely canvassed. Rather, the dominant claim is that a mature market will produce a capable, skilled, diverse and sustainable workforce (DSS 2019; Senior Officials Working Group for the

Disability Reform Council 2015)—including as service providers become more efficient by reducing their current operating costs (McKinsey and Company 2018; NDIA 2019e).

Documents on NDIS market development and pricing strategy repeat the assertion that many disability support service provider organisations are operating inefficiently (McKinsey and Company 2018; NDIA 2019e, p. 15). They present efficiency gains as *the key* to reducing the social care system costs in the long term. NDIA policy considers the 'efficient' price of disability support and care in a future 'mature' market to be lower than the price would have been before the introduction of individualised funding (NDIA 2019e, p. 7, Figure 1). While many service providers are struggling to remain viable under the NDIS individualised pricing model and current funding level (Carey et al. 2020; McKinsey and Company 2018), the NDIA regards the problem to be one of service provider inefficiencies, referring to existing low levels of NDIS funding as reflecting 'sustainable' levels or 'the price at which the average current firm is viable (even if inefficient)'[2] (NDIA 2019e, p. 36).

When efficiency gains are contemplated in NDIS texts, service providers' employment arrangements, the spotlight is directed to labour utilisation and overheads. Efficient providers are seen to be those providers that can increase their labour utilisation by increasing their use of a casualised workforce, using sole trader care workers and adopting 'lean operating models' (McKinsey and Company 2018, p. 25). Service providers 'with more qualified specialist or experienced workforces' or with '(collective agreements) that are more generous' in offering pay over the regulated minimum rate are the service providers who find the NDIS pricing 'challenging' (McKinsey 2018, p. 25).

The NDIA present the ideal as a market in which consumer choice will drive down prices, as suggested here: 'Already in parts of the NDIS market, self-managing participants, as empowered consumers, are seeking value for money, which is driving competitive pricing, greater flexibility and a quality workforce' (NDIA 2018b, p. 5). Further, the NDIA's guidance for people self-managing their supports and directly employing their own personal care and support workers distances the notion of an appropriate pay rate for workers from the regulated minimum pay rates that are set in the industry award by Australia's Fair Work Commission (Fair Work

[2] Brackets are in the original text.

Commission 2020). For example, the NDIA guide for directly engaging support workers advises only that: 'You are able to negotiate the pay rate that you pay your staff, however it is worth keeping in mind the rate of pay for a support worker as outlined in the (SCHCDS Industry Award)' (NDIA 2019b).

Minimisation of the cost of individual supports is built into the *NDIS Act 2013* (Cth), which stipulates that a funded support must represent 'value for money in that the costs of the support are reasonable relative both to the benefits achieved and to the cost of alternative support'. The NDIA interprets this to refer to reasonable costs 'relative to the market cost of the support' (NDIA 2019e, p. 16). Already the evidence suggests that an NDIS employment model of disability support workers in permanent jobs with paid sick and annual leave, some access to employer-supported training, adequate supervision and peer support, and remuneration for work-related travel, is beyond the scope of what is considered a reasonable cost in the NDIS (Carey et al. 2019; Cortis and van Toorn 2020). If the NDIA continue to take their direction on the pricing model from the so-called efficient provider, an approach to the workforce that supports decent jobs may no longer fit with the requirement to offer 'value for money' as conceived within the NDIS.

In one government-commissioned report, self-employed support workers (who are not protected by minimum pay standards) are themselves described as a new category of 'efficient' service provider. 'Sole trader care attendants' are referred to as one of the 'profitable and successful operating models' of service provision (McKinsey and Company 2018, p. 27). As detailed in subsequent chapters, the available evidence suggests self-employed care and support workers can be engaged very cheaply in the NDIS care and support market as their 'price' often does not include provision for the on-costs and overheads associated with employment security, other employment protections and benefits, training, or access to supervision and support.

The Consumer Choice Narrative: Who You Want and When You Want Them

Alongside the NDIS cost reduction narrative a consumer choice narrative requires that social care and support must meet consumer desires and preferences (including for value for money). This is not to suggest that the NDIS does in fact meet everyone's needs. Rather, policy documents concerned with the NDIS market present responsiveness to consumer choice as something that obliges service providers (and, implicitly, workers) to do whatever it takes. They portray direct employment of care and support workers as the best consumer choice as it 'may give (the service user) the ultimate control over the people who work with you, the hours they work and the tasks that they perform' (NDIA 2019b, p. 3).

A common concern raised by service providers in interviews and focus groups for this and other research concerned how to balance responsiveness to consumers with workforce stability, sustainability and workers' rights (e.g. not to be discriminated against) (see also Macdonald 2019). However, such concerns are not very apparent in NDIS market-related policy documents in which the focus is more likely to be on flexibility to meet consumer demands at any cost. Similarly these texts often present anything that constrains the ability to provide preferred support on demand as a problem. For instance, provisions in employment regulations that provide working time security or compensation to workers for variability in hours are described as 'impediments' to achieving consumer choice that need to be removed (Productivity Commission PC 2017, p. 325). The NDIA suggest, somewhat euphemistically, that employers should adopt 'more mature rostering and staff management practices' (NDIA 2017, p. 98) while, less euphemistically, consultants to the NDIA have called for employers to make greater use of a more casualised workforce (McKinsey and Company 2018).

NDIS policy links both consumer choice and efficiencies to 'innovative' models of service provision. Such models are those that have lower overheads, maximise productivity and staff utilisation and offer better value for money, while also providing greater choice and control over who provides services and when and how they provide them (DSS 2020, p. 4; McKinsey and Company 2018, p. 28; NDIA 2017, p. 19). In these texts references to innovation are usually references to gig economy digital care platforms. NDIS managers welcome these organisations into the NDIS disability care and support marketplace, primarily for their potential to reduce costs. For instance, the NDIA (2018d, p. 66) note 'in general contexts, eMarket platforms may be able to reduce unit costs by between 15–30%'. McKinsey and Company (2018, pp. 92–93) assert the digital platforms' 'innovation' is in 'leverag(ing) technology to minimise overhead costs' (see also Hoffman 2020).

These discussions of platforms' innovation are almost always silent on the fact that cost savings are likely to be made through avoidance of many costs of employment that a service provider or direct employer has to pay, including wages and labour on-costs such as the costs of supervision and training (NDIA 2019c). As time has passed, NDIS managers appear to have elevated the role and importance of digital platforms in the publicly-funded social system from being a replacement for—or version of—a service provider to being sector infrastructure, as suggested by the NDIA (2019e, p. 23) in referring to 'appropriate support infrastructure for the sector, such as digital platforms…'. This is a significant shift given that, as examined in detail in subsequent chapters, the business and service models of the digital care platforms rely on shifting many of the costs and risks of both service provision and employment away from their organisations to individual service users and social care workers.

Regulating with Care? Quality, Safety and Skills in the Managed Market

The second set of NDIS documents, concerned with regulating care for quality and safeguarding, is much more explicitly concerned with care and support workers and their skills and practice. Like the market-related documents these NDIS documents also contain many implicit assumptions about workers, employers, the organisation of work and the nature of care and support jobs. There is clear tension in the NDIS between the NDIA goals for self-management and keeping down unit costs, on the one hand, and the state's multiple responsibilities for ensuring safe and quality care, and for worker health and safety, on the other. These tensions are evident when considering the business and employment models promoted in the market policies described above and the expectations placed on workers for skilled and safe practice in quality and safeguarding documents. The structural conditions of casualised work, direct employment and self-employed contracting in low-paid jobs and the characterisation of the work as low-skilled and requiring no formal training do not sit comfortably alongside the responsibilities and expectations that are evident in the quality and safeguarding obligations placed on workers in the NDIS.

As explained, disability service providers only have to be registered with the NDIS Quality and Safeguards Commission if they are providing services to people whose NDIS funding is managed by the NDIA. Only registered providers are required to meet NDIS practice standards and apply basic worker screening checks (e.g. police checks). As NDIS goals and key performance indicators are for increases in self-management of supports which does not require the use of registered providers (NDIA 2018d), it is likely that an increasing share of care and support funded by the NDIS will be extremely lightly regulated in this system.

An *NDIS Code of Conduct* does apply to all workers and to registered and unregistered service providers. It is unclear what education, support, monitoring or enforcement activities the NDIS Commission can, or will, engage in to support compliance with this code, or how they will ensure that workers who are directly engaged or employed will even know about its existence (Joint Standing Committee 2018, p. 65). A more general concern about the likely effectiveness of the quality and safeguarding system is a concern that it is a reactive system as it is largely complaints-based. In addition, doubts have been raised about whether the NDIS Quality and Safeguards Commission is adequately resourced to even manage complaints (Schulz 2020).

The *NDIS Code of Conduct—Guidance for Workers* provides information and examples about what the *NDIS Code of Conduct* means in practice (NDIS Commission 2019b). The guidance and examples provided in the document are instructive, as they bring to the fore the significant disconnect between, on the one hand, expectations placed on workers in relation to quality and safe practice in providing supports and, on the other, the circumstances of workers directly employed or engaged as self-employed or independent contractors. In many places the guidance document contains an implicit assumption that there is a service provider-employer, yet a growing number of workers are outside organisation-based employment relationships. For example, the document includes 22 scenarios as examples of required practice. In 21 of these scenarios, problem or issue resolution involves either one or the other of the person being supported or their support worker seeking advice or assistance from a service co-ordinator, manager or supervisor. The document also directs workers to their employers' policies, procedures and training, for example, in making sure workers avoid conflicts of interest, and in preventing and identifying violence, abuse and neglect and exploitation (NDIS Commission 2019b).

Limited accountability for workers is apparent in the NDIS approach to quality and safeguarding. For example, the *NDIS Code of Conduct—Guidance for Service Providers* requires that service providers must ensure their workers are appropriately trained, skilled and supervised. The guidance document reinforces providers' duty to comply with relevant work health and safety regulations (NDIS Commission 2019a). However, otherwise it is not concerned with workers.

Poor accountability at the system level for both NDIS funding recipients and workers became very apparent in 2020 when the COVID-19 pandemic struck. While government responses including lockdowns commenced in March 2020, it was not until the end of July that the NDIA announced people could spend their disability support funds on personal protective equipment such as masks and gloves (Michael 2020).

Service provider and other stakeholder accounts and the interviews with workers undertaken for this research suggest there are many inexperienced and untrained workers being recruited to provide support to people in the NDIS. There is emerging evidence of the potential risks this changing workforce composition may bring to service users (Cortis et al. 2017; Cortis and Van Toorn 2020). The NDIS Commission (2020c) is leading the development of an NDIS Workforce Capability Framework that will identify core capabilities workers are expected to have. However, as argued above, the NDIS pricing structure and levels and the broader market approach provide few resources to support training, they assume basic levels of worker skills, do not provide for worker progression, and support workforce casualisation strategies. All of these pressures appear to be in direct tension with system aspirations for worker capabilities to support quality and safeguarding.

The requirements placed on individuals who choose to engage their own care and support workers with their NDIS funds do not include any obligations to follow good employment or procurement practices. There are provisions in the NDIS Act to prohibit self-management of NDIS support funds in some circumstances, including insolvency and where self-management would present an 'unreasonable risk to the participant' (NDIS Act 2013, s. 44(2)(a)). However, there is no provision for the NDIA to withdraw access to self-management of funds where a person does not comply with employment laws. Guidance offered to direct employers about their responsibilities and obligations as employers is generally restricted to the need to meet legal obligations (NDIA 2019b; NDIA 2019d).

Conclusion

The analysis summarised in this chapter revealed some of the underlying ideas and values embedded in NDIS policies and motivating the market approach as well as some inherent tensions and apparent contradictions with system aspirations for quality and safety. Two strong themes emerge as capturing the character of the new scheme as it is likely to shape the nature of work and the employment conditions and arrangements for the frontline social care workforce. These themes are *consumer choice and control* and *the market as the basis for fair pay and conditions*.

Consumer choice and control concerns the ways in which the NDIS defines and expresses person-centred support and puts it into practice. Consumer choice and control as a normative ideal provides a key rationale for the absence of any formal qualifications and skills framework for care and support work in the care system, and for the absence of care regulation in much of the market. Consumer choice and control provides the basis for viewing care and support workers as flexible services rather than as people with rights as workers, and the minimisation of labour costs as necessary to achieve value for money.

Acceptance and promotion of *the market as the basis for fair pay and conditions* (as an ideal) is underpinned by the NDIS cost reduction imperative and is operationalised in the pricing arrangements and value for money principles. It is evident in the light-touch approach to regulation of the social care market. This theme captures how care and support workers' labour is viewed as a commodity in a services market and how the minimisation of labour costs is seen as essential for efficiency and value for money. In the next chapter I show how gaps and limitations of labour market and employment regulation establish the spaces and opportunity for social care work and employment to be re-fashioned to align with these themes and the NDIS' ideals.

References

Alakeson, V. (2016). Self-direction in long-term services and supports: International differences and current challenges. *Public Policy & Aging Report, 26*(4), 143–148. https://doi.org/10.1093/ppar/prw018.

Australian National Audit Office. (2016). *National Disability Insurance Scheme—Management of the transition of the disability services market*. The Auditor-General ANAO Report No. 24 2016–17 Performance Audit. Canberra: Australian National Audit Office.

Bottery, S., & Babalola, G. (2020). *Social care 360*. https://www.kingsfund.org.uk/publications/social-care-360#a-fragile-sector. Accessed May 2020.

Buckmaster, L., & Clarke, S. (2018). *The national disability insurance scheme: A chronology*. Research Paper Series, 2018–19 (Vol. 2020). Canberra: Parliament of Australia.

Carey, G. (2019). *What happened to the NDIS?* https://www.csi.edu.au/news/director-update-what-happened-ndis/. Accessed 14 June 2020.

Carey, G., Dickinson, H., Malbon, E., & Reeders, D. (2018a). The vexed question of market stewardship in the public sector: Examining equity and the social contract through the Australian National Disability Insurance Scheme. *Social Policy & Administration, 52*(1), 387–407. https://doi.org/10.1111/spol.12321.

Carey, G., Malbon, E., Marjolin, A., & Reeders, D. (2018b). National disability markets: Market stewardship actions for the NDIS. Sydney: Centre for Social Impact, University of New South Wales. https://www.csi.edu.au/research/project/market-stewardship-actions-ndis-new-report/. Accessed 13 August 2020.

Carey, G., Weier, Malbon, E., Dickinson, H., & Duff, G. (2020). *How is the disability sector faring? A report from National Disability Services' annual market survey*. Sydney: Centre for Social Impact, University of New South Wales. https://www.unsw.adfa.edu.au/public-service-research-group/reports. Accessed 13 August 2020.

Cortis, N., Macdonald, F., Davidson, B., & Bentham, E. (2017). *Reasonable, necessary and valued: Pricing disability services for quality support and decent jobs*. Sydney: Social Policy Research Centre, University of New South Wales. https://www.arts.unsw.edu.au/sites/default/files/documents/NDIS_Pricing_Report.pdf. Accessed 17 September 2020.

Cortis, N., & van Toorn, G. (2020). *Working in new disability markets: A survey of Australia's disability workforce*. Sydney: Social Policy Research Centre, University of New South Wales.

Department of Social Services (DSS). (2019). *Growing the NDIS market and workforce*. Canberra: Commonwealth of Australia.

Department of Social Services (DSS). (2020). *Australian government department of social services submission to the joint standing committee on the national disability insurance scheme inquiry into implementation, performance and governance of the National Disability Insurance Scheme (NDIS): The NDIS workforce Parliament of Australia*.

Dickinson, H. (2017). Individual funding systems: what works? *Evidence Base, 3*(3), 1–18. https://doi.org/10.21307/eb-2017-003.

Dickinson, H., Needham, C., & Sullivan, H. (2014). Individual funding for disability support: What are the implications for accountability? *Australian Journal of Public Administration, 73*(4), 417–425. https://doi.org/10.1111/1467-8500.12106.

Duffy, S., & Waters, J. (2008). *A report on In Control's second phase, evaluation and learning 2005–2007*. London: In Control Publications.

Fair Work Commission. (2020). *Social, community, home care and disability services industry award 2010* (PR721438). Fair Work Commission. https://www.fwc.gov.au/documents/documents/modern_awards/award/ma000100/default.html. Accessed 19 August 2020.

Fleming, P., McGilloway, S., Hernon, M., Furlong, M., O'Doherty, S., Keogh, F., et al. (2019). Individualised funding interventions to improve health and social care outcomes for people with a disability: A mixed-methods systematic review. *A Campbell Systematic Review 2019:3*. Oslo: Campbell Collaboration.

Fletcher, P., & Henderson, S. (2018). Morrison Government strategy to boost NDIS workforce. *Joint Media Release*. Canberra: Australian Government.

Gash, T., Panchamia, N., Sims, S., & Hotson, L. (2013). *Making public service markets work: Professionalising government's approach to commissioning and market stewardship*. London: Institute for Government.

Gillard, J. (2013). *Locking in a fairer future for Australians with disability*. Canberra: Treasury Portfolio Ministers. https://ministers.treasury.gov.au/ministers/wayne-swan-2007/media-releases?page=1. Accessed 22 September 2020.

Glendinning, C., Challis, D., Fernandez, J., Jacobs, S., Jones, K., Knapp, M., et al. (2008). *Evaluation of the individual budgets pilot programme: Final report*. York: Individual Budgets Evaluation Network (IBSEN).

Green, J., & Mears, J. (2014). The implementation of the NDIS: Who wins, who loses? *Cosmopolitan Civil Societies, 6*(2). https://doi.org/10.5130/ccs.v6i2.3915.

Hoffman, M. (2020). *CEO address to the Council for Economic Development of Australia, NDIA*. https://www.ndis.gov.au/news/4413-ceo-address-council-economic-development-australia. Accessed 15 March 2020.

House of Commons Committee of Public Accounts (UK Parliament). (2016). Personal budgets in social care: second report of Session 2016–17. In House of Commons (Ed.), *Report, together with formal minutes relating to the report* (p. 67). London, UK: Her Majesty's Stationery Office (HMSO).

IFF Research. (2008). Employment aspects and workforce implications of direct payments. *Skills for care* (p. 253). London: IFF Research.

Independent Advisory Council to the NDIS. (2017). *IAC report on enhancing self-direction and self-management in the NDIS*. Canberra: NDIA. https://www.ndis-iac.com.au/advice. Accessed 12 May 2020.

Joint Standing Committee on the National Disability Insurance Scheme. (2018). *Market readiness for provision of services under the NDIS* (Parliament of Australia, Ed.). Canberra.

Macdonald, F. (2019). *Where secure employment meets client needs: Greenacres disability services workforce innovation fund project*. Sydney: National Disability Services.

Macdonald, F., & Charlesworth, S. (2016). Cash for care under the NDIS: Shaping care workers' working conditions? *Journal of Industrial Relations, 58*(5), 627–646. https://doi.org/10.1177/0022185615623083.

Malbon, E., Carey, G., & Reeders, D. (2019). Mixed accountability within new public governance: The case of a personalized welfare scheme in early implementation. *Social Policy & Administration, 53*(1), 156–169. https://doi.org/10.1111/spol.12446.

McKinsey and Company. (2018). *Independent pricing review. National Disability Insurance Agency*. The Board of the NDIA. https://www.ndis.gov.au/providers/price-guides-and-pricing/independent-pricing-review#key-documents. Accessed 11 November 2019.

Meagher, G., & Goodwin, S. (2015). Introduction: Capturing marketisation in Australian social policy. In G. Meagher & S. Goodwin (Eds.), *Markets, Rights and Power in Australian Social Policy* (pp. 1–27). Sydney: Sydney University Press.

Michael, L. (2020, July 29). NDIS makes it easier for participants to get face masks. *Pro Bono Australia*.

Miller, P., & Hayward, D. (2017). Social policy 'generosity' at a time of fiscal austerity: The strange case of Australia's National Disability Insurance Scheme. *Critical Social Policy, 37*(1), 128–147. https://doi.org/10.1177/0261018316664463.

National Disability Insurance Agency (NDIA). (2016). *NDIS market approach: Statement of opportunity and intent—November 2016*. Canberra: National Disability Insurance Agency.

National Disability Insurance Agency (NDIA). (2018a). *NDIA Annual Report 2017–18*. Canberra: National Disability Insurance Agency.

National Disability Insurance Agency (NDIA). (2018b). *Independent pricing review NDIA response*. NDIA. Accessed from https://www.ndis.gov.au/providers/price-guides-and-pricing/independent-pricing-review#final-report-and-ndia-response.

National Disability Insurance Agency (NDIA). (2018c). *NDIS market enablement framework*. Canberra: National Disability Insurance Agency.

National Disability Insurance Agency (NDIA). (2018d). *NDIA submission to the Joint Standing Committee on the National Disability Insurance Scheme*. Market readiness for provision of services under the NDIS. Canberra: National Disability Insurance Agency.

National Disability Insurance Agency (NDIA). (2018e). *Ways to manage your funding*. https://www.ndis.gov.au/participants/creating-your-plan/ways-manage-your-funding. Accessed January 2019.

National Disability Insurance Agency (NDIA). (2019a). *National Disability Insurance Scheme annual report 2018–2019*. Canberra: National Disability Insurance Agency.

National Disability Insurance Agency (NDIA). (2019b). *Directly engaging your own staff*. Canberra: National Disability Insurance Agency.

National Disability Insurance Agency (NDIA). (2019c). *National Disability Insurance Scheme cost model for disability support workers*. Canberra: National Disability Insurance Agency.

National Disability Insurance Agency (NDIA). (2019d). *National Disability Insurance Scheme guide to self-management*. Canberra: National Disability Insurance Agency.

National Disability Insurance Agency (NDIA). (2019e). *National Disability Insurance Scheme pricing strategy*. Canberra: National Disability Insurance Agency.

National Disability Insurance Agency (NDIA). (2020a). *COAG Disability Reform Council NDIS Quarterly Report, 31 March 2020*. Canberra: National Disability Insurance Agency.

National Disability Insurance Agency (NDIA). (2020b). *Support budgets in your plan*. https://www.ndis.gov.au/participants/using-your-plan/managing-your-plan/support-budgets-your-plan. Accessed 10 September 2020.

NDIS Quality and Safeguards Commission. (2019a). *The NDIS code of conduct—Guidance for service providers*. Canberra: NDIS Quality and Safeguards Commission.

NDIS Quality and Safeguards Commission. (2019b). *The NDIS code of conduct—Guidance for workers*. Canberra: NDIS Quality and Safeguards Commission.

NDIS Quality and Safeguards Commission. (2020a). NDIS Commission homepage. https://www.ndiscommission.gov.au. Accessed 15 March 2020.

NDIS Quality and Safeguards Commission. (2020b). *NDIS Commission start dates*. NDIS Quality and Safeguards Commission. https://www.ndiscommission.gov.au/about/start-dates. Accessed 15 March 2020.

NDIS Quality and Safeguards Commission. (2020c). *NDIS workforce capability framework*. NDIS Quality and Safeguards Commission. https://www.ndiscommission.gov.au/workers/ndis-workforce-capability-framework. Accessed 15 July 2020.

Naufal. (2020). *NDIA gaslighting group providers*. DSC Consulting. https://teamdsc.com.au/resources/ndia-gaslighting-group-providers?rq=gaslighting. Accessed 27 June 2020.

Needham, C., & Dickinson, H. (2018). 'Any one of us could be among that number': Comparing the policy narratives for individualized disability funding in Australia and England. *Social Policy & Administration*, *52*(3), 731–749. https://doi.org/10.1111/spol.12320.

Needham, C., Hall, K., Allen, K., Burn, E., Mangan, C., & Henwood, M. (2018). *Market shaping and personalisation in social care: a realist synthesis of the literature*. Birmingham: Health Services Management Centre, University of Birmingham. https://www.thinkbigpicture.co.uk. Accessed 10 September 2019.

Nevile, A., Malbon, E., Kay, A., & Carey, G. (2019). The implementation of complex social policy: Institutional layering and unintended consequences in the National Disability Insurance Scheme. *Australian Journal of Public Administration*. https://doi.org/10.1111/1467-8500.12380.

Productivity Commission. (2010). *Contribution of the not-for-profit sector, research report*. Canberra: Productivity Commission.

Productivity Commission. (2011). *Disability care and support* (Report No. 54). Canberra: Productivity Commission.

Productivity Commission. (2017). *National Disability Insurance Scheme (NDIS) Costs: Position paper*. Melbourne: Australian Government.

Robert, The Hon S. (MP). (2019, November 14). *The NDIS plan*. Speech delivered to the National Press Club. Canberra.

Schulz, T. (2020, August 12). *'People are bursting into tears': Inside the troubled NDIS watchdog*. Crikey.com. https://www.crikey.com.au/2020/08/12/nidis-watchdog-complaints-commission/. Accessed 12 August 2020.

Senior Officials Working Group for the Disability Reform Council. (2015). *National Disability Insurance Scheme integrated market, sector and workforce strategy*. Canberra: Department of Social Services. https://www.dss.gov.au/sites/default/files/documents/07_2015/ndis_integrated_market_sector_and_workforce_strategy_june_2015.pdf. Accessed 17 October 2016.

The Senate Standing Committee on Community Affairs. (2007). *Funding and operation of the Commonwealth State/Territory Disability Agreement*. Canberra: Parliament of Australia.

Van Toorn, G. (2018). *The new political economy of disability: Transnational networks and individualised funding in the age of neoliberalism* (Doctoral dissertation). University of New South Wales and University of Glasgow.

Webber, M., Treacy, S., Carr, S., Clark, M., & Parker, G. (2014). The effectiveness of personal budgets for people with mental health problems: A systematic review. *Journal of Mental Health, 23*(3), 146–155. https://doi.org/10.3109/09638237.2014.910642.

CHAPTER 5

Regulating Work, Constructing Workers

Introduction

Social care work and employment are shaped within the intersections of care and employment regimes. In Chapter 4, I examined the social care system established by the NDIS and the ways in which frontline social care workers are considered and treated in the new cash-for-care scheme. In this chapter, I explore the characterisation and treatment of social care workers in Australia's labour market regulation and, in particular, in labour laws.

I have shown how the mechanisms of the individualised NDIS characterise social care workers as flexible services, the value of which is best determined by the individual consumer who knows what they want and what they want to pay. In the pursuit of consumer choice and cost containment (through reductions in the unit costs of care), the NDIS market managers encourage lean organisations that are able to devolve the costs (and risks) of service provision and of employment to individual service users and workers. This is the logic of the market mechanism. Labour market regulation also encompasses ideas and values about who is a worker, what work is and when a working person should be protected in the labour market and employment and these ideas are reflected in the scope and mechanisms of regulation including labour laws. As shown in the discussion that follows, there is plenty of room to accommodate, and even enable and reinforce the NDIS's preferred constructions of social

F. Macdonald, *Individualising Risk*,
https://doi.org/10.1007/978-981-33-6366-3_5

care workers under Australia's systems of employment and labour market regulation.

Labour Market Regulation: Failing Care Workers?

While Australia's industrial relations system has its own unique character, the problems and challenges for an effective system that protects the rights and conditions of all workers in this country are similar to those faced by many other nations with similarly well-developed employment regulation (Arup et al. 2006; Davidov and Langille 2011; Marshall 2019). Many of these problems arise from the limitations of laws for effectively regulating work in the context of changing institutional and market arrangements (Arup et al. 2006). Australia's care and support workers in the NDIS individualised funding market are highly exposed to many of the failings of contemporary labour laws, despite Australia having a comprehensive safety net of pay and conditions standards.

Many of the ways in which labour laws are failing to protect low-paid and vulnerable workers are well documented. One shortcoming is the inadequate coverage of minimum standards that apply to employees. In Australia, exceptions and gaps in employment minimum standards mean that a large proportion of the workforce, especially casual employees, work with fewer benefits than other workers and without protection against job loss and against working time and other insecurities (Campbell et al. 2019, Fair Work Ombudsman 2018). A second aspect in which labour laws fail is in the absence of regulation for setting standards for the pay and conditions of dependent and/or vulnerable workers who are outside of dependent employment relationships (Stewart and Stanford 2017). Such workers include, but are not limited to, workers in employment that has been disguised as independent contracting or self-employment. A proliferation of market actors utilising these forms of employment when securing and organising social care labour has occurred under the NDIS, as I describe in Chapter 6 that follows. A third problem for the effectiveness of labour laws is the absence of legal mechanisms to ascribe responsibility for workers' pay and conditions to organisations in supply chains that have control over work organisation (Johnstone et al. 2012). In the NDIS social care market, in addition to employers, there can be a number of other organisations with some control over disability support workers' jobs, employment arrangements and/or pay and working conditions. These organisations include the national authority, the National Disability Insurance Agency (the NDIA), that sets the prices and rules for provision of care and support and a variety of third party intermediaries, such as digital care platforms and labour hire agencies that broker care and support services and/or employment. Two other significant shortcomings of regulation concern lack of access to collective representation and bargaining and ineffective enforcement of labour regulation (Clibborn 2020; Macdonald et al. 2018b).

Some long-standing problems with the effectiveness of labour laws arise from the fact that regulations are reflective of and may reinforce existing inequalities and divisions in the labour market and society (Fudge and Owens 2006, Peck 2016). Gender divisions and inequalities are especially important when the feminised social care workforce is under consideration.

Gendering Work in Australian Industrial Relations

A historical perspective on Australia's labour market institutions provides insight into how and why the contemporary system fails to provide decent work for care and support workers. Australia's labour market is highly segmented by gender, with women overrepresented in many occupations and industry sectors, including social and community services, that have lower pay rates than prevail in most male-dominated industries and occupations. Women's labour force participation is comparatively high (OECD 2020) and women make up half of all employed persons. However, women make up 68% of all part-time employees and only 38% of all full-time employees (ABS 2020b). Such statistics highlight the fact that women continue to do a disproportionate amount of unpaid work and care in heterosexual couple households. Traditional gendered social norms persist in such households, where a 'one-and-half earner' model is dominant; men are in full-time employment while women combine part-time work with unpaid care (Charlesworth et al. 2011).

Historically, employment regulation has played a critical role in defining gender norms in Australia's labour market (O'Connor et al. 1999). In Australia's so-called 'wage-earner's welfare state' (Castles 1985), labour and social protections were built around a male breadwinner model. From early in the twentieth century, state and federal wage tribunals set 'basic wages' based on the needs of an unskilled male worker supporting a wife and three children living in 'frugal comfort' (Isaac 2008). 'Women's work' was undervalued within the broader industrial relations system, a fact reflected in low wages in feminised industries (Frances 2000). Much has changed—including that (male) minimum wages are no longer living wages, and a principle of equal remuneration for work of equal value has been established in the main federal industrial relations legislation, the Fair Work Act (2009 Cth). However, Australia has made little progress towards closing a large gender pay gap, and the institutionalisation of women's economic dependence on men continues to be supported by employment regulation that has largely failed to address systemic undervaluation of women's work (Smith and Whitehouse 2020). Employment regulation continues to privilege workers in full-time employment and to construct much part-time employment as insecure (Charlesworth and Macdonald 2017; Tham 2007).

Around half of all part-time female employees in Australia are casual employees (Gilfillan 2018, p. 7). Casual employees are without many of the protections and benefits provided to other employees, including paid annual and sick leave. Casuals receive a pay loading of 25% on their base hourly pay rates, but this monetary compensation is not equivalent in dollar terms to the benefits accruing to permanent employees. Further, as casuals have little or no working time certainty or security, they can be treated as on-demand workers in zero-hours work arrangements. Casuals can be engaged by employers to work on an as-needs basis—in short: whenever, wherever and for however long as needed. With the exception of employees who have had regular work with the same employer for a long period, casuals have no job security including any rights to claim unfair dismissal (Campbell et al. 2019). Historically, casual employment was established as an exception to the norm to enable employers to fill short-term vacancies (Hunter 2006). Now, the phenomenon of the 'long-term casual' is not unusual. One in five employees in Australia is employed on a casual basis (ABS 2019, Table 1b.3). Women are more likely to be in casual employment than men, although their long-standing over-representation has declined in recent years, as casual employment in male and youth labour markets has expanded.

In the female-dominated disability services workforce, in 2009, prior to the NDIS, only 14% of the direct care workforce of disability support workers was in a full-time job with permanent employee status, while 55% were employed on a permanent part-time basis and 31% were employed on a casual basis (Martin and Healy 2010, p. 113). With the implementation of the NDIS, casual employment of frontline care and support workers has increased relative to permanent employment (NDS 2017).

Unlike casual employees, workers in permanent part-time employment generally *do* have formal rights to the same benefits and protections as full-time employees. Permanent part-time jobs are often considered to be better quality jobs than casual jobs and historically have been promoted as good for women who are balancing work and family. Nevertheless, some problems remain with working time rules for part-time employees (Campbell et al. 2019), and there are also other ways in which some part-time employees are treated less favourably in labour and other regulation than full-time employees. This poorer treatment in regulation has implications for the social and community services workforce, particularly for lower paid, frontline social care workers including disability care and support workers, as explained below.

Social and Community Services Employment

Historically, most social care workers, including workers providing care and support to people with disability, have been employed by not-for-profit organisations in what is known in Australia as the social and community services or SACS industry sector. Gender divisions in employment are enormously significant in this highly feminised industry sector where many care and other social and welfare services are located. Racialised divisions have emerged more strongly in the last decade or so under a migration regime that has rapidly increased the pool of vulnerable migrant workers on temporary visas (Brennan et al. 2017).

Employees in the highly feminised SACS workforce were on the margins of the industrial relations system until late in the twentieth century. It was only in the mid-1980s that social care and community services workers gained 'industrial citizenship' with the creation of an industry-based 'award' which, like industrial awards for workers in other industries and occupations, sets out a classification structure, and pay and conditions of employees (Briggs et al. 2007, p. 497). Historically, under Australia's centralised wages systems, wages specified in industrial awards rose for employees in all industries as gains were made by employees in some parts of the economy. However, soon after SACS workers were recognised in the industrial relations system and workers gained award coverage, Australia's centralised system started to be dismantled, beginning with the replacement of industry or sector-wide bargaining with individual enterprise-based bargaining. From the 1990s, along with most other industrial awards, SACS industry awards eventually became a 'safety net' of minimum pay and conditions standards for employees who are unable to benefit from enterprise bargaining (Macdonald and Pegg 2018).

Enterprise bargaining in the SACS sector has been limited and has generally resulted in only small gains for workers, meaning most employees have been paid at levels on or just above the minimum safety net pay rate specfied in the industrial award. Low levels of government funding presented a major constraint to trade union bargaining for pay increases (Charlesworth 2012). In general, unions' attempts to engage government bodies—as the 'lead employers' with control over the purse strings—in bargaining processes have been unsuccessful (Macdonald et al. 2018b).

In 2012, a historic federal equal pay decision awarded significant wage increases to most SACS workers, to address acknowledged gendered undervaluation. The equal pay win followed a strong campaign by the social and community sector unions, led by the Australian Services Union. While most of the not-for-profit employers supported the equal pay campaign, peak bodies representing a much smaller group of for-profit employers opposed it (Macdonald and Charlesworth 2013).

A critical factor in the success of the unions' equal pay claim was a commitment made by the Labor Federal Government, led by Australia's first female prime minister, to fund organisations employing SACS workers to cover any pay increases that might be awarded by the federal tribunal determining the outcome of the equal pay case (Macdonald and Charlesworth 2013). However, while the outcome of the equal pay case remedied historically gendered undervaluation, SACS sector wages remain well below those of comparable public sector workers' wages and below average weekly wages in Australia. In 2019, under what is now called the Social, Community, Homecare and Disability Services Industry Award (the SCHCDS Industry Award) (Fair Work Commission 2020), a disability support worker's hourly wage was about two-thirds of the average hourly wage of all workers in Australia, and a home care worker's wage was about half the average (ABS 2020a; Fair Work Ombudsman [FWO] 2019).

Some of the lowest-paid social care workers in the SACS sector did not receive the equal pay increases at all. These are the employees classified as 'home care' workers in the SCHCDS Industry Award. The home care classification does not, on paper, apply to all disability support workers. However, as described in Chapter 6, in practice under the NDIS, some workers providing personal care and support to people with disability in their homes are being misclassified and employed on the (lower) 'home care' pay scale and conditions.

Sara Charlesworth has researched and written extensively about how the legal construction of home care work in the SCHCDS Industry Award reproduces gender inequalities. Charlesworth observes that not only are social care workers' minimum conditions and pay lower than those of workers in male-dominated occupations and industries (Charlesworth and Heron 2012), but a hierarchy in the treatment of social care workers exists in the standards set out in the SCHCDS Industry Award (Charlesworth 2012). The minimum conditions and pay standards are lower for employees undertaking the paid care work that most closely resembles women's unpaid personal care and domestic work in families. Thus, home care workers are the lowest-paid social care workers in the SCHCDS Industry Award classification structure. They also have much shorter minimum shift periods than other workers, meaning there is less restriction on the working time flexibility that employers can require of them. Workers classified as disability support workers are next up from the bottom of the SCHCDS Industry Award hierarchy, as their minimum shift periods are shorter than other social care workers covered by the Award (two hours compared with three hours for other social and community services workers).

A key differentiating factor in this hierarchy of pay and working conditions is the location of work. Under the SCHCDS Industry Award, employees who perform their work in private homes or other non-organisational settings (i.e. all home care workers and many disability support workers) are lower-paid and less well protected from very short shifts than other employees whose work is undertaken in organisational settings. Their work is more easily organised as on-call work, with unpredictable work schedules and fragmented working time than is the case for other social and community services workers (Charlesworth 2012). Home care workers' pay and conditions standards are also lower than those of aged care workers in institutional residential aged care settings whose pay and conditions are covered by the Aged Care Award (Charlesworth 2017).

While social care workers with casual employment status can be engaged on zero-hours arrangements and called in to work for a period as short as one hour, permanent part-time social care workers are not protected from such 'on-demand' work arrangements or short shifts either (Campbell et al. 2019). The SCHCDS Industry Award, like other industrial awards, contains a complex set of working time standards. However, as noted, the SCHCDS Industry Award standards are poorer than in many awards covering employees in other industries (Charlesworth and Heron 2012).

The SCHCDS Industry Award specifies that part-time employees must have a 'regular pattern of work' (Clause 10.3 (c)). However, an employee can work additional hours above their regular roster by agreement. This means that part-time workers can be engaged on regular rosters of very short hours for the week and treated as flexible on-demand labour for other work hours. Some employers of disability support workers have adopted this practice (Macdonald et al. 2018a). Further, it is a practice that appears to have grown under the NDIS pricing model, with significant negative impacts on workers' pay and working time security. These problems with working time and unpaid work that appear to be fairly widespread arise, not just from poorly regulated working time, but also from employer non-compliance with working time regulation in the SCHCDS Industry Award (Macdonald et al. 2018a). Employer organisations representing the interests of the private-for-profit employers have opposed unions' claims to strengthen working time protections for care and support workers, arguing that NDIS funding arrangements and levels demand more flexible arrangements and that working time standards are already too restrictive (Australian Industry Group 2019).

In addition to divisions and hierarchies within the SCHCDS Industry Award, as the main industrial instrument that regulates most social care employment, other exceptions and exclusions in regulations exist that establish poor treatment of care and support workers relative to other workers. These exceptions and exclusions relate to working time, work location, type of work, work relationship and nature of the employer.

In Australia employers are required to pay superannuation contributions for their employees but are exempt where employees earn less than AUD 450 a month (Austen and Mavisakalyan 2018). This exemption affects workers who are employed for only a few hours a week for any single organisation, including frontline social care workers who, under the

NDIS, are more likely than previously to be employed in multiple short-hours low-paid jobs (NDS 2018). Although their total monthly earnings may be well above $450 a month, employees may have no eligibility for employer superannuation contributions with any single employer. These exemptions have direct consequences for workers' retirement savings. As with this exemption based on the part-time/full-time work division, the bases for poorer treatment in other regulations both reflect and reproduce societal gendered norms and inequalities. They reinforce divisions between male breadwinner full-time productive work that is regulated as employment and female reproductive care work that is not regulated quite like other work. This gendering in regulation specifically affects workers who are employed by individuals and in private homes, situations likely to apply to a growing number of care and support workers in Australia's individualised funding scheme.

Part-Time 'Private', 'Domestic' and 'Personal' Work: Not Quite Like Other Work

> Demarcating the boundaries of work and home has historically been, and continues to be, a key function and effect of labour law. (Fudge 2014, p. 11)

> While there are certain activities that lend themselves more to informalization than others, it is not the intrinsic characteristics of activities which determine informalization, but rather the boundaries of state regulation. (Sassen 1997, p. 2)

The home has been separated from the market and treated as the private sphere of the family, to be protected from state interference, even where governments have created public markets for care (Anderson 2007). The treatment of employment in the home as a matter for labour law remains contested in many countries (Fudge 2014), despite attempts to change this through the establishment of international labour standards, including the recent *Domestic Workers Convention 2011* (No. 189) (International Labour Organization).

In Australia, exceptions in regulatory protections and benefits exist where jobs are only short hours, where work is located in private households and/or considered to be of a domestic or personal nature, and where employers are not running a business. NDIS regulation and market mechanisms provide incentives for care and support work to be organised in ways that place the work into these categories, distancing care and support workers from organisational work settings, from organisational employers and from collective organisation and representation. In all of these situations, risks and costs that would normally be shared with or borne by the employer, and/or pooled among workers, are devolved to the individual worker and/or indivdual service user. The work is also to some extent informalised (Delaney and Macdonald 2018).

Australian Federal and states' anti-discrimination laws contain some very significant exceptions where employment involves providing personal or domestic services in private homes. These exceptions make it *not unlawful*—under the specific law, although possibly under other laws—to discriminate against care and support workers on the basis of a very large number of attributes that, for other workers, are the bases for protection against discrimination. In the State of Victoria, for example, the *Equal Opportunity Act 2010* (Vic) (EO Act Vic) prohibits discrimination in employment on the grounds of age, breastfeeding, employment activity, gender identity, disability, industrial activity, lawful sexual activity, marital status, parental status or status as a carer, physical features, political belief or activity, pregnancy, race, religious belief or activity, sex, sexual orientation, an expunged homosexual conviction and association with a person identified by any of the listed attributes. However, the EO Act Vic contains an exception such that 'an employer may discriminate in determining who should be offered employment in relation to the provision of domestic or personal services' (EO Act Vic s.24(1)). This exception applies, not only to individuals who directly employ care and support workers in their own homes, but to service provider organisations that employ support workers to deliver support to clients, where these clients wish to discriminate. In many circumstances, individual employers may also be exempt from the obligation to pay employer contributions to workers' superannuation. This exemption exists for employers who are householders and their employees are employed 'to do work wholly or principally of a domestic or private nature for not more than 30 hours per week' (Australian Taxation Office Superannuation Guarantee Ruling SGR 2005/1).

While direct employment of workers by individual service users is usually still within the scope of many of the protections offered by employment regulation, in this situation compliance with regulated pay and conditions standards may be a significant problem. The private and informal nature of personal support and care relationships and the distance from organisational structures and supports as well as collective representation are factors in this. Neither workers nor their employers may be aware of the full range of conditions specified in the SCHCDS Industry Award or have good knowledge of their respective rights and obligations as employees and employers (Macdonald 2020; Purcal et al. 2016). Prior to the introduction of the NDIS, an Australian study of individualised funding pilots found that, where workers were hired directly by people with disabilities or their families, workers' conditions were 'poorly protected', and 'some people were concerned with getting the most hours of support possible, employing carers willing to work at below the industry award' (Fisher et al. 2010, p. 42).

Self-Employment, Gig Work and 'On-Hired' Labour

In Australia, as in many other countries, the distinction between employment and self-employment is the basis for labour regulation. Workers legally characterised as self-employed or independent contractors—also referred to as sole traders and freelancers—do not have the same entitlements and protections that apply to employees under labour laws. It follows that most self-employed contractors in Australia work with no regulated minimum rate of pay, nor any standards relating to hours of work (Stewart and Stanford 2017). Unlike employees who are economically dependent on an employer and whose labour is performed under their control, self-employed workers are assumed to be autonomous, independent and able to work for multiple clients and choose how they perform their work.

Very little scope exists for self-employed workers to bargain collectively, and they are without access to the supports, advice or forms of assistance available to employees (Industrial Relations Victoria [IRV] 2020; Johnstone et al. 2012; McCrystal 2009). Coverage under the Fair Work Act, the National Employment Standards and industrial awards is confined to employees (Fair Work Ombudsman 2018). Other worker entitlements and protections (and employer obligations) in superannuation, workers' compensation, occupational health and safety and discrimination laws also apply 'first and foremost' to workers who have employee status (IRV 2020, p. 101). Sham contracting legislation is in place to prevent employees being intentionally misrepresented by employers as independent contractors so as to avoid employment responsibilities (Roles and Stewart 2012). This legislation does not, however, address the problems of the absence of entitlements and protections for low-paid and other vulnerable workers from the high levels of risk and insecurity associated with independent contractor status (Johnstone et al. 2012).

Engagement of self-employed contractor care and support workers is promoted by the national authority for the NDIS as an option for people self-managing their care and support funding who do not wish to take on the responsibilities of being an employer (NDIA 2019). With the introduction of large-scale individualised care funding, then, it might have been expected that some self-employed care and support workers would appear in the market. However, with the NDIS coinciding with the emergence of 'gig economy' digital platform companies that broker care labour, it is possible that workers will be engaged on this basis on a large scale (McKinsey and Company 2018, p. 28). As I argued in Chapter 4, self-employed care and support workers are strongly promoted by NDIS managers and policymakers as providers of an efficient service option, and the business of digital care platforms in the NDIS market is being actively supported by government.

Along with other third parties or care work intermediaries, care platforms provide a service supplying care labour to service users. However, unlike traditional labour hire (or on-hire) firms that supply care labour to *service provider businesses*, platforms supply workers directly to *individual service users*. Also, unlike labour hire agencies, many platforms take ongoing payments from workers as well as from the service users. With few exceptions, care platforms do not employ workers, thereby avoiding employment costs and devolving the economic risks of employment to the self-employed workers (De Stefano 2016; Flanagan 2019). As platforms are not service providers, they also do not bear the costs or risks of service provision. While very little research has been conducted into platforms for care work, there are concerns that, as with platforms in other industries, they exert significant control over the social relations of work and the labour process—setting terms and conditions of work and standardising services while also controlling access to work, pushing pay rates down and increasing working time insecurity in on-demand work (Flanagan 2019, McDonald et al. 2020, Trojansky 2020).

Labour hire firms are other third parties in the care and support labour market, employing or engaging the workers and hiring them out to service providers to work in their businesses. Labour hire arrangements allow 'host' organisations to access on-demand flexible labour without having to concern themselves with ongoing employees (IRV 2016) and with 'no requirement to consider their pay and conditions' (IRV 2020, p. 22). Workers engaged through labour hire companies are mostly employed as casuals, although they can also be engaged as self-employed contractors (IRV 2016). Workers can be employed on lower wages and conditions than the people they work alongside, even though they are doing the same work.

Other grey areas exist where labour hire workers do not have access to the same employment protections as other workers in the host organisations (IRV 2020). Recently, legislation has been enacted in a number of Australian states to regulate labour hire, in response to evidence of problems of exploitation of vulnerable workers in a number of sectors (IRV 2020). National legislation has also been proposed. Under recently-established labour hire licensing schemes, host organisations can only access workers through licensed labour hire firms (IRV 2016, p. 17). However, labour hire licensing regulation may not apply where firms 'on-hire' workers to individuals or households, as the workers are not being hired to perform work *in and as part of a business* (author's emphasis) (Labour Hire Licensing Authority 2020). Once again it seems the household work location is deemed to be a private realm and the householder or individual's employment practices are treated as a private matter, not to be regulated as work. However, where a labour hire firm provides workers to a care or disability services provider, the firm would be covered by this type of labour hire licensing regulation.

Conclusion

Australia's labour market regulation allows for the *transformation of the relations of work and care* under individualised funding in ways that are likely to informalise social care jobs, reinforce gendered undervaluation and undermine prospects for decent work. The boundaries of inclusion and exclusion established by labour laws and labour market regulation and the gendered character of many regulatory gaps provide space for transformation to take place that potentially radically changes the character of social care work and jobs.

NDIS service provision rules and funding arrangements provide for direct employment of workers by individuals. This places workers in the poorly regulated private household realm where labour laws have long failed to ensure decent work for women. The limited scope of labour laws makes possible the transformation of care and support workers into apparently independent entrepreneurial service providers, deemed not to need protection and free to work for whatever the market will pay. Workers in these arrangements face legal barriers to collective organisation and bargaining.

Few regulatory barriers stand in the way of the organisation of work by service providers and third parties in ways that distance them from the responsibilities, risks and costs of employment. Such practices usually devolve these responsibilities and risks to workers and service users. While, for now, the majority of NDIS support workers remain employees in service provider organisations, individual hourly-based funding at low levels and the shifting market conditions are placing pressures on their pay and conditions. The industrial relations tribunal, the Australian Fair Work Commission, has faced pressures to erode the working conditions of these social care workers. There is no capacity within the industrial relations system to ensure the funder—the NDIA—establishes NDIS pricing that is adequate to meet regulated minimum employment standards, let alone to provide for wages and conditions above the minimums.

So, what changes are occurring in the NDIS care and support market? In the next chapter, I explore how the composition and configuration of employers and other market actors are changing under the NDIS and examine the business and employment strategies and practices being adopted by service providers, employers and brokers and their implications for social care workers.

References

Anderson, B. (2007). A very private business: Exploring the demand for migrant domestic workers. *European Journal of Women's Studies, 14*(3), 247–264. https://doi.org/10.1177/1350506807079013.

Arup, C., Gahan, P., Howe, J., Johnstone, R., Mitchell, R., & O'Donnell, A. (2006). *Labour law and labour market regulation*. Sydney: Federation Press.

Austen, S., & Mavisakalyan, A. (2018). Gender gaps in long-term earnings and retirement wealth: The effects of education and parenthood. *Journal of Industrial Relations, 60*(4), 492–516. https://doi.org/10.1177/0022185618767474.

Australian Bureau of Statistics (ABS). (2019). *Characteristics of employment*, Australia, August 2019, Cat. No. 6333.0. Canberra: Australian Bureau of Statistics.

Australian Bureau of Statistics (ABS). (2020a, November). *Average weekly earnings, Australia*, Cat. No. 6302.0. Canberra: Australian Bureau of Statistics.

Australian Bureau of Statistics (ABS). (2020b, February). *Labour Force Australia*, Cat. No. 6202.0 Canberra: Australian Bureau of Statistics.

Australian Industry Group. (2019, November 18). 4 yearly review of Modern Awards. Final submission Social, Community, Home Care and Disability Services Industry Award 2010 (AM2018/26). https://www.aigroup.com.au/policy-and-esearch/mediacentre/submissions/workplacerelations/. Accessed 14 August 2020.

Brennan, D., Charlesworth, S., Adamson, E., & Cortis, N. (2017). Out of kilter: Changing care, migration and employment regimes in Australia. In S. Michel, & I. Peng (Eds.), *Gender, migration, and the work of care. A multi-scalar approach to the Pacific Rim* (pp. 143–165). New York: Palgrave Macmillan.

Briggs, C., Meagher, G., & Healy, K. (2007). Becoming an industry: The struggle of social and community workers for award coverage, 1976–2001. *Journal of Industrial Relations, 49*(4), 497–521. https://doi.org/10.1177/0022185607080319.

Campbell, I., Macdonald, F., & Charlesworth, S. (2019). On-demand work in Australia. In M. O'Sullivan, J. Lavelle, J. McMahon, L. Ryan, C. Murphy, T. Turner, et al. (Eds.), *Zero-hours and on-call work in Anglo-Saxon countries* (pp. 67–90, Work, Organisation and Employment). Singapore: Springer Press.

Castles, F. (1985). *The working class and welfare: Reflections on the political development of the welfare state in Australia and New Zealand, 1890–1980.* Sydney and Wellington: George Allen & Unwin in association with the Port Nicholson Press.

Charlesworth, S. (2012). Decent working conditions for care workers? The intersections of employment regulation, the funding market and gender norms. *Australian Journal of Labour Law, 25*, 107.

Charlesworth, S. (2017). Partial protection? The regulation of home care workers' working conditions. In C. Fenwick, & V. V. Goethem (Eds.), *Regulating for equitable and job-rich growth* (pp. 125–150). Edward Elgar.

Charlesworth, S., Strazdins, L., O'Brien, L., & Sims, S. (2011). Parents' jobs in Australia: Work hours polarisation and the consequences for job quality and gender equality. *Australian Journal of Labour Economics, 14*(1), 35–57.

Charlesworth, S., & Heron, A. (2012). New Australian working time minimum standards: Reproducing the same old gendered architecture? *Journal of Industrial Relations, 54*(2), 164–181. https://doi.org/10.1177/0022185612437840.

Charlesworth, S., & Macdonald, F. (2017). Employment regulation and worker-carers: Reproducing gender inequality in the domestic and market spheres? In D. Peetz & G. Murray (Eds.), *Women, labor segmentation and regulation* (pp. 79–96). New York: Palgrave Macmillan.

Clibborn, S. (2020). Australian industrial relations in 2019: The year wage theft went mainstream. *Journal of Industrial Relations, 62*(3), 331–340. https://doi.org/10.1177/0022185620913889.

Davidov, G., & Langille, B. (Eds.). (2011). *The idea of labour law.* Oxford: Oxford University Press.

Delaney, A., & Macdonald, F. (2018). Thinking about informality: Gender (in)equality (in) decent work across geographic and economic boundaries. *Labour & Industry, 28*(2), 99–114. https://doi.org/10.1080/10301763.2018.1475024.

De Stefano, V. (2016). *The rise of the 'just-in-time workforce': On-demand work, crowdwork and labour protection in the 'gig-economy.'* Geneva: International Labour Office.

Fair Work Commission. (2020). *Social, community, home care and disability services industry award 2010* (PR721438). Fair Work Commission. https://www.fwc.gov.au/documents/documents/modern_awards/award/ma000100/default.htm. Accessed 19 August 2020

Fair Work Ombudsman (FWO). (2018). *Introduction to the National Employment Standards Canberra: FWO.* https://www.fairwork.gov.au/how-we-will-help/templates-and-guides/fact-sheets/minimum-workplace-entitlements/introduction-to-the-national-employment-standards.

Fair Work Ombudsman (FWO). (2019, November 28). *Pay guide social, community, home care and disability services industry award 2010* [MA000100]. Canberra: Fair Work Ombudsman.

Fisher, K. R., Edwards, R., Gleeson, R., Purcal, C., Sitek, T., Dinning, B., et al. (2010). *Effectiveness of individual funding approaches for disability support*. Canberra: Department of Families, Housing, Community Services and Indigenous Affairs.

Flanagan, F. (2019). Theorising the gig economy and home-based service work. *Journal of Industrial Relations, 61*(1), 57–78. https://doi.org/10.1177/0022185618800518.

Frances, R. (2000). One hundred years of women's wage-fixing. *Journal of Interdisciplinary Gender Studies, 5*(2), 84–93.

Fudge, J. (2014). Feminist reflections on the scope of labour law: Domestic work, social reproduction, and jurisdiction. *Feminist Legal Studies, 22*(1), 1–23. https://doi.org/10.1007/s10691-014-9256-2.

Fudge, J., & Owens, R. (Eds.). (2006). *Precarious work, women and the new economy: The challenge to legal norms*. Oxford: Hart Publishing.

Gilfillan, G. (2018). Characteristics and use of casual employees in Australia. *Research Paper Series, 2017–2018*, Department of Parliamentary Services, Parliament of Australia.

Hunter, R. (2006). The legal production of precarious work. In J. Fudge & R. Owens (Eds.), *Precarious work, women, and the new economy: The challenge to legal norms* (pp. 283–304). Portland, Oregon: Hart Publishing.

Industrial Relations Victoria (IRV). (2016). *Victorian inquiry into the labour hire industry and insecure work, final report*. Melbourne: Industrial Relations Victoria. https://engage.vic.gov.au/inquiry-labour-hire-industry-and-insecure-work. Accessed 12 November 2020.

Industrial Relations Victoria (IRV). (2020). *Report of the inquiry into the Victorian on-demand workforce*. Melbourne: Industrial Relations Victoria.

Isaac, J. (2008). The economic consequences of harvester. *Australian Economic History Review, 48*(3), 280–300. https://doi.org/10.1111/j.1467-8446.2008.00242.x.

Johnstone, R., McCrystal, S., Nossar, I., Quinlan, M., Rawling, M., & Riley, J. (2012). *Beyond employment: The legal regulation of work relationships*. Sydney: The Federation Press.

Labour Hire Licensing Authority. (2020). *General definition of labour hire services*. State Government of Victoria, Labour Hire Licensing Authority. https://labourhireauthority.vic.gov.au/provider/general-definition-of-labour-hire-services/. Accessed 6 November 2020.

Macdonald, F. (2020). 'Personalised risk' in paid care work and the impacts of 'gig economy' care platforms and other market-based organisations. *International Journal of Care and Caring*, 1–17. https://doi.org/10.1332/239788220X15966470624270.

Macdonald, F., & Charlesworth, S. (2013). Equal pay under the 'Fair Work Act 2009' (Cth): Mainstreamed or marginalised? *The University of New South Wales Law Journal, 36*(2), 563–586.

Macdonald, F., & Pegg, M. (2018). Contracting out community services, marketisation and wages. In A. Stewart, J. Stanford, & T. Hardy (Eds.), *The wages crisis in Australia: What it is and what to do about it* (pp. 129–142). Adelaide: University of Adelaide Press.

Macdonald, F., Bentham, E., & Malone, J. (2018a). Wage theft, underpayment and unpaid work in marketised social care. *The Economic and Labour Relations Review, 29*(1), 80–96. https://doi.org/10.1177/1035304618758252.

Macdonald, F., Charlesworth, S., & Brigden, C. (2018b). Access to collective bargaining for low-paid workers. In S. McCrystal, B. Creighton, & A. Forsyth (Eds.), *Collective bargaining under the Fair Work Act* (pp. 206–227). Sydney: The Federation Press.

McDonald, P., Williams, P., & Mayes, R. J. W. (2020). Means of control in the organization of digitally intermediated care work. *Work, Employment and Society*, Online first, 1–19. https://doi.org/10.1177/0950017020969107.

McCrystal, S. (2009). Is there a "public benefit" in improving working conditions for independent contractors? Collective bargaining and the Trade Practices Act 1974 (Cth). *Federal Law Review, 37*(2), 263–293. https://doi.org/10.1177/0067205X0903700204.

McKinsey and Company. (2018). *Independent pricing review: National Disability Insurance Agency* (p. 103). The Board of the NDIA.

Marshall, S. (2019). *Living wage: Regulatory solutions to informal and precarious work in global supply chains* (1st ed.). Oxford: Oxford University Press.

Martin, B., & Healy, J. (2010). *Who works in community services? A profile of Australian workforces in child protection, juvenile justice, disability services and general community services*. Adelaide: National Institute of Labour Studies, Flinders University.

National Disability Insurance Agency (NDIA). (2019). *Directly engaging your own staff*. Canberra: NDIA.

National Disability Services (NDS). (2017). *Australian disability workforce report July 2017*. Sydney: NDS.

National Disability Services (NDS). (2018). *Australian disability workforce report February 2018*. Sydney: NDS.

O'Connor, J. S., Orloff, A. S., & Shaver, S. (1999). *States, markets, families: Gender, liberalism and social policy in Australia, Canada, Great Britain and the United States*. Cambridge: Cambridge University Press.

OECD Data. (2020). *Labour force participation rate*. https://data.oecd.org/emp/labour-force-participation-rate.htm. Accessed 15 September 2020.

Peck, J. (1996). *Work-place: The social regulation of labor markets*. New York: Guilford Press.

Purcal, C., Zmudzki, F., & Fisher, K. R. (2016). *Direct funding trial: Final evaluation report*. SPRC Report 10/16. Sydney: Social Policy Research Centre, University of New South Wales.

Roles, C., & Stewart, A. (2012). The reach of labour regulation: Tackling sham contracting. *Australian Journal of Labour Law, 25*(3), 258–283.

Sassen, S. (1997). *Informalization in advanced market economies* (Issues in development discussion paper 20). Geneva: International Labour Office.

Smith, M., & Whitehouse, G. (2020). Wage-setting and gender pay equality in Australia: Advances, retreats and future prospects. *Journal of Industrial Relations, 62*(4), 533–559. https://doi.org/10.1177/0022185620926220.

Stewart, A., & Stanford, J. (2017). Regulating work in the gig economy: What are the options? *The Economic and Labour Relations Review, 28*(3), 420–437. https://doi.org/10.1177/1035304617722461.

Tham, J.-C. (2007). Towards an understanding of standard employment relationships under Australian labour law. *Australian Journal of Labour Law, 20*(2), 123–158.

Trojansky, A. (2020). *Towards the 'Uberisation' of care? Platform work in the sector of long-term home care and its implications for workers' rights*. Brussels: European Economic and Social Committee.

CHAPTER 6

The Emerging Market for Individualised Support and Care

Introduction

In Chapters 4 and 5, I examined how disability care and support workers are regarded and accounted for in the design, management and regulation of the individualised and marketised NDIS and I considered how care workers are characterised and treated in labour laws and labour market regulation. In practice, the ways in which the individualisation and marketisation of social care transform work and employment depend also on the power, preferences and strategies of service users, service providers and other market actors, and on the composition and configuration of these actors in the market. In this chapter, I explore the developing structure and operations of the market for individualised care and support services under the NDIS, to understand the emerging organisation of work and what it might mean for the future of decent work for the care and support workforce.

Who's Who in the New Market for Care and Support

The establishment of the individualised NDIS social care consumer market has seen a massive expansion in the number and diversity of disability service providers. As Australia's new disability support system has rolled out nationally, an increasing share of NDIS funding is going to,

F. Macdonald, *Individualising Risk*,
https://doi.org/10.1007/978-981-33-6366-3_6

firstly, services providers that are not registered with the NDIS (unregistered providers) and, secondly, a rapidly expanding assortment of brokers and other market intermediaries. Businesses in both categories have few obligations to meet quality standards under the NDIS quality and safeguarding regulatory arrangements. They exert significant influence and control in the market and over care quality and care work processes, yet they are not subject to monitoring, and may not even be counted, in the oversight and management of the NDIS.

Prior to the NDIS, in 2011–2012, there were 2,277 organisations providing government-funded disability services under federal/state government agreements. At that time, the majority of services were provided by not-for-profit organisations, with not-for-profits providing 69% of services, government bodies providing 20% and private-for-profit businesses providing 11% (AIHW 2013). By mid-2020, with the NDIS rolled out nationally, over 14,800 registered disability service providers had provided supports to people with social care funding managed by the National Disability Insurance Agency (NDIA) (NDIA 2020d, p. 62). By this time, state governments had sold their disability support services to the private sector and most local government authorities had also ceased providing public social care services to people with disability.

Under the NDIS, not-for-profit providers remain the dominant *registered* service providers; however, there are many new organisations in the individualised social care market. Some of these organisations provide services to people with disability as *unregistered* NDIS service providers, while many others are intermediaries in care and support work relationships and work arrangements, including care/labour brokers, service co-ordinators and financial managers. The business and service models adopted by these market actors impact on the nature of frontline disability care and support workers' jobs and employment. Mostly, third parties' business models depend on, and/or facilitate, the employment of support workers in highly casualised and insecure forms of employment.

In the NDIS, only people whose support funding is *NDIA-managed* must purchase their supports from registered service providers. People with *self-managed* or *plan-managed* funds can choose to purchase their supports from unregistered providers. The number of organisations acting as unregistered service providers of NDIS-funded services is not known. Many unregistered providers are 'mainstream providers' that are providing services to the community generally—for example, a gym, a swimming pool or a theatre (Productivity Commission 2011,

p. 237). However, there are unregistered providers that provide *personal care and support* services to people with disability in the new NDIS market also, for example a non-NDIS-registered home care company. As explained in Chapter 4, people with support plans and funding managed by the NDIA—whose support services must be purchased from registered service providers—now account for only a minority (28%) of all NDIS participants. Another 31% of people with NDIS funding partly or fully self-manage their support funding and around 40% use registered plan managers (financial managers). Self- and plan-managing groups are permitted to purchase their supports from unregistered providers (NDIA 2020d, p. 139, Table E53). There are only a few types of specialist services that cannot be provided by unregistered providers, such as specialist disability accommodation and care and support that involves restrictive practices (NDIS Quality and Safeguards Commission, n.d.).

By 2020, the landscape of the supply side of the disability support services market had changed so significantly that, when the COVID-19 pandemic hit Australia in March, it was to a group of unregistered support and care labour brokers, mainly digital care platforms, rather than to the dominant not-for-profit NDIS-registered service providers, that the NDIA turned to as the source of a 'contingency' workforce in the face of a feared labour shortage (Hoffman 2020; NDIA 2020b).

For-profit digital care platforms first appeared in Australia around about the same time as the NDIS implementation, targeting people with disability who self-manage their NDIS funding as well as aged people who self-fund their home care services. Like other digital platforms brokering labour such as Uber, Deliveroo and, in Australia, AirTasker (Stewart and Stanford 2017), most care platforms maintain they are neither service providers nor employers. Workers who use the platforms to find jobs are treated as self-employed contractors, contracted directly to service users. Some digital platforms also act as intermediaries between service provider organisations that seek to provide NDIS-funded services via self-employed contractor social care workers.

A significant proportion (43%) of NDIS-registered providers are 'sole trader' service providers (NDIA 2020d, p. 143). While some of these sole traders would be people in professional or para-professional occupations—with the largest number of sole traders registered to provide therapeutic supports—the available data suggests a growing number and proportion of sole traders among registered service providers are providing lower-paid categories of personal support and care services, including support for daily personal activities; support for participation in community and social activities, and assistance with household tasks (NDIA 2019b, pp. 103–104; 2020d, p. 143).

While there has been massive growth in small providers, there is a concentration of business in the NDIS disability support market, with some large service providers dominating. In June 2020, between 86 and 93% of NDIS payments went to the top 25% of providers (NDA 2020d, p. 141). On average, across all Australian regions, 62% of NDIS payments go to the 10 largest providers in a region. In over a third of the total 76 regions—with many of this third being rural or remote regions—more than two-thirds of all NDIS business goes to the ten largest providers (NDIA 2020a, p. 56). No publicly available data currently exists on unregistered providers.

Transformation of the *disability services workforce* by the NDIS has also been significant. The new system was expected to lead to a doubling of the size of the workforce from 73,000 full-time equivalent jobs before the scheme began to 162,000 equivalent full-time jobs when fully rolled out, with one in five of all new jobs created in Australia over the first few years of the NDIS being in disability services (Joint Standing Committee on the National Disability Insurance Scheme 2017, p. 4). While growth has been the headline in relation to workforce, the new NDIS market is also having major impacts on the work and employment arrangements of disability support workers. Disability support workers are now working shorter hours on average and, in smaller organisations, a shift to casual employment has occurred (National Disability Service [NDS] 2017). This social care workforce now includes workers who are employed directly by the people to whom they provide care and support, and it includes self-employed contractors who carry all the business and employment risks associated with their work and service provision as explained in detail in Chapter 5 (McKinsey and Company 2018; Stewart and Stanford 2017). The vast majority of employees in the various Australian states' public sector disability support workforces have been moved to the private sector (Macdonald and Pegg 2018). All of these changes are examined in more detail in the discussion in the remainder of the chapter. A gap in this discussion concerns the individual NDIS consumers. There is no reliable data on the diversity of consumer approaches to purchasing NDIS supports in the new market beyond information about planning arrangements and categories of supports. There is emerging evidence to indicate the NDIS market may be increasing social and economic inequalities

(Warr et al. 2017), and it is clear some businesses aim to provide services to consumers who do not have complex needs and consumers who may be able to supplement their NDIS funds with private money. However, more information is needed about how different consumer groups fare in different parts of the NDIS care and support market.

The Demise of Public Sector Disability Services

Prior to the NDIS, most Australian states and territories had some publicly-owned and operated disability services and, in some jurisdictions, they and/or local government bodies were the main providers of certain types of services or services to particular groups of people. Governments were often the providers of last resort, delivering where there were few or no other providers, and they were dominant providers of services such as supported accommodation and respite services in some states (NDIS Senior Officials Working Group for the Disability Reform Council 2015). Once the NDIS implementation got underway, privatisations occurred in most jurisdictions. For example, in New South Wales (NSW)—Australia's most populous state—the NSW government had been the largest provider of in-home support and personal care services to the aged and people with disability, accounting for about 70% of all service provision.

In 2016, the NSW government sold the public home care service to a large health insurance mutual and, by mid-2018, they had also sold off all other publicly-owned and operated disability services, leading to an estimated loss of over 14,000 public sector jobs (Belardi 2015; Macdonald and Pegg 2018). In other states, many local authorities also discontinued provision of home and community care services to people with disability under the new NDIS arrangements, including in areas where there had been few other providers (Municipal Association of Victoria 2017). They cited NDIS pricing as a key problem; prices were too low to provide for the wages and conditions of care and support workers who were employed under union-bargained agreements that had delivered some pay parity with other local government employees (Macdonald and Pegg 2018; Municipal Association of Victoria 2017; Trotter et al. 2018).

The loss of public sector services has already had significant negative impacts on disability care and support worker pay and conditions and is likely to do so in the future. Most workers in the states and territories' public sectors were employed in permanent full-time jobs with pay rates set by collective union-negotiated enterprise agreements. These union-negotiated pay rates were significantly higher than the regulated minimum rate that most disability care and support workers in the not-for-profit community sector were paid (Macdonald and Pegg 2018). In addition, public sector workers often received higher penalty rates or loadings to compensate for shifts in unsocial hours and had a range of other benefits, such as better access to employer-supported training and career pathways and better paid leave provisions (Baines et al. 2019, Douglas 2019). With privatisation of services, unions have negotiated for former public service employees to maintain their pay and conditions. However, these agreements are for limited periods only (Macdonald and Pegg 2018).

The presence of a public sector social care workforce was extremely important in the success of the equal pay case for Australian social and community services (SACS) workers in 2012 detailed in Chapter 5. The SACS Equal Pay Case—the only successful equal pay case in any industry under Australia's federal industrial relations laws—led to pay increases for SACS workers of between 19 and 41% over eight years (Cortis and Meagher 2012; Macdonald and Charlesworth 2013). In the case, the higher-paid public sector workforce provided the comparator used by unions to demonstrate that care work within the not-for-profit sector was undervalued on the basis of gender (Cortis and Meagher 2012). In the absence of a public sector workforce performing what is clearly equivalent work, it may have been much more difficult for unions to win this case.

The Changing Fortunes of the Not-For-Profits Under a Billable Hours Regime

Prior to the introduction of the individualised market, the main providers of publicly-funded support and care services to people with disability were specialist disability service providers in the not-for-profit social and community services sector. Most service providers were reliant on government funding as their main source of income. However, they were consistently under-funded for the services contracted by governments, and they were not usually allowed to retain any surplus funds from government contracts (Productivity Commission 2010). So, in the event efficiencies led to surplus funds, the not-for-profit providers were not able to accumulate these as savings to invest in their operations. As a consequence of government funding shortfalls, many disability service providers came into the NDIS with little spare capital to invest in the additional administrative and marketing capabilities required in the new system, or to carry the costs of transition and adaptation to the increased risks of individualised services—let alone to innovate or grow.

Not-for-profit specialist disability service providers continue to be the main providers of most disability support services in the new system, but many have struggled to survive under the individualised funding model and low prices set for disability support work (Carey et al. 2020, Cortis et al. 2017; NDS 2019). An industry report released in September 2020 indicates profitability is projected to continue to decline under the NDIS, due to 'intensifying competition' (Harrison 2020, p. 8). As detailed elsewhere, registered providers cannot compete with unregistered providers on the basis of price.

Generally, the relationship between service providers and the NDIA, the manager of the new system, has been poor. Fewer than 20% of respondents to a 2019 survey undertaken by the provider peak body, National Disability Services (NDS), agreed that the NDIA was working well with providers to implement the individualised system, and only 22% believed the NDIA demonstrated a high level of respect for them and their work (Carey et al. 2020, p. 15). These responses had barely changed from an earlier survey (NDS 2019, p. 13).

As was anticipated by the Productivity Commission (2011) in their report recommending the individualised system (see Chapter 4), the implementation of the NDIS has caused major disruption to the disability services sector. With NDIS funding tied to the person, rather than the provider, disability service providers are paid *after* delivering a service to an individual, rather than being paid in bulk in advance for months of service provision to multiple people as was the case before individualised funding was introduced. Providers have had to adapt their finance and administration arrangements to manage payments by the hour of service in the individualised billable hours regime. They have had to ensure the labour time of all staff can be charged to a funded episode of service provision to an individual. Providers now also have to spend more money on marketing in the competitive market. In addition, survey research suggests the not-for-profits are doing a lot of unfunded work preparing individuals and their families and carers for the NDIS support planning and review processes that determine what individual support funding they will receive (Carey et al. 2020). More generally, it appears that service providers—along with families and service users—now bear many more of the administrative costs of service provision. The shifting of these costs away from government is a phenomenon seen also in the UK personalisation experience (Glasby and Littlechild 2016).

Under-pricing of government funding for care and support services leading to loss-making services has been a key concern for providers since the full rollout of the new system (Cortis et al. 2017). In 2018, a third of not-for-profit disability service providers made a loss (Gilchrist and Knight 2018, p. 7). In 2019, three years after the commencement of full implementation, the sector 'continue(d) to be characterised by uncertainty' (Carey et al. 2020, p. 4). While a half (55%) of the service providers responding to a national survey believed that the NDIS reforms were heading in the right direction, a similar proportion (55%) were worried they wouldn't be able to provide NDIS services at current prices. Workforce development was service providers' number one concern (Carey et al. 2020, pp. 4–5).

The NDIS has brought about mergers between some large not-for-profit organisations and winding up of small ones (Carey et al. 2020). Reduced collaboration between not-for-profit organisations in the sector has been observed (Carey et al. 2020), suggesting that providers are adopting 'a private sector operational ethos' in the competitive market and under pressure for greater efficiency (van Toorn 2018, p. 157).

Many examples can be found of not-for-profit disability service providers looking for ways to adapt to the new market model and doing so on the basis of a skilled workforce with secure jobs (see, for example, Macdonald 2019; NDS 2018). However, many service providers struggle to provide secure jobs and adopt high-road employment strategies under the NDIS (Cortis et al. 2017; Macdonald 2019). There are equally as many examples of providers adopting strategies that distance their organisations from the costs and risks of service provision, including by devolving these to workers. As already noted, disability support workers employed in the not-for-profit sector are now working shorter hours on average and, in smaller organisations, a shift to casual employment has occurred (NDS 2017).

Strategies that devolve costs and risks to workers are often among those promoted by the NDIA and government as innovative. For example, the federal government's 'boosting the local care workforce' website promotes the approach adopted by one NDIS-registered provider of home care services as using an 'innovative contractor workforce model to manage its workforce successfully' (Department of Social Services [DSS], n.d., p. 1). The not-for-profit service provider, referring to itself as a 'host employer', vets and 'registers' contractor care workers, who can then be matched on their website with people seeking care. The workers must organise their work themselves and submit invoices for payment via the company's mobile app (DSS, n.d., p. 1). Contractor care workers are required to have their own insurance, access and log their work and submit their invoices through the organisation's mobile app, while the service provider offers them information and promotional materials and delivers training materials to their mobile devices (West Coast Homecare, n.d.).

Where Are the New For-Profit Registered Service Providers?

In early 2017, an article in the *Australian Financial Review* referred to 'the new breed of entrepreneurs chasing NDIS profit' ... 'positioning themselves for a slice of the $22 billion National Disability Services pie' (Whyte 2017, p. 25). At odds with this headline, the author of the article also noted there had not actually been any large flow of investors into the NDIS services market and it was not easy to make a profit in many parts of the new market. While there has been an increase in the number of for-profit service providers registered to provide individualised disability support services, many of these businesses are very small organisations (Gilchrist and Knight 2018, p. 6). It is possible there are new large for-profit disability support providers in the market that have chosen to be NDIS-registered providers; however, the visible new for-profits in the market are not registered providers.

There have been reports of strong growth in for-profit providers of home care services for the aged and there are indications many of these businesses are also providing disability supports in the NDIS market. For example, in mid-2017, it was reported that new providers made up a third of all home care providers in metropolitan locations, with 70% of them being for-profit companies and 40% also providing NDIS disability support services (Doyle and Morris 2017). Among the new providers were several USA-based care franchise firms and some labour hire agencies that were expanding into direct service provision. New entrants to the home care market were reported to be 'using price as a competitive advantage' (Doyle and Morris 2017, p. 1). Other overseas-owned care franchise companies have acquired or merged with Australian businesses to offer care and support services in the new NDIS market. For example, Just Better Care, an Australian home care franchise established in 2004, is now part of the global Caring Brands International group, which includes USA-based home care franchise Interim HealthCare, and the UK and Republic of Ireland-based home care group Bluebird Care (Levine Leichtman Capital Partners 2015).

While NDIS pricing regulation sets caps on the fees registered service providers can charge for care and support, there are no caps on unregistered providers' fees. As the number of people who self-manage and plan-manage their NDIS funding grows, so do the opportunities for unregistered service providers. In 2020, 31 and 38% of people with NDIS support funding self and plan-managed, respectively (NDIA 2020a, Appendix E, p. 118, Figure E.17). One observer has suggested that, under NDIS funding levels and pricing caps, more providers may choose not to be registered, stating: 'As the new pricing guidelines become the new normal, we are expecting more providers to look at the Price Guide and seriously pose the question: "do we really have to be registered?"' (Woolley 2020, p. 1).

One large new service provider that entered the NDIS care and support market in 2016 as a *registered* provider was the member-owned Australian Unity, following the mutual's purchase of the NSW government's home care service. Social and community sector bodies and trade unions were reported to be relieved that a mutual organisation had purchased the privatised home care service, rather than some other private-for-profit company, including because of their concerns that service provision in rural and regional areas might not continue under privatisation (Easton 2015). However, confidence in Australian Unity appears to have been misplaced as, in mid-2019, the mutual announced the progressive scaling down of their NDIS services in all locations except metropolitan Sydney (Australian Unity 2019). Apparently, the organisation found some NDIS services were not viable under NDIS pricing (Australian Unity 2017).

Another service provider that has attracted some attention is the digital platform, HireUp, that offers service users an individualised service in which they choose their workers from online platform profiles (HireUp 2020a). Unlike the more common Uber-style digital care platforms that have emerged in the new disability care and support market—and that require workers to be self-employed contractors—HireUp is an NDIS-registered service provider organisation that employs the care and support workers who are matched with clients through its online platform.

HireUp is notable for its service and business model that utilises a digital platform to provide market access and offer service users greater choice and control without transferring all of the risks of care and employment to individual service users and workers. However, as appears to be the case with many other providers in the NDIS disability support market, HireUp employees are engaged as casuals, without job security, guaranteed hours or paid sick and annual leave. Furthermore, HireUp workers are paid at a rate that is at the bottom of the classification scale (Level 1) of the regulated minimum pay rates set in the Social, Community, Home Care and Disability Services (SCHCDS) Industry Award (Fair Work Commission 2020; HireUp 2020b). This is lower than a disability support worker would be paid as an employee in the not-for-profit sector (Cortis et al. 2017) and, arguably, is lower than a disability worker *should* be paid under the regulation. The SCHCDS Industry Award describes the Level 1 classification used by HireUp as applying to inexperienced home care workers performing basic domestic tasks and requiring close supervision (Fair Work Commission 2020).

In sum, there is little evidence that providing personal care and support services as an NDIS-registered provider is an attractive proposition to potential new market entrants. There are new providers and there are many for-profit businesses in the NDIS market, organising and brokering services but, in the main, they are operating outside the scope of the system quality and safeguarding regulation.

Getting a Slice of the NDIS Pie: Labour Hire, Digital Platforms and Other Brokers

> Already in parts of the NDIS market, self-managing participants, as empowered consumers, are seeking value for money – which is driving competitive pricing, greater flexibility and a quality workforce. (NDIA 2016, p. 26)

Labour Hire, Recruitment Firms and Other Third Parties

People with self-managed and plan-managed support funding can directly employ or contract their own care and support workers. There is no readily accessible data on the extent of direct engagement of workers in these individualised employment arrangements and workers are almost entirely invisible within the systems governing the publicly-funded NDIS. An increasingly complex array of third parties are involved in these individual service user–support worker care and employment relationships. Third parties also operate as intermediaries and labour brokers where service provider organisations are involved in care and support provision.

Third parties in employment and work arrangements include new and old types of labour brokers, along with intermediaries who coordinate supports and/or manage people's NDIS finances. Some third parties—mainly NDIS plan managers and service co-ordinators—are paid with NDIS funding that is allocated to individuals for them to purchase assistance with managing their NDIS funds or with organising, procuring and paying for their support services. Other third parties, like labour hire firms and digital platforms, take a portion of the hourly-based NDIS funding that is paid to individual NDIS service users to purchase their care and support.

Sourcing care and support staff from labour hire agencies to fill casual vacancies was a fairly widespread practice among service providers before the introduction of the individualised funding scheme (Fattore et al. 2010). Some service providers used labour hire extensively to access an on-demand care workforce as an alternative to employing their own staff. Labour hire firms in Australia employ workers—usually as casuals—and send them out to work in host organisations. So, labour hire employees are likely to have less knowledge of the host organisation's processes and poorer access to organisational supports than other employees. Workers employed via labour hire firms may also be employed on lower rates and have no rights to convert to permanent employment with the host organisation, rights that other workers would have. In the NDIS market, labour hire firms are highly visible and their numbers are likely to be growing given overall growth in demand and the increasingly 'on-demand' character of care and support work. Economy-wide growth in the combined healthcare and social and community services sectors (the healthcare and social assistance industry) is one of the main drivers of growth in the temporary staffing industry (Allday 2020).

Care and support workers employed by labour hire firms have less access to training than employees of service providers and, where there is heavy reliance on labour hire, there have been concerns about service quality (Fattore et al. 2010). Worker accounts tell of the use of inadequately trained and inexperienced casual and agency staff, leading to safety and care risks and to more, rather than less, work for organisations' own care and support workforces (Cortis et al. 2017; Cortis and van Toorn 2020). More generally, the employment practices of labour hire operators have attracted the attention of federal and state governments, although not particularly in this industry, as noted in Chapter 5.

Labour hire companies and recruitment firms have traditionally charged employers for recruiting workers and/or providing workers to labour in their organisations. In contrast, most digital platforms in the NDIS care market have business models whereby they take ongoing fees from care and support workers and from employers. In the NDIS context, this model has been lauded as innovative, as detailed in Chapter 4. However, while the digital platform-based market portal may be an innovation, many aspects of the model are not new in home-based services in Australia and other countries. In Australia, from the nineteenth century, domestic servant agencies have matched workers and householders and operated on a similar business model to the digital platforms of today (Flanagan 2019).

Digital Platforms: The Uberisation of Social Care?

Digital platforms for care and support are very visible in the NDIS support marketplace; and the NDIA has promoted and supported them (Hoffman 2020, NDIA 2020b). Some platforms act as strong lobbyists in public policy processes, arguing for their place in individualised care markets and against state regulation of digital platforms (Industrial Relations Victoria [IRV] 2020). Mable, a highly visible platform in the Australian NDIS market, has attracted public attention as a company backed by high-profile shareholders and, more recently, because it was awarded a very large federal government contact for the provision of a COVID-response 'surge' aged care workforce without an open tender process (Hardaker 2020).

The presence of platforms in the disability support and care market facilitates the creation of short-term gig care and support jobs. While the platform companies have emphasised their recognition of the relational aspects of care and support work and the importance of relationships to continuity and quality of support (IRV, p. 89), they promote the idea of support workers as an on-demand *service* to be provided for as short or as long a time as needed. In mid-2020, one platform launched a 'last-minute jobs' service to enable people to engage care and support workers who are to be available 'within as little as 4 hours' (Mable Technologies 2020b).

The platform presents support workers as being available to people who might, in the morning, realise they have forgotten to organise a worker for the afternoon.

Keeping track of the number of platforms brokering care and support work is no simple task. Monitoring for this research project identified several platforms listing disability support and care workers that appeared and then disappeared in the Australian market between 2015 and 2020. Over the same period, significant growth has occurred in the number and assortment of labour hire firms, service providers, financial intermediaries, service directories and other information sites that perform some or all of the same functions as the digital platforms via online interfaces but adopting slightly different business models.

Digital platforms broker care and support labour by providing an online platform on which workers post their profiles listing experience and skills, the services they provide and their hourly rates. Service users choose workers on the basis of their profiles, and actual terms are negotiated. Workers are engaged by service users as self-employed contractors. Work is organised and payments are made through the platform. The platform charges each party a fee that is a percentage of the agreed fee for the care service for every hour of work booked through the platform. Most platforms manage all financial transactions and some require work schedules to be organised via the platform and also encourage communications between the worker and service user to be undertaken via their portals or apps. Most platform firms perform basic worker screening, requiring workers to upload clearance documents. Some organise public liability insurance cover for workers and some offer group rates on other insurances. An internet scan of care and support platforms advertising their services to individuals with NDIS funding conducted in August 2020 for this research found most platforms charged service users ongoing fees of around five per cent of the hourly fee the service users agreed to pay their workers and they charged workers ongoing fees of between 15 and 25%. The internet scan identified a dozen digital care platforms using this model and operating in one or more large metropolitan cities. Other digital platforms carry disability care and support workers listings, such as AirTasker (2020), a widely-used Australian platform that covers a wide range of mainly one-off, on-demand domestic and business services. Care platforms encourage service users to rate workers on their star rating systems and they make worker ratings available to potential consumers/service users. Thus, they monitor service quality/worker performance via customer satisfaction ratings (McDonald et al. 2020).

There is no reliable data on the extent to which care and support work under the NDIS is intermediated by third parties, including digital platforms. Australian national labour force surveys do not capture the extent to which people use digital platforms to obtain work. Based on Australian Bureau of Statistics (ABS) labour force estimates of self-employed contractors in all occupations, there does not appear to have been any significant growth in workers who obtain their primary or main jobs through platforms. The reason for this is that there has been little change in the proportion of employed people who are self-employed contractors in their main job, at just under 10% of the workforce in December 2019 (ABS 2019, Table 10). However, there are some problems with using labour force data to identify the extent of contracting, including in obtaining accurate estimates of contractors where they are people who hold multiple jobs (IRV 2020, pp. 27–28). This is very likely to be an issue in disability care and support, given the high number of workers whose jobs offer only short part-time hours (NDS 2019) and indications of high levels of multiple job-holding (Macdonald et al. 2018).

A survey of disability support workers conducted in early 2020 found five% of respondents had used platforms to seek disability support work (Cortis and van Toorn 2020). However, this sample was of workers who were invited to participate in the survey by their trade unions, a sample possibly skewed towards older disability support workers employed in more secure jobs. Such workers are less likely to be seeking work on platforms than workers in more insecure and part-time hours jobs (Cortis and van Toorn 2020). Across the entire Australian labour market in all occupations, 13% of people responding to a survey said they had used a platform to obtain work at some time (McDonald et al. 2019, p. 5). This national survey found the median hourly rate earned by care workers on platforms was $23.50 (McDonald et al. 2019, p. 43), several dollars below the minimum rate for a casual employee who is paid at the very bottom of the pay scale of minimum rates for care and support workers (Fair Work Ombudsman 2019, p. 7).

The impact of platforms in some labour markets in Australia is certainly not negligible (Industrial Relations Victoria 2020) and platforms do appear to be having significant impacts in the NDIS support market. For example, findings of this research suggest the presence of platforms in the market may be influencing judgements of appropriate or acceptable prices for care and support. In focus groups and interviews with service providers and other stakeholders in the industry, people reported that care platforms were influencing service users' expectations that NDIS-funded care and support prices should be unreasonably low. Service providers, NDIS support and care service users and family carers reported that some service users considered the fees charged by traditional not-for-profit service providers to be, in one family carer's words, 'exorbitant'. Often this view was based on a belief that the service provider took as profit most or all of the difference between a support worker's hourly wage and the capped NDIS price.

In fact, if a worker is paid the minimum wage under the SCHCDS Industry Award, around two-thirds of the NDIS funding (and capped price) is accounted for by wages and *direct* labour on-costs (i.e. leave, superannuation, workers' compensation). The NDIS pricing includes provisions for corporate overheads and for training and supervision, leaving a very small profit margin (2% in 2019–2020) (NDIA 2019a). As explained elsewhere, there is a good deal of evidence suggesting the price is too low for many providers to provide services without making a loss.

Although platforms maintain they are neither service providers nor employers they present their services as being provided on the same basis as services provided by registered service providers except as are more flexible and much cheaper services. For example, Mable, one of the most high-profile care and support platforms in Australia, displays a bar chart on their website comparing the price of care and support services purchased via the platform with the much higher fee for services charged by registered service providers. While the registered service provider's fee includes the labour on-costs, supervision, training, quality assurance and other overheads, Mable labels the difference as the provider's 'fee/margin' and state: 'As a Mable customer, you simply and clearly receive better value which translates to more support hours for you' (Mable Technologies 2020a). In line with the NDIS conception of value for money, discussed in Chapter 4, 'value' is a matter of price alone.

Representing Workers in the NDIS

Industrial representation of employees undertaking disability care and support work in Australia is a patchwork arrangement involving multiple trade unions. Key unions representing employees in disability support services are the Australian Services Union (ASU), the United Workers Union (UWU) and the Health and Community Services Union (HACSU). Historically, trade union representation of these social care workers was organised on a state-by-state basis (Douglas 2019). Until the 1990s and 2000s, the Australian states had primary responsibility for industrial relations laws and state governments had primary responsibility for most publicly-funded disability support services and many other social and community services. Contemporary trade union coverage of disability care and support workers reflects these historical arrangements among other factors.

When the then Labor Federal Government announced the NDIS, the unions representing disability workers were to be represented on a workforce advisory body that was to provide advice to the federal minister and administer a national workforce innovation fund (Macklin 2012). However, following a change of federal government soon after this, the NDIS was implemented by a conservative Liberal-National Coalition government that abandoned the idea of the workforce advisory body before it had been formed. In 2018, when an NDIS Industry Reference Group was finally established, worker representatives were not given a seat at the table (NDIA 2020c).

As I explained in Chapter 5, the main way for social care, and other waged-workers, to gain better pay and conditions is through union-led enterprise-based bargaining. Prior to the establishment of the NDIS individualised funding arrangements, the low level of government funding for social care services was a major constraint to bargaining for better pay and conditions for disability care and support workers. Under the NDIS, the barriers to union organising and to gaining positive outcomes for workers from enterprise-based bargaining have multiplied. Funding is much tighter and workforces are more casualised and dispersed.

The three main unions representing disability care and support workers have worked independently and collaboratively to argue for better working time and other protections in reviews by Australia's industrial tribunal, the Fair Work Commission of the SCHCDS Industry Award.

They have attempted to influence NDIS pricing and employment arrangements through research and submissions to government inquiries. The ASU, the union with broad coverage of social and community services sector in the most populous states, has attempted to re-vitalise an occupational association and the UWU has attempted online organising of dispersed care workers. While workforce growth, along with mergers and acquisitions in the not-for-profit sector, has consolidated and strengthened union membership in some areas, unions may be struggling to organise and represent workers not employed in the large not-for-profits, let alone workers employed as self-employed contractors.

Prior to the NDIS, the unions and not-for-profit employers of social care workers in disability services were frequently in agreement about the need for a better-paid and skilled workforce. Under NDIS policy, the politics of industrial relations have changed. Peak employer bodies representing for-profit employers have been at the forefront of attempts to change the SCHCDS Industry Award employment conditions in ways that would reduce employees' working time security (Workplace Express 2018).

Consumer Choice, the Market Rules and the Transformation of Work Relations

As labour market actors respond to the introduction of the individualised consumer market, they are transforming the organisation of work and employment arrangements and conditions of frontline social care workers. Organisations' strategies align with NDIS consumer choice and control mechanisms and goals, and the new system's free market emphasis and pricing arrangements. Ineffective labour market regulation provides ample opportunity for organisations in this market to maximise labour flexibility and minimise costs—whether to survive or to profit—by minimising or avoiding obligations and responsibilities as employers. For experienced disability support workers, there may be new opportunities to work with more independence and autonomy and better pay. However, the emerging picture suggests a trend in disability support jobs to more precarious forms of employment, pressures to lower wages and the informalisation of work. The NDIS and its emerging market are transforming care and work relationships. Boundaries between regulated employment and informal privatised and personal work are blurring. Care and support labour is being commodified as workers are engaged as services. In the next two chapters, I explore workers' experiences in the NDIS to identify how these changes make a difference to working lives, to care and support work and relationships, and to care quality.

References

AirTasker. (2020). *Homepage: Connect with experts to get the job done on Airtasker*. Airtasker. https://www.airtasker.com/. Accessed 11 February 2020.

Allday, A. (2020). 'Temporary Staff Services in Australia' *Industry (ANZSIC) Report N7212*. Melbourne: IBIS World.

Australian Bureau of Statistics (ABS). (2019). *Characteristics of employment*, August 2019, Cat. No. 6330.0. ABS. https://www.abs.gov.au/statistics/labour/earnings-and-work-hours/characteristics-employment-australia/latest-release#data-download. Accessed 23 June 2020.

Australian Institute of Health and Welfare. (2013). *Disability support services: Services provided under the National Disability Agreement 2011–12* (Bulletin 118, July). Canberra: Australian Institute of Health and Welfare.

Australian Unity. (2017). *Submission to the Productivity Commission issues Paper on NDIS Costs*. Australian Unity. https://www.australianunity.com.au/~/media/corporate/documents/thoughtplus/australian%20unitys%20view%20on%20ndis%20cost.pdf. Accessed 2 February 2021.

Australian Unity. (2019, May 31). *Statement on NDIS Services* [Media release]. https://www.australianunity.com.au/media-centre/news-and-media/statement-on-ndis-services.

Baines, D., Macdonald, F., Stanford, J., & Moore, J. (2019). *Precarity and job instability in NDIS support work*. Canberra: The Centre for Future Work at the Australia Institute. https://www.futurework.org.au/reports_from_the_front_lines_of_the_ndis. Accessed 1 October 2020.

Belardi, L. (2015, August 28). NSW govt strikes deal with Australian Unity for sale of home care service. *Community Care Review*. https://www.australianageingagenda.com.au/executive/nsw-govt-strikes-deal-with-australian-unity-for-sale-of-home-care-service/. Accessed 23 July 2019.

Carey, G., Weier, M., Malbon, E., Dickinson, H., & Duff, G. (2020). *How is the disability sector faring? A report from National Disability Services' annual market survey*. Sydney: Centre for Social Impact, University of New South Wales. https://www.csi.edu.au/research/project/how-disability-sector-faring-2020-report/. Accessed 30 April 2020

Cortis, N., & Meagher, G. (2012). Recognition at last: Care work and the equal remuneration case. *Journal of Industrial Relations, 54*(3), 377–385. https://doi.org/10.1177/0022185612442278.

Cortis, N., Macdonald, F., Davidson, B., & Bentham, E. (2017). *Reasonable, necessary and valued: Pricing disability services for quality support and decent jobs*. Sydney: Social Policy Research Centre, University of New South Wales. https://www.arts.unsw.edu.au/sites/default/files/documents/NDIS_Pricing_Report.pdf. Accessed 17 September 2020.

Cortis, N., & van Toorn, G. (2020). *Working in new disability markets: A survey of Australia's disability workforce*. Sydney: Social Policy Research Centre, University of New South Wales.

Department of Social Services (DSS). (n.d.). *Contractor workforce model helping providers and participants*. DSS. https://blcw.dss.gov.au/articles/contractor-workforce-model-helping-providers-and-participants/. Accessed 30 July 2020.

Douglas, K. L. (2019). *Addressing trade union barriers to organising devalued and labour-intensive workforces: A study of disability support workers in Victoria* (Australia, PhD thesis). Melbourne: RMIT University.

Doyle, N., & Morris, S. (2017). *Home care market competition: Who's new?* https://home.kpmg/au/en/home/insights/2017/10/home-care-market-competition.html. Accessed 24 June 2020.

Easton, S. (2015). NSW home care sell-off 'demonstrates trust' in public sector mutual. *The Mandarin*. Melbourne: Private Media 4 September. https://www.themandarin.com.au/50806-everyones-happy-nsw-home-care-sell-demonstrates-trust-public-sector-mutuals/. Accessed 1 November 2019.

Fair Work Commission. (2020). *Social, community, home care and disability services industry award 2010* (PR721438). Fair Work Commission. https://www.fwc.gov.au/documents/documents/modern_awards/award/ma000100/default.htm. Accessed 19 August 2020.

Fair Work Ombudsman. (2019). *Pay guide: Social, community, home care and disability services industry award* [MA000100], 1 July 2010. Fair Work Ombudsman. https://www.fairwork.gov.au/pay/minimum-wages/social-and-community-services-industry-pay-rates#pay-guides. Accessed 12 October 2019.

Fattore, T., Evesson, J., Moensted, M., & Jakubauskas, M. (2010). *An examination of workforce capacity issues in the disability services workforce: increasing workforce capacity*. Community Services and Health Industry Skills Council.

Flanagan, F. (2019). Theorising the gig economy and home-based service work. *Journal of Industrial Relations, 61*(1), 57–78. https://doi.org/10.1177/0022185618800518.

Gilchrist, D., & Knight, P. (2018). *Disability services market report 2018. A report for National Disability Services*. Canberra: National Disability Services.

Glasby, J., & Littlechild, R. (2016). *Direct payments and personal budgets: putting personalisation into practice* (3rd ed.). Policy Press.

Hardaker, D. (2020, September 21). *Revealed: The liberal, Murdoch networks making millions delivering 'Uber for aged care'*. https://www.crikey.com.au/

2020/09/21/aged-care-mable-liberal-news-corp-connection/. Accessed 19 October 2020.

Harrison, L. (2020). *National Disability Insurance Scheme providers in Australia*. Industry (ANZSIC) Report X0029. Melbourne: IBIS World.

HireUp. (2020a). *Become a support worker*. https://www.hireup.com.au/become-a-support-worker/. Accessed 27 May 2020.

HireUp. (2020b). *Support worker pay rates*. HireUp. https://www.hireup.com.au/pay-rates/. Accessed August 20, 2020.

Hoffman, M. (2020). *CEO address to the Council for Economic Development of Australia, NDIA*. https://www.ndis.gov.au/news/4413-ceo-address-council-economic-development-australia. Accessed 15 March 2020.

Industrial Relations Victoria. (2020). *Report of the inquiry into the Victorian on-demand workforce* (Industrial Relations Victoria, Ed.). Melbourne: Victorian Government.

Joint Standing Committee on the National Disability Insurance Scheme. (2017). *Progress report in Parliament of Australia*. Canberra.

Levine Leichtman Capital Partners. (2015, October 1). *Levine Leichtman capital partners and management acquire Caring Brands International* [Press release]. https://www.llcp.com/news/entry/levine-leichtman-capital-partners-and-management-acquire-caring-brands-inte. Accessed 16 September 2020.

Mable Technologies. (2020a). *Clients pay less. Support people earn more*. Mable Technologies. https://mable.com.au/faqs/. Accessed 12 October 2020.

Mable Technologies. (2020b). *Last minute jobs*. Mable Technologies. https://mable.com.au/last-minute-jobs/. Accessed 12 October 2020.

Macdonald, F. (2019). *Where secure employment meets client needs: Greenacres disability services innovative workforce fund project*. Sydney: National Disability Services.

Macdonald, F., & Charlesworth, S. (2013). Equal pay under the 'Fair Work Act 2009' (Cth): Mainstreamed or marginalised? *The University of New South Wales Law Journal, 36*(2), 563–586.

Macdonald, F., & Pegg, M. (2018). Contracting out community services, marketisation and wages. In A. Stewart, J. Stanford, & T. Hardy (Eds.), *The wages crisis in Australia: What it is and what to do about it* (pp. 129–142). Adelaide: University of Adelaide Press.

Macdonald, F., Bentham, E., & Malone, J. (2018). Wage theft, underpayment and unpaid work in marketised social care. *The Economic and Labour Relations Review, 29*(1), 80–96. https://doi.org/10.1177/1035304618758252.

McDonald, P., Williams, P., & Mayes, R. J. W. (2020). Means of control in the organization of digitally intermediated care work. *Work, Employment and Society*, Online first, 1–19. https://doi.org/10.1177/0950017020969107.

McDonald, P., Williams, P., Stewart, A., Mayes, R., & Oliver, D. (2019). *Digital platform work in Australia: Prevalence, nature and impact*. https://eprints.qut.edu.au/203119/. Accessed 23 June 2020.

McKinsey and Company. (2018). Independent Pricing Review: National Disability Insurance Agency. (pp. 103): NDIA.

Macklin, J. (2012). Engaging the disability sector to build a National Disability Insurance Scheme. *Joint Media Release with Senator Jan McLucas*. https://formerministers.dss.gov.au/13513/engaging-the-disability-sector-to-build-a-national-disability-insurance-scheme-2/. Accessed: 30 June 2020.

Municipal Association of Victoria (MAV). (2017). *National Disability Insurance Scheme (NDIS) costs, response to Productivity Commission issues paper on NDIS costs*. Melbourne: Municipal Association of Victoria.

National Disability Insurance Agency (NDIA). (2016). *NDIS market approach: Statement of opportunity and intent—November 2016*. NDIA. https://www.ndis.gov.au/media/448/download. Accessed 24 February 2020.

National Disability Insurance Agency (NDIA) (2019a). *Disability support worker cost model*. June 2019. NDIA. https://www.ndis.gov.au/providers/price-guides-and-pricing. Accessed 7 January 2020.

National Disability Insurance Agency (NDIA). (2019b). *National Disability Insurance Scheme pricing strategy*. NDIA. https://www.ndis.gov.au/providers/price-guides-and-pricing. Accessed 5 April 2020.

National Disability Insurance Agency (NDIA). (2020a, March 31). *COAG Disability Reform Council NDIS Quarterly Report*. NDIA. https://www.ndis.gov.au/about-us/publications/quarterly-reports. Accessed 8 April 2020.

National Disability Insurance Agency (NDIA). (2020b). *Finding support workers*. NDIA. https://www.ndis.gov.au/coronavirus/finding-support-workers. Accessed 16 September 2020

National Disability Insurance Agency (NDIA). (2020c). *NDIS industry reference group*. NDIA. https://www.ndis.gov.au/about-us/reference-group-updates/industry-reference-group. Accessed 15 September 2020.

National Disability Insurance Agency (NDIA). (2020d, June 30). *NDIS quarterly report to disability ministers*. NDIA. https://www.ndis.gov.au/about-us/publications/quarterly-reports. Accessed 8 August 2020.

NDIS Quality and Safeguards Commission (n.d.). *Unregistered providers*. NDIS Quality and Safeguards Commission. https://www.ndiscommission.gov.au/providers/unregistered-providers. Accessed 13 December 2019.

NDIS Senior Officials Working Group for the Disability Reform Council. (2015). *Consultation paper. Proposal for a National Disability Insurance Scheme quality and safeguarding framework*. Canberra: Australian Government.

National Disability Services (NDS). (2017). *Australian Disability Workforce Report July 2017*. Sydney: NDS.

National Disability Services (NDS). (2018). *Innovative Workforce Fund*. NDS. https://workforce.nds.org.au/category/trialling-teams-and-new-contexts/. Accessed 6 December 2019.

National Disability Services (NDS). (2019). *State of the Disability Sector Report 2019*. Sydney.

Productivity Commission. (2010). *Contribution of the not-for-profit sector, research report*. Canberra: Productivity Commission.

Productivity Commission. (2011). *Disability care and support* (Vols. 1–2 Report No. 54). Canberra: Australian Government.

Stewart, A., & Stanford, J. (2017). Regulating work in the gig economy: What are the options? *The Economic and Labour Relations Review, 28*(3), 420–437. https://doi.org/10.1177/1035304617722461.

Trotter, J., Myhill, J., & Wate, T. (2018) *Final Report. The impact of the rollout of the NDIS on metropolitan local governments in South Australia*. Adelaide: Local Government Professionals Association.

Van Toorn, G. (2018). *The new political economy of disability: Transnational networks and individualised funding in the age of neoliberalism* (Doctoral dissertation). University of New South Wales and University of Glasgow.

Warr, D., Dickinson, H., Olney, S., Arstein-Kerslake, A., Wilson, E., Hargrave, J., et al. (2017). *Choice, control and the NDIS: Service users' perspectives on having choice and control in the new National Disability Insurance Scheme*. Parkville: University of Melbourne. https://socialequity.unimelb.edu.au/__data/assets/pdf_file/0010/2364499/Choice-Control-and-the-NDIS-Report-Melbourne-Social-Equity-Institute.pdf. Accessed 13 October 2020.

West Coast Homecare. (n.d.). *Homecare business solutions*. West Coast Homecare. https://westcoasthomecare.com/homecare-business-solutions/. Accessed 12 June 2020.

Whyte, J (2017, July 15). Entrepreneurs make steady NDIS progress: Disabled care. *Australian Financial Review*, p. 25.

Woolley, R. (2020, July 12). Is now the time to become an unregistered provider? DSC *NDIS News*. Melbourne. https://teamdsc.com.au/resources/unregistered-provider. Accessed 12 July 2020.

Workplace Express. (2018, September 25). *Employers respond to casuals ruling with "perma-flexi" bid*. Workplace Express. https://www.workplaceexpress.com.au/. Accessed 12 December 2020.

CHAPTER 7

Care Work, Individualisation and Risk

Introduction

The introduction of an individualised quasi-market for disability care and support in Australia has created new risks for social care workers. In this chapter and in Chapter 8 that follows, the idea of ***individualised risk*** is used to describe different types of risks for workers associated with the broader structural changes occurring under the NDIS. The NDIS policy, the marketisation approach and the emerging social care market have produced changes that have significant negative implications for the nature and valuing of frontline social care work and for the quality of social care employment.

In previous chapters, I identified three themes as capturing some of the key ideas underlying the broader changes, including how frontline social care work is characterised and organised in the NDIS managed care system and market. In this chapter and in Chapter 8, I explore some of the multiple ways in which risks for frontline social care workers are produced in the day-to-day experience of work.

The chapter commences with a brief consideration of the nature of adult social care work, before introducing the concept of individualised risk. Then, I explore workers' experiences in the NDIS, drawing primarily on analysis of individual interviews conducted with 62 frontline disability support and care workers and data from focus groups with another 32 workers employed across a great diversity of support and care relationships

F. Macdonald, *Individualising Risk*,
https://doi.org/10.1007/978-981-33-6366-3_7

and employment arrangements. The chapter also draws on interviews and discussions with smaller numbers of service providers (executive, management and human resources staff), individual service users and family carers. Its focus is on how the individualised funding system introduces *new risks that reinforce the gendered undervaluation of care and support work*. Other types of individualised risk are examined in Chapter 8.

What's Special About Personal Support and Care Work?

Michael Fine offers a conception of care involving three distinct but intertwining elements: (i) care as work providing practical assistance to a person, (ii) care as a social and personal relationship of interpersonal support and (iii) care as a disposition or a cognitive or emotional concern for another's well-being (Fine 2004, pp. 224–225). This understanding of care recognises all three elements as present in paid care work and accounts for the complexities and contradictions of the work. Many care and support workers express deep commitment to the work of care as a vocation, and many develop very close relationships with the people they support. It is not uncommon for care and support workers to say they love their work because of the relational and emotional aspects of it, though these can also be sources of tension and difficulty.

As an illustration of some of the complexity and tensions of adult social care work, the remark below, made by a disability support worker with many years' experience, is instructive. For this worker, both the joy and the 'burden' of work arose from the emotional concern for others it involved. Helen said she 'loved' her job but she was now looking for work in which she could do 'something less client focused':

> The burden of—the burden, that's not a good word. To do something a bit more robotic rather than having to care so much about what you do. (To do something that's) not about people. I know customer service is about people, but not about people's welfare. (Helen)[1]

[1] Pseudonyms are used and other information that could identify people or organisations has been changed or removed.

Another worker felt the social and personal relationships she developed were the rewards of her work, but that this aspect of care was not sanctioned as part of her job by her employers:

> There's certainly a bit of everything in this job. That's what I love about it. ... And I love that you build an attachment to people, although you're not supposed to. I shouldn't say an attachment; you build a friendship. You're not supposed to ... but that's totally unrealistic. I mean, you're a carer, you're going to care. (Christine)

For many workers, the relationship and emotional aspects of care are sources of great satisfaction, but they can also be sources of guilt, stress and overwork. Most often, however, the problems workers experience with their work are not aspects of care; they are pay and conditions. Despite saying she loved her work, Christine—the worker quoted above—was actively looking for another job because of the long workdays, on-demand work, lack of recognition from her managers, poor pay and impacts on her health:

> ... (Before I cut back my hours) I was really stressed, really stressed all the time; I was tired all the time, my back was hurting all the time ... I didn't know how to say no, and these (service managers), like I used to think, but if I don't go, maybe they can't find someone else to do it – as if they can't! Like I thought I was quite indispensable. No, I didn't think that; I just thought, well I don't want to let anybody down. And so I put my own health at risk, and would do everything that was asked of me, and get paid peanuts, and come home buggered. Pay the bills, and off I'd go again the next day. ... Apparently, there's jobs out there that you can earn money the same as what I'm earning while I'm working days and nights. (I am) applying for jobs left right and centre. (Christine)

Individualised Risk

Consumer choice and control, *market determination of fair pay and conditions* and *transformation of the relations of work and care* are the three interconnected and overlapping themes identified in analyses in earlier chapters. These themes capture some of the key ideas, drivers and organising principles embedded in the institutional structures and processes of the individualised social care system which shape the supply side of the new individualised social care market. In my analysis of workers' experiences below and in Chapter 8, I draw on these themes to explore the ways in which the individualised funding arrangements are changing disability care and support work.

Focusing on the micro-level of day-to-day care and support work relationships and employment and drawing primarily on interviews with workers, I employ the idea of *individualised risk* to describe different types of risks common in workers' accounts of their experiences and that are associated with the NDIS institutional changes. Individualised risks play out at the micro-level of individual work and care and support relationships, in the labour process, in working time arrangements and in rewards and protections attached to individuals' employment.

I identify three broad intersecting categories of individualised risk as (i) risks of *reinforcing gendered undervaluation*; (ii) risks of *isolating and individualising workers*; and iii) risks of *fragmenting work, working time and working lives*. Risks in each of these categories are influenced by a combination of structural changes and system and market operations and practices associated with the three themes of consumer choice and control, market determination of fair pay and conditions and transformation of the work and care relations.

The idea of individualised risk encompasses and extends Christensen and Manthorpe's (2016) concept of 'personalised risk', which focuses on three changes in the public/private dimensions of social care work under individualisation policies. Christensen and Manthorpe (2016, pp. 140–141) identify (i) reduced public accountability when workers are directly employed or engaged by people requiring care and support, (ii) increased employment in home-based care and (iii) the blurring of employer/employee relationships with service user/care worker relationships. These lead, they argue, to, respectively, risks of 'informality and insecurity of employment conditions and rights', risks of 'emotionalised relationships' not mediated by organisations and risks of 'intimacy' through crossing the boundaries of employer/employee roles. The concept of individualised risk encompasses these changes and risks and broadens the focus to include other new and heightened risks for workers arising from significant changes occurring through the NDIS individualisation.

Individualised risk includes a focus on market ideas and principles in the NDIS, providing insight into how the ways in which the market is governed, managed and funded influence and shape care and support work and employment to create risks for workers. So, one question guiding exploration of workers' experiences is: Are the two themes *consumer choice and control* and *market determination of fair pay and conditions* reproduced and represented in the micro-level of day-to-day labour market and care practices and, if so, are they implicated in creating risks for workers? Investigation of individualised risk associated with the third theme *transformation of the relations of work and care* is concerned with any risks associated with the institutional changes to the organisational and legal relations of work that structurally distance workers from organisational control and change their employment status.

The discussion that follows commences with an examination of the production of individualised risks of the first type: *reinforcing gendered undervaluation*, exploring workers' experiences to show how these risks are produced in the new social care system. Chapter 8 continues the exploration of workers' experiences and individualised risks of *isolating and individualising workers*, and *fragmenting work, working time and working lives*.

Risks of Reinforcing Gendered Undervaluation

The ways in which the NDIS heightens the risks of gendered undervaluation of care and support work can be linked to each of the themes of *consumer choice and control*, *market determination of fair pay and conditions* and *transformation of the relations of work and care*.

First, risks are heightened by transforming the location of, and the parties to, work and care relations. Care and support work is moved to private home settings and performed within private individualised employment relationships. In Chapter 2, I noted Ungerson's (2004) key findings from her comparative studies of individualised social care. Ungerson found that outcomes for workers are poor where both care provision is poorly regulated *and* care work is able to be constructed and treated as care (rather than work). The NDIS places poorly regulated care and support provision in individualised direct employment relations that is subject to little oversight. Employees are provided with fewer protections than other workers under law and in practice due to personal nature and household location of the work. The 'partial protection' under labour law of home-based work in privatised relationships (Charlesworth 2017) leaves this work open to characterisation as informal help akin to unpaid care.

Second, risks of gendered undervaluation are heightened in the NDIS as frontline workers are often characterised as *services*. This is achieved structurally through the mechanisms of self-employed contracting and direct employment relationships with people requiring supports, and through the treatment of the work as unskilled. The self-employed contractor workforce is a 'value for money', flexible workforce that can fulfil the consumer choice and control ideals for self-directed support by providing the support people want when they want it at a lower cost to the consumer—at the expense of workers who are re-fashioned as on-demand services. Digital care platforms facilitate the development and growth of a self-employed contractor workforce while also supporting the fragmenting of care and support jobs into small micro-jobs or incidences of service.

Third, intersecting and overlapping with the first two processes that heighten risks is the creation of risks through various structural and ideational changes that extol the market as the (best) basis for determining fair pay and conditions. In the next three sections, I show how risks of reinforcing gendered undervaluation are heightened associated with these three themes, through an exploration of disability care and support workers' experiences.

Transforming Relations: Informalised Work and the Very Private Business of Care

> It takes a special kind of person to work as a care assistant: one who almost innately puts others' needs before their own and does so with compassion. (Indeed.com [jobs website] Indeed.com 2020)

> Lend a helping hand ... *Like Family* is more than just a job. Build friendships, strengthen your community and improve people's lives — including your own. (Like Family [digital platform] 2020)

The notion that women work selflessly for love rather than money (Folbre and Nelson 2000) continues to underpin the undervaluation of support and care work in Australia. As described in Chapter 5, employment regulation supports this stereotype in multiple ways through its differential treatment of work located in private homes and personal relations. The design of the individualised social care and support system also supports this characterisation of the highly feminised workforce by constructing care and support work as unskilled—and, as has been noted elsewhere, sometimes as not really work at all (Delaney and Macdonald 2018). So, in the individualised funding system, the relations of work and care are transformed in ways that blur the lines between care work as paid employment in the formal labour force and care as informal and unpaid private or personal work.

Complex power relations exist in support relationships, influenced by the social relations of gender and disability as well as other relations of class, age, ethnicity and migrant status. Analysis of workers' experiences suggests the norms of traditional gendered and classed relations of household, family and 'help' in the home may be much stronger in private family spaces and individualised work relations than in organisations. These dynamics can play out in multiple ways that devalue care and support work, leading to downward pressure on pay. Where workers are directly engaged or employed by the people they support, ideas about work value are developed—and negotiations around pay occur—in individualised, private and informal transactions and relationships. The potential for collective representation is weakened, and organisational oversight of work is often negligible. Anderson (2007) has referred to the 'very private business' of domestic work, and the term is apt for describing care and support in individualised relations, relations characterised by informality and distanced from regulation.

Workforce shortages are cited by NDIS policymakers and market managers in suggesting care and support workers might be able to pick and choose their preferred work in the growing market for individualised care and support (McKinsey & Company 2018; Productivity Commission 2011; Senior Officials Working Group for the Disability Reform Council 2015). However, this is not how individual workers experience the labour market. Workers are able to exercise some choice, but this is often highly constrained in a labour market that offers many insecure, short hours' on-demand jobs that provide little certainty, predictability or guaranteed income. Workers juggle multiple jobs to get adequate hours, and they make many trade-offs to get and keep jobs that provide some certainty and stability. People stay in jobs they are dissatisfied with, and some stay in jobs in which they feel exploited or unsafe, because the work is close to home or the hours suit. For example, Aurora thought her employer was paying her the 'wrong' rate but did not want to raise this in case it led to her losing her job in a region where there were few jobs on offer:

> And I didn't really know whether I should say anything yet to the boss … and I didn't really want to rock the boat because it's kind of hard to get work here in (regional city). And I actually really enjoy what I'm doing, I really like it, so I didn't want to make any waves or just, yeah, I don't know. It's a problem. (Aurora)

Similarly, another worker, Gabrielle, knew she was being underpaid by her direct employer but she agreed with him to hide this by adjusting her timesheets to make it look like she worked shorter hours than she actually did. She did this at her employer's request to 'help him' because he wanted to make his support funds stretch to more hours of support, and because she valued her job. She had a regular weekend shift that fitted with her own family responsibilities. Gabrielle said her employer was 'a good employer', as he didn't cancel or shorten her shifts with little notice, as she had experienced previously.

Workers cite informality in the relations of work in direct employment and contracting arrangements with service users as a source of difficulties they experience in changing jobs to get better paid, or safer, or less stressful work. In direct care and support relations, the emotional aspects of care can be significant in determining employment arrangement and working conditions. Workers' commitments to their employers and clients are sometimes based on friendship or family relations which involve strong beliefs about obligations and interpersonal dependency and often lead to undervaluation through extra unpaid work.

For example, Dimitra was employed by a neighbour and family friend. She felt very conflicted in her job as she wanted to leave but felt she could not do so. She struggled with the idea that providing support to her friend was 'work'. Dimitra felt 'guilty' for being paid for some of her work and, to compensate for this, she worked many unpaid hours for her neighbour. Sometimes she felt unable to decline requests to work at times that clashed with her university classes, feeling obliged to be available whenever she was 'needed'. Dimitra said she was 'very stressed'. She could not talk to her parents about the situation as they were also relying on her to support her client who was also their friend and neighbour.

Some directly engaged workers worried that they were not taking enough care or responsibility for people's safety but felt unable to challenge people engaging in unsafe or highly risky behaviours. Dimitra assisted her client with showering but, after two incidents when her client had almost fallen, suggested a shower chair be used. However, her client did not want to use a chair and Dimitra did not raise the suggestion again as she did not want to 'upset' her.

For directly employed and contracted workers, ambiguities and uncertainties about employers' and clients' expectations of care and support relationships were intertwined with lack of clarity about aspects of employment. A recurring theme in interviews concerned the absence of clear expectations about roles and responsibilities, which often fed into uncertainty for workers about whether they were doing enough to earn their wages or contractor fees. This often played out in gendered ways that devalued the work of social care.

One young worker, Vincent, bringing his ideas of what 'proper' work is to the support relationship, dealt with this problem by defining his role as 'getting stuff done'. He limited his paid work time to task time, avoiding spending time on the emotional aspects of care, so he could feel he was earning his wage doing legitimate work. He explained his approach:

> I'm here to work for you rather than just be there. I'm here to do a job. I'm here to take care of your needs. So that (my employer) doesn't, so that he gets the most out of what I'm providing, I suppose. Which is important because he can often not, he may at certain stages say, 'that's ok, I'll just get you to sit down for a little bit, don't really need anything right now'. But I think I find that I'd prefer to be constantly working and constantly doing something to help him because I'm getting paid, it's my job. So, yeah, I think that's important. … When I'm done, I'll say 'is there anything else I can do?' And if there's not, then I'll go. (Vincent)

Other workers spoke of feeling guilty or grateful for being paid because of the emotional aspects of care in their work in informalised support relationships; feeling guilty or grateful for being paid to care about people, or for being paid when enjoying the company of people they supported. Ethan, who was in his early 20s, spoke of sometimes feeling guilty that he was paid for accompanying people to community activities because he had fun and felt like he was going out with a friend. As in a friendship relationship, he felt he needed to reciprocate so he often paid for drinks and snacks for both of them, something he said was 'not really affordable' on his income.

Undervaluation of the work was an issue for some highly experienced and skilled workers who might have been expected to be less likely to have this problem. Judith had taken up a role as the main support worker for a young man who had recently moved out of his parent's home for the first time. Judith was committed to helping the young man and his parents. She said the man and his family were determined they could self-manage the man's support arrangements, and to do this, they needed to make the NDIS funding stretch to as much support as possible. However, Judith felt they had not really anticipated how much work was involved in self-management of personal supports and that, consequently, a lot of that work fell to her to do. She said the family were not paying her 'anything like what they'd be paying an organisation', but were asking a lot of her:

> It's not difficult, it's... it's just intense work. Because you discover things ..you discover even just little things that go on that need to be supported. ... So basically I'm creating policies and procedures, you know. And yeah, sometimes a little bit of resentment creeps in because I think I'm doing this and it's really, it's complex work and I don't feel like I'm being rewarded properly for it. ... if I don't do it, no-one else has the capacity to do it unless it's outsourced to an organisation and then you're bound by their policies and procedures. Therefore the whole model can potentially just fall apart. So I'm invested in making sure this model works, so there is this personal investment as well, so there's a lot of these factors pulling and to and from, so sometimes it can be quite overwhelming. I haven't had a holiday in 18 months, haven't had time off. And I can't, there's no prospect of me taking time off for quite some time. (Judith)

A small and growing body of qualitative studies in the UK has explored the complexity and difficulty of establishing self-directed and self-managed support arrangements (see Chapter 3) and studies are emerging in Australia (Fisher et al. 2010; Purcal et al. 2016). However, these studies rarely examine either the roles or experiences of support workers in self-managed arrangements or they rely solely on information provided by employers to draw conclusions about workers' experiences and employment conditions, which are generally positive. As argued in Chapter 4, in Australia, the NDIS pricing structures, work organisation and developing approach to consumer service are redefining support work as unskilled personal assistance. Judith's experience suggests there may be some large gaps in understandings of the contributions of support workers and of the judgement and other skills they are required to apply in their jobs in the individualised system.

Workers employed by service provider organisations also experienced the devaluing of their work with the introduction of NDIS individualised funding, due to the move to pricing care and support by the hour. Workers and service providers spoke of the individualised funding model and pricing levels encouraging the use of casual employment and engagement of workers at lower classification levels than previously, and service providers and workers spoke of removing team meetings and training from employees' paid work time. Similar findings are present in recent survey research under NDIS arrangements (Cortis and van Toorn 2020; Cortis et al. 2017).

Workers experienced undervaluation as part of the daily practice of their work and employment. They spoke of feeling devalued and not respected *as skilled workers* and of losing autonomy, as their employers no longer allowed them time in their jobs to do what they felt they needed to provide good quality care and support. They had inadequate time to support people properly, communicate with supervisors, hand over essential information to the next worker on a care shift or communicate with family members about a person's well-being. There were consequences for quality of care and support including not meeting people's needs and preferences, reduced well-being and risking health and safety. Workers raised concerns with employers that appeared to go unheard. These included, for example, that two people were needed to operate a hoist to lift a person or that a client's current health issues required better monitoring. Workers reported greater inconsistency and less continuity of care and support, arising from more fragmented shift schedules and greater use of casuals. Clients' well-being and safety were affected by, for example, mis-use and unsafe use of medical equipment, reduced time and opportunity for organising activities in line with people's preferences, and casual workers' inability to communicate with clients or lack of understanding of their needs. The consequences for working time fragmentation are discussed in Chapter 8.

Workers felt devalued and poorly treated *as employees* as they were expected to undertake more and more of their work unpaid, including completing required administrative and reporting tasks. Their experiences suggest care and employment relationships in the NDIS are now taking on the 'time and task' character seen to be the basis of much adult social care work in England. This type of work 'exclude(s) the costs of the emotional labour needed to build a relationship with the user' (Lewis and West 2014, p. 3) by excluding the time needed for the relational work of care from paid work time. Along with this informalisation of the social care and support role, the centrality of consumer choice in individualised care and support also supports processes that re-shape expectations of care and support relations. The next section examines how care and support is being reshaped to be much more transactional.

Consumer Choice and Control: Master–Servant Relations and Humans as Flexible Services

Tensions and contradictions prevail in the ways in which individualised care and support work arrangements reproduce gendered undervaluation in direct employment and engagement relationships. On the one hand, as outlined above, the distinctions between unpaid care and paid care work can be blurred as informalised relationships heighten the emotional aspects of adult social care work. On the other hand, the idea of consumer choice and control—central to individual empowerment in the NDIS system and market—can entail a rejection of paid support work as *care*. In rejecting the treatment of people with disability as passive recipients of care, individualisation also challenges the power and expertise of professional care providers, as described in the discussion of debates about personalisation in Chapter 3 (Beresford 2014; Glasby and Littlechild 2016). The very concept of care may be rejected as patronising or disabling (Mladenov 2015).

In direct employment arrangements, the rejection of care can be achieved in part through a shift in power relations where care relationships also become employment relationships in which the person being supported, as employer, has control over the labour process. Sometimes this can lead to relationships taking on a master–servant character—something observed by Christensen (2012) in similarly unregulated direct care and employment relationships in England. In the Australian individualised system, consumer choice and control are often given structural form through workers being engaged as self-employed contractors; disability support work is cast as a consumer service and workers are cast as service. However, workers may have little autonomy despite this being an assumption in the legal status of contractors. Their work is a commodity purchased for as long as required, with no responsibility placed on the purchaser for training, security or protection (Prassl 2018).

It is worthwhile noting that most self-employed contractor workers interviewed for this research had not chosen to work in this employment arrangement in preference to being in an employment relationship. It was even more rare to come across a worker who was motivated by ideas of self-employed contracting as offering freedom from subordination and the constraints of dependent employment—ideas that have been strong in Australian public discourse promoting entrepreneurialism and enterprise workers since the early 2000 s (Howard 2004; Johnson 2007). In this study, people did not take up contracting to be in control of their work. Workers engaged as self-employed contractors often referred to their clients as 'my employer' or 'my boss'; many had little autonomy or control over their work. Jobs were often described as, in one worker's words, 'being there when they want and doing whatever they want me to do' (Marie). Promotion of self-employed contractor support workers by digital care platforms and some care labour brokers to people with disability is often on the basis that they are *cheaper and more flexible services* than are provided by traditional service provider organisations that employ support workers (Like Family 2020; Mable 2020).

Mostly, people in this study became contractors because this was the arrangement that was on offer to them, irrespective of whether they found their jobs through informal networks, internet searches, digital platforms, student job boards or other means. The exceptions were a few comparatively older and very experienced workers who did welcome the prospect of working outside of large organisations, often in anticipation of having more control over working time arrangements, rather than having control over the labour process. Among employees, some had chosen to seek work in employment relationships with service provider organisations or individuals in preference to self-employed contracting. People sought to be employees to ensure they received superannuation contributions, because they wanted paid leave, and/or to make sure they had the support and backup of an organisation, including to have backup to provide support to service users if they couldn't work due to illness or wanted time off.

Low levels of funding and the individualised market ideal of 'value for money' are key to the treatment of care and support work as unskilled in Australia's NDIS. However, as noted earlier, it is also the case that undoing the idea of adult social care work as professional work is an important project for some self-directed support advocates. In England, for example, the idea of using registers of care workers seeking direct employment to contact workers to offer them training has been rejected by some people with disability who regard these types of initiatives as removing control from them as employers and managers of their own supports. This has also been the case with proposals for worker registers to obtain pre-employment background checks on workers (Woolham et al. 2019).

In Australia, as in England, much is made in the NDIS of the importance of workers having the 'right' values and attitudes. Often this is expressed in terms of attitudes and values being more important than qualifications (ARTD Consultants 2015, p. iv). Some individuals and advocacy groups for people with disability have argued strongly against proposals for mandatory systems of worker registration on the basis that these would undermine choice and control; they also argued against the establishment of formal skills requirements for NDIS-funded care and support workers on the same basis (ARTD Consultants 2015; Productivity Commission 2011). These ideas also underpin the NDIS as a social care system that neglects worker training, and in which there is an implicit expectation that workers should not expect skill development, because person-centred support requires only that they present as required and take direction from service users.

Several workers spoke of their employers and clients insisting they did not want formally qualified workers to support them, and that they did not want their support workers to undertake training. Like a number of support workers interviewed, Cassie said she would 'appreciate some sort of training' and would feel more confident supporting her client if she had basic first aid training and training in how to use the equipment—including hoists and oxygen pumps—she was required to use in her job. She related a recent incident where her client had experienced an acute health problem and she had to assist him. She said '(t)hat was pretty confronting … I had no idea what I was doing'. Asked how she felt about this, Cassie said it was 'very stressful because I don't want to hurt him or do it wrong'. Like other workers interviewed, Cassie wanted to feel she was competent to do her job, but she also accepted it was her client's prerogative to determine what training she had and how she would perform her role, as shown in these interview excerpts:

> I have asked quite a few times if he'd like me to do some training but he's always been very adamant that he doesn't want me to be trained, I think because he doesn't want me to, I get the sense that he doesn't want me to learn things in the training that he won't really want me to do.

> … I think it also might be to do with he doesn't want someone to come in and be patronising or come in and think they know what to do whereas I can kind of go in and blend into the background of his day-to-day life … So yeah, I think it's possibly that's why he doesn't want me to be trained if you know what I mean.
>
> … I feel like, if there was good training to go and do, and that he wanted me to do it, I'd be more than happy to do it but because he's so reticent for me to do it, I feel if I went away and did it, he would find it frustrating possibly. (Cassie)

There was a common narrative in interviews of jobs being primarily about doing what people wanted. When asked what she needed to do as a support worker to do 'a good job', Samantha responded 'mainly just anticipating what she wants me to do and being aware if she's had a bad day'. Asked if she felt she had support in her job, Cassie said 'it would be good to be able to ask someone questions sometimes'. She also explained she would like to have a better sense of how well her employer thought she was doing:

> *Cassie*: I asked for feedback a while ago as to whether I was doing a good job and [he] just kind of brushed it off, was like, 'Yeah, you're great, you're the best. Never had anyone better'. *Interviewer:* Ok. That sounds good. *Cassie*: But some sort of constructive feedback as to what I could do to improve or how I could be better at the job would be really helpful because a lot of the time I'm second-guessing what I'm doing. (Cassie)

The emphasis on care and support as consumer service may be encouraging more instrumental and transactional approaches to the work as a market-based exchange. Other studies have identified what has been called a 'utilitarian' approach adopted by some people with disability to their personal support workers, involving taking a view of workers as depersonalised 'arms and legs' or as servants. In this approach, support workers are subordinated and not permitted to exercise agency or 'personhood' in the relationship (Shakespeare et al. 2018, pp. 171–172).

While an inclination to this approach is present in the denial of skill in the NDIS, it was also apparent in some very poor treatment experienced by a few workers. For example, Beatriz felt her employer was using her as an outlet for her frustrations. Beatriz said she thought the woman treated her badly 'just because she *can* be rude to me instead of being rude to (family members), as she knows I won't do anything about it'. Beatriz had started 'dreading going to work' and said:

> I don't have an expectation that people are nice to me all the time because I feel as if you can be in a bad mood in your own house and that's okay, but I should be able to have an expectation that they're not indirectly or directly rude or aggressive. (Beatriz)

Another characterisation of directly employed workers is as 'paid friends', something that has also been observed in individualised support relationships in England. Shakespeare et al. (2018) have noted that the reciprocity that friendship entails in a support relationship is not an equal exchange between worker and the person with a disability, as the worker has more choice about preserving their privacy. However, the strong consumer choice and control ideal promoted for support relationships in the Australian system may entail some different or strengthened expectations of what workers should give of themselves as support services.

In interviews with workers in this study, there were many examples of what Christensen and Manthorpe (2016) have referred to as the 'risks of intimacy', risks arising through crossing the boundaries of employer/employee roles. Some workers experienced people with disability treating the support relationship as, in the words of one young woman, 'buying a friend'. This was described as a phenomenon that was quite different from the 'paid friend' identified in the English research—as it was about being paid to be the kind of friend the service user wanted. Some workers felt they were expected to have little or no say in how and when the friendship aspects of the relationship were expressed or how the relationship was presented to others. This was a highly gendered phenomenon, with female workers often experiencing these issues as connected to the representation of masculinity and male sexuality of the men they supported. For example, young women spoke of being 'paraded about' in public or 'displayed' on men's social media pages, as in Tisha's case 'making it look like I'm his girlfriend'. Stephanie said she was asked to 'wear something special, something sexy' to accompany her employer to a business function to support him. She felt demoralised by this and said it 'was not really for looking professional … more for him to use me to impress people'. Prior to this, Stephanie had believed she was valued by her employer for her knowledge and expertise as a postgraduate student in an allied health field, something she now questioned.

In traditional service provider organisations, a consumer choice and control imperative was highly evident as a driver of changes that led to the devaluation of support work. The NDIS has challenged disability support service providers to diversify their workforces as well as their service offerings and models; diversity is promoted as a way for providers to be more responsive to the diversity of people, needs, preferences and types of supports required in a system that upholds the rights of people with disability. Meeting these challenges could lead to more inclusive workforces, with new opportunities for people from groups who are poorly represented in the support and care workforce, including people with disability. However, consumer choice and control also entails a demand for increased flexibility. When this is combined with the financial pressures created by the pricing model, the easiest way for service providers to respond to calls for greater diversity can be to take a low-road approach. Flexibility and diversity are achieved by engaging an on-demand workforce of low-paid, less-skilled and trained staff employed in short-hours, insecure casual work. From the available data on support workers' employment arrangements, it would appear this has been the approach that has dominated the individualised market (NDS 2019a).

Time, effort, safety and 'good practice' were experienced by some workers to be less respected and/or valued by their service provider organisations under individualised funding. Some workers reported that their managers required them to be more flexible, abandon some safety procedures and put up with poor treatment from organisations' clients to maximise responsiveness to consumer demands. Heather was rostered to support a person who frequently changed the time of his personal support visits on the same day with as little as an hour's notice. Heather expected her employer would agree it was unreasonable for her to have to accommodate frequent shift changes with very short notice.

However, when Heather raised the issue with her employer, she said his response was 'Oh well this is what the client has requested and he is your client, he's on your roster. That's what we have to do'. Heather felt she was treated unfairly, saying:

> It's the assumption being that my time is so flexible that I can change it within an hour ... I don't get an explanation as to why. ... (Later) it'll come up in conversation (that the person) was out having lunch with friends and having such a good time (they) didn't realise the time, that sort of thing. And I don't think that's terribly fair. (Heather)

Market Determination of Fair Pay and Conditions: Value for Money

> Self-management maximises choice and control, as participants can opt for bespoke or innovative supports outside of the specialist disability services and negotiate their own prices. (NDIA 2019b, p. 27)

> Clients pay less. Workers earn more. (Mable 2020)

> Well you see what other people are charging. I didn't want to price myself out of the market so I started out low, but not at the bottom because I didn't want to look like a loser. (Michael, disability support worker)

NDIS fund holders directly employing or engaging their own support staff can use a plan manager to manage their funding, or they can manage it themselves (self-management). Self-managers are advised to seek advice on their obligations as employers but they may not be provided with much information at all about these unless they actively seek it out. Even where there is some organisational support for self-management, it seems it is not uncommon for people directly employing workers to be unaware of their obligations and responsibilities as employers or of the risks involved (Purcal et al. 2016, Appendix B).

A belief that the market sets the prices for disability support work was common among workers interviewed. Directly employed and workers using platforms cited various notions of accepted practice as the basis for their pay—including 'what [individuals seeking support] will pay', 'what other people are charging' or the 'going rate'. Workers' understandings of how much they should be paid sometimes included reference to the regulated minimum rates in the industry award. However, unless they were very experienced workers, their understanding of employment regulation and of minimum standards applying to conditions and pay was often poor. Workers cited the hourly rate for the lowest classification level for weekday times for a permanent employee, not including the pay loading a casual employee would receive in lieu of paid leave. Nor did they make reference to any minimum engagement period or compensation for late cancellations and some did not account for loadings for evening and weekend work. The accounts of workers who were directly employed by people with NDIS funding suggest some employers do not observe or are unaware of minimum pay and conditions standards. Self-employed contractors rarely accounted for the additional costs of self-employment such as workers' compensation and superannuation in considering the rates they were paid.

Arguably, the main innovation of the digital care platform model for the individualised system is in providing an avenue for development of a self-contractor workforce and the transformation of work relations on a large scale whereby care and support work is almost completely delinked from labour laws and minimum standards and benefits accruing to employees including minimum pay rates, working time and other standards. Some care and support platforms present their rates as maintaining a link to regulated minimum pay rates but, as noted in Chapter 6, the connection is usually to a low classification without additional regulated loadings and does not take account of the absence of employer superannuation contributions. The other main innovation of platforms is in creating 'a new version of Taylorism' whereby labour is broken up into small tasks (Aloisi 2016, p. 653). The relational nature of social care might suggest it would be more difficult to Taylorise this work than it is with other types of work allocated by platforms including, for example, clerical and writing tasks. However, workers' experiences show this is occurring with care and support work.

The experiences of one young worker presented below illustrate some of the many ways in which the organisation of work through self-employed contracting and digital platforms in an individualised social care market leaves workers open to exploitation and ongoing insecurity with no certainty of work or income. While Oscar's story suggests a naïve young worker, many elements of his story were echoed in the experiences of other workers interviewed.

Oscar's experience of seeking and gaining disability support work through two digital platforms over almost a year had been mixed. He enjoyed supporting different people in a variety of settings, assisting people to participate in different activities in the community and seeing people achieve their goals. However, he had struggled to work out how he could make a living from this work. He spent 'a lot' of unpaid time obtaining work, including travelling to and attending meetings and pre-employment interviews with people who only wanted a worker to support them on a single occasion or needed someone very infrequently. He was 'losing money' as he didn't get reimbursed for many expenses that arose when he was at work. He said: 'I can put on the website that I charge for this and that but that doesn't cover everything, and, anyway, I don't want to put people off'. Oscar said his 'biggest problem' with his pay was that he couldn't negotiate reimbursement of expenses in advance, as these were very unpredictable—for example, when his client decided at the last minute that he wanted Oscar to transport him across town.

In addition, Oscar found he spent money when at work. Sometimes this was because he didn't want to 'ruin the spontaneity' when, for example, his client decided they should go out for fast food or to the cinema, which meant Oscar had to pay to participate in the shared activity. Another way Oscar thought he lost money was by spending several hours a week of unpaid time doing administration work to get paid. He said one platform company that he relied on for work treated him 'badly' as, often, he was not paid until several weeks after he submitted his timesheet. Oscar thought he probably needed to charge people for late cancellations but he wanted to keep a good rating on a platform and believed charging might damage his rating. At the time of the interview, he was looking for a part-time customer service job that would give him a 'regular pay packet' so he could continue his disability support work but worry less about his income.

Care and support workers who gained their work through platforms or who were in direct employment arrangements commonly reported having their work cancelled at very late notice without pay. While there is some protection against loss of income from last minute cancellations for employees under the industrial award and in the NDIS pricing, workers employed or contracted directly or through third parties were often not aware of this. Having shifts cancelled and changed with little notice was one of the worst aspects of the job for many. However, it was also often thought of as just 'part of the deal', as Marie put it, rather than as not 'fair' as Heather, the worker mentioned above who was employed by a service provider, believed.

The difference in this appears to be that Heather had an expectation that consideration of her rights and treatment is part of the deal in her employment relationship, whereas people who were working outside organisations often didn't have these expectations. For example, Nicole had worked with one client for about four months when the client said she was reducing Nicole's hourly rate by a substantial amount. According to Nicole, this was so her client could use the money to 'get extra support when she goes on holiday'. Nicole was disappointed but hadn't protested as said she could understand why the woman made the decision.

Other workers, many who had very positive relationships with their clients, did expect they had a right to fair treatment, but when faced with being treated poorly or with a lack of consideration, didn't act or raise issues, considering it was out of their control. As Meg put it, 'it's not really fair but it's the nature of the industry'. Others were similarly resigned to being given little consideration, especially when it came to employers treating them as on-demand services.

> Often, I have my shift cancelled ... Yeah, she'll just be like 'Oh, I don't need you today'—in the morning and that's pretty bad. ... but that's why she employs her own workers... . (Louise)

> ... and with (client), I go on a shift and I have to leave because he says 'oh, it's okay, you've done what you should do' and I've only been there half the time. That happens regularly. (Gabrielle)

Employees with traditional not-for-profit service provider organisations expressed very mixed emotions about how their work was valued under individualisation. While being optimistic that, in the individualised system, their support for people could be better directed to supporting individual empowerment, this was not the workers' experience in the first few years of the NDIS. Direct support workers and service co-ordinators spoke of how the billable hours model was shifting the logic of their work to a time and task basis, leaving no opportunity to provide support in ways they felt would be empowering or enabling.

With reduced capacity to invest in workers and increased use of casual employment, from workers' accounts, it appears that some service providers are adopting some of the practices more commonly used by labour hire agencies including reliance on casual workforces and outsourcing work to self-employed contractors. Workers reported they had to pay for police checks, working with children checks and first aid certificates together costing around $500 in total before gaining employment that may be only part-time work of very short hours a week.

Since the NDIS, labour hire agencies and service providers have introduced recruitment and pre-employment practices that include requiring potential employees to participate in full day and longer company-run, and/or online training and orientation in their own time with no guarantee of work. Some Australian states' training authorities provide certificate-level training in disability work at no-cost through public providers. Nevertheless, workers who been unemployed had been recruited into expensive privately-run training courses by companies that were both private training providers and labour hire agencies or registered service providers, on the promise of a job on completion of training.

Dumi became a support worker after responding to a job vacancy notice on a jobs website. The company advertising for employees recruited Dumi into their own four-day training course for a fee of almost $1000. Dumi also completed a 'mandatory' unpaid work placement with the company after the formal training course. At the time of his interview for the research, Dumi was employed by the company on a casual basis and he had fairly regular shifts of about 10 hours a week, usually working these over four or five days. He was still paying off his course fees which were deducted from his wages. He said the company had him 'tied down to them' as he couldn't get the training certificate to find more work elsewhere until he had worked off the fees he owed the company. Dumi felt he was 'just breaking even', given his short shifts involved a lot of unpaid time travel time in inner city traffic and because he was still paying off his training fees. He wondered if he had been 'cheated' by the company as they gave him so few hours of work after he had paid for their training.

Conclusion

This chapter has examined how the individualised funding system introduces new risks that reinforce the gendered undervaluation of care and support work. The consequences for workers are both material and social. The broader consequences for gender equality in the Australian labour market and for gendered social relations are still to play out.

The individualised funding scheme heightens the risks of gendered undervaluation in two ways. It removes access to many of the mechanisms and avenues that might be used to tackle undervaluation of the work *and* it reverses past gains made towards recognition and valuing of the work. The work is being redefined as low-skilled and task-based, or as informal 'help'; jobs are increasingly casualised, with little opportunity for skill development and access to career pathways; employment is moving away from the reach of regulation that protects incomes and conditions; and workers are isolated from opportunities for collective organisation and representation. The risks of reinforcing gendered undervaluation also have consequences for the quality of care and support provided and for the well-being and recognition of rights of people being supported. These risks are interconnected and overlapping with other individualised risks for workers that are considered in Chapter 8.

References

Aloisi, A. (2016). Commoditized workers: Case study research on labor law issues arising from a set of on-demand/gig economy platforms. *Comparative Labor Law and Policy Journal, 37*(3), 653–690. https://heinonline.org/HOL/LandingPage?handle=hein.journals/cllpj37&div=40&id=&page=.

Anderson, B. (2007). A very private business: Exploring the demand for migrant domestic workers. *European Journal of Women's Studies, 14*(3), 247–264. https://doi.org/10.1177/1350506807079013.

ARTD Consultants. (2015). *NDIS Quality and Safeguarding Framework consultation paper.* Canberra: Department of Social Services. https://engage.dss.gov.au/wp-content/uploads/2015/11/consultation_report_ndis_quality_safeguarding_framework.pdf. Accessed 16 July 2020.

Beresford, P. (2014). Advancing the positives of personalisation/person-centred support: A multi-perspective view. In C. Needham & J. Glasby (Eds.), *Debates in personalisation* (pp. 153–166). Bristol: Polity Press.

Charlesworth, S. (2017). Partial protection? The regulation of home care workers' working conditions. In C. Fenwick & V. V. Goethem (Eds.), *Regulating for equitable and job-rich growth* (pp. 125–150). Edward Elgar Publishing. https://doi.org/10.4337/9781788112673.00013.

Christensen, K. (2012). Towards sustainable hybrid relationships in cash-for-care systems. *Disability & Society, 27*(3), 399–412. https://doi.org/10.1080/09687599.2012.654990.

Christensen, K., & Manthorpe, J. (2016). Personalised risk: New risk encounters facing migrant care workers. *Health, Risk & Society, 18*(3–4), 137–152. https://doi.org/10.1080/13698575.2016.1182628.

Cortis, N., Macdonald, F., Davidson, B., & Bentham, E. (2017). *Reasonable, necessary and valued: Pricing disability services for quality support and decent jobs*. Sydney: Social Policy Research Centre, University of New South Wales. https://www.arts.unsw.edu.au/sites/default/files/documents/NDIS_Pricing_Report.pdf. Accessed 17 September 2020.

Cortis, N., & van Toorn, G. (2020). *Working in new disability markets: A survey of Australia's disability workforce*. Sydney: Social Policy Research Centre, University of New South Wales. https://www.arts.unsw.edu.au/sprc/our-projects/NDIS-workforce. Accessed 16 September 2020.

Delaney, A., & Macdonald, F. (2018). Thinking about informality: gender (in)equality (in) decent work across geographic and economic boundaries. *Labour & Industry, 28*(2), 99–114. https://doi.org/10.1080/10301763.2018.1475024.

Fine, M. (2004). Care: Renewing the social vision. *Journal of Social Issues, 31*(3), 217–32. https://doi.org/10.1002/j.1839-4655.2004.tb01173.x.

Fisher, K. R., Edwards, R., Gleeson, R., Purcal, C., Sitek, T., Dinning, B., et al. (2010). *Effectiveness of individual funding approaches for disability support* (Occasional Paper no. 29). Department of Social Services. Canberra: Department of Families, Housing, Community Services and Indigenous Affairs. https://www.dss.gov.au/sites/default/files/documents/05_2012/op29.pdf. Accessed 29 November 2018.

Folbre, N., & Nelson, J. (2000). For love or money–or both? *The Journal of Economic Perspectives, 14*(4), 123–140. https://doi.org/10.1257/jep.14.4.123.

Glasby, J., & Littlechild, R. (2016). *Direct payments and personal budgets: Putting personalisation into practice*. Bristol: The Policy Press.

Howard, J. (2004). *Transcript of the Prime Minister's address to the Sydney Institute. Workplace relations reform: The next logical step*. Sydney: Sydney Institute. https://pmtranscripts.pmc.gov.au/release/transcript-21818. Accessed 14 September 2020.

Indeed.com. (2020). *Indeed.com [jobs website]* https://www.indeed.com/hire/interview-questions/care-assistant. Accessed 17 September 2020.

Johnson, C. (2007). John Howard's 'values' and Australian identity. *Australian Journal of Political Science, 42*(7), 239–256. https://doi.org/10.1080/10361140701319986.

Lewis, J., & West, A. (2014). Re-shaping social care services for older people in England: policy development and the problem of achieving 'good care'. *Journal of Social Policy, 43*(1), 1–18.

Like Family. (2020). *Why work with Like Family?* https://likefamily.com.au/social-carers/onboardings/new. Accessed 10 October 2020.

Mable. (2020). *Clients pay less. Workers earn more.* https://mable.com.au/pricing/. Accessed 16 September 2020.

McKinsey & Company. (2018). *Independent pricing review: National Disability Insurance Agency*. The Board of the NDIA. https://www.ndis.gov.au/providers/price-guides-and-pricing/independent-pricing-review#key-documents. Accessed 11 November 2019.

Mladenov, T. (2015). Neoliberalism, postsocialism, disability. *Disability & Society, 30*(3), 445–459. https://doi.org/10.1080/09687599.2015.1021758.

National Disability Insurance Agency (NDIA). (2019a). *COAG Disability Reform Council NDIS quarterly report*, 31 December. National Disability Insurance Agency. https://www.ndis.gov.au/about-us/publications/quarterly-reports. Accessed 17 September 2020.

National Disability Insurance Agency (NDIA). (2019b). *National Disability Insurance Scheme pricing strategy*. Canberra: National Disability Insurance Agency. https://www.ndis.gov.au/providers/price-guides-and-pricing. Accessed 16 September 2020.

Prassl, J. (2018). *Humans as service: The promise and perils of work in the gig economy*. Oxford: Oxford University Press.

Productivity Commission. (2011). *Disability Care and Support*. (Report no. 54). Canberra.

Purcal, C., Zmudzki, F., & Fisher, K. R. (2016). *Direct funding trial: Final evaluation report*. Sydney: Social Policy Research Centre, University of New South Wales. http://handle.unsw.edu.au/1959.4/unsworks_40538. Accessed 22 September 2020.

Senior Officials Working Group for the Disability Reform Council. (2015). *National Disability Insurance Scheme integrated market, sector and workforce strategy*. Canberra: Department of Social Services. https://www.dss.gov.au/sites/default/files/documents/07_2015/ndis_integrated_market_sector_and_workforce_strategy_june_2015.pdf. Accessed 26 July 2018.

Shakespeare, T., Stöckl, A., & Porter, T. (2018). Metaphors to work by: The meaning of personal assistance in England. *International Journal of Care and Caring, 2*(2), 165–179. https://doi.org/10.1332/239788218X15187915600658.

Woolham, J., Norrie, C., Samsi, K., & Manthorpe, J. (2019). *Roles, responsibilities, and relationships: hearing the voices of personal assistants and directly employed care workers*. London: NIHR Policy Research Unit in Health and Social Care Workforce, The Policy Institute, King's College London. https://doi.org/10.18742/pub01-005. Accessed 11 May 2020.

CHAPTER 8

Individualised Risk: Isolation and Fragmentation

Introduction

In Chapter 7, I identified three types of *individualised risk* arising from the institutional changes established by Australia's new National Disability Insurance Scheme (NDIS) and I showed how the individualised system heightens the risk of *reinforcing gendered undervaluation* of frontline social care work. In this chapter, I explore how the NDIS creates new risks of two other types: *isolating and individualising workers*, and *fragmenting work, working time and working lives*.

Risks are created through the shaping of work and employment that occurs in the intersections of the social care system and employment regulation. Changes established by the NDIS leading to individual risks are associated with three broad themes: *consumer choice and control*, *market as the basis for fair pay and conditions* and *transformation of the relations of work and care*. These themes were explained in some detail in earlier chapters. They are visible as ideas and organising principles for social care work in the exploration of risks that follows. The chapter first explores risks of isolating and individualising workers before turning to risks of fragmenting work, working time and life.

F. Macdonald, *Individualising Risk*,
https://doi.org/10.1007/978-981-33-6366-3_8

Risks of Isolating & Individualising Workers

Risks of isolating and individualising workers encompass some of the risks referred to by Christensen and Manthorpe (2016) as 'risks of emotionalised relationships' and 'risks of intimacy'. These are, respectively, increased risks where emotion work is not mediated by organisations, arising from shifts to home-based work, and increased risks of intimate emotional and physical encounters that cross the boundaries of what is normally expected of employer/employee roles—the latter arising from changes that blur employer (user)/employee (care worker) roles. Risks of isolating and individualising workers are broader and include risks arising from various transfers of responsibility that devolve decision-making and duty to individual people with disability and to workers. These risks do not necessarily involve emotion work or blurred roles, although they can.

Within service provider organisations, the approach taken to the quality of care and support is to a considerable extent determined by the individualised funding model (and low price). Funding strongly constrains the amount and type of resources that organisations can direct to care and makes it hard for service providers to be responsive to changing needs, increasing risks of neglect. Previously, under aggregate block-funding providers could redirect resources on a day-to-day basis as needed (Cortis et al. 2017). The pricing model creates a billable hours regime for service provision in which every expense needs to be tied to a funded hour of support for each particular individual. This appears to have increased the practice of care and support provision being atomised or redefined as hourly units of funded support, as is evident in workers' experiences described in this chapter.

Employees working for service providers experience the consequences of atomisation in two ways: first, through the loss of collective responsibility for the well-being of people with disability, and second, through the loss of paid work time for the 'articulation' or 'linking work' of care and support—that is, the work involving all the activities required to provide continuity of care (Hampson and Junor 2010, p. 531).

The NDIS promised more holistic and person-centred care and support that would provide for the diversity of individual needs, preferences and aspirations. However, workers experience the changes as being towards more fragmented and partial care due to less time, less collective effort, less skill and less planning for support, preventing good quality and personalised support and increasing risks of neglect and abuse, as others have found (Cortis et al. 2017). Workers describe organisations placing increased expectations on them to take responsibility for ensuring consumer choice and control. At the same time, they find it harder to provide good care and support and are more physically isolated and unsupported.

In care and support work *organised outside of service provider organisations,* risks of isolating and individualising workers arise in two ways—through devolution of responsibility to people with disability for determining their supports and employing their workers, and through devolution to workers of responsibility for managing their work and employment. The absence of service oversight is built into the NDIS as a mechanism for enabling people with disability to choose and control their support. It is acknowledged that this creates risks for people with disability, especially where they choose to self-manage their NDIS funds and directly engage or employ their own workers (NDIA 2019). However, this risk is regarded as acceptable as it is balanced by greater empowerment; it is referred to as the 'dignity of risk' (ARTD Consultants 2015, p. 11). As I have already noted, the experiences of workers in these arrangements have not been given much attention.

Workers' accounts in this chapter highlight how responsibilities and risks assumed to be borne by self-managing NDIS participants can be borne by their support workers as well. This can occur as people with disability actively devolve responsibilities to workers; it can occur by default as workers attempt to fill gaps to ensure people are safe, their support needs are met, and/or their well-being is enhanced. In some cases, workers become co-managers of supports. Sometimes clients/employers acknowledge and appreciate this but at other times isolated and unsupported workers 'just manage'. The devolution of responsibility and risk to individual care and support workers is not recognised or acknowledged in the NDIS structures and funding. The risks to people with disability employing their own workers and to workers managing their own employment are significant and varied.

In Chapter 3, I identified a small but growing body of evidence from England's personalised social care experience suggesting direct employment and engagement is creating unacceptable risks for workers. However, in that country, until recently, only a small number of eligible social care users had taken up the option of direct payments (the equivalent to self-management in Australia's NDIS). It is possible that different risks will emerge in an individualised social care scheme where it is the norm for people to directly engage their own workers, as may turn out to be the case in the NDIS, as explained in earlier chapters. In Australia, the rapid transition to a competitive, very lightly regulated individualised market has seen the rapid development of an on-demand or gig economy social care workforce in precarious work.

One finding of this research is that the market for individualised disability support in Australia includes the kind of temporary and short hours, often one-off work engagements that were described as 'gig work' before the term became associated with digital platforms (Prassl 2018, p. 2). In the NDIS, many of these jobs do come through digital care platforms. Scans of digital care platform sites suggest this new gig economy of temporary and on-demand care and support work includes many younger workers, although there is no reliable data against which to test this impression. In 2017, a national survey of service provider organisations reported people aged between 16 and 24 years made up 11% of disability support workers (National Disability Services 2017, p. 5); however, the survey only captured workers employed by registered service providers. In interviews, youth, employment inexperience, lack of knowledge and experience of disability support work and recent migrant status were all evident as factors that alone and in combination increased worker vulnerability.

The risks of *isolating* work for workers in organisational employment are explored in the next section, followed by exploration of risks for workers in individualised self-managed arrangements. The creation of risks of *individualising* work and their impacts on workers in the two types of employment are then considered.

Isolation and Individualisation in the Disappearing Organisation

The Atomisation of Social Care and Support

Many workers welcomed the opportunity to be part of a new system and contribute to 'making a difference' by assisting people with disability to realise their aspirations for greater control over their day-to-day living and greater independence. Further, numerous workers expressed the view that their disability support work was not only support for individuals, but also service to the broader community. However, workers with long experience in the sector and some newer workers felt these rewarding aspects of their work were being eroded in the NDIS. Workers employed in service provider organisations experienced personal and professional isolation; many also believed the NDIS was lowering the quality of supports being provided to people. They saw this as occurring through reductions in time and resources, and through the erosion of collective effort. In relation to the latter, Tanya, a support service co-ordinator, explained: 'all the little bits that held it altogether, like the glue, it's all that. That's what's been taken away'.

Isolation and lack of support recur as themes in the experiences of employees of traditional not-for-profit and other service provider organisations. Workers experienced these as organisational disrespect for them and their work, and as lack of professionalismand care for clients. Workers felt frustration and even despair due to feeling unable to provide quality care and support, have anyone listen to their concerns, and in some cases prevent and respond to threats to their own and others' safety and well-being. Workers spoke of there being less organisational capacity to provide person-centred support while risks of client neglect increased.

To minimise costs that are not accounted for in the individualised pricing model, some service providers have reduced staff supervision, training and professional development, shift handovers and debriefings. Some organisations have Taylorised work, splitting supervision from rostering to save money and reducing supervisors' time and contact with support staff. Notably, these are strategies suggested in a consultant's pricing review report for the NDIA for achieving more efficient service provision (McKinsey and Company 2018). In service provider organisations, these changes leave employees feeling unsupported, unvalued and sometimes unsafe, especially when combined with casualisation strategies through which many workers' paid hours are reduced almost entirely to the time they spend providing face-to-face supports, as illustrated in the account provided by an experienced disability worker who provided home-based support.

> Working full-time … I actually felt quite isolated. Because, when you do one on one support work, this is the thing with the NDIS, it's like there's, I don't think there's much funding left for office time, so you don't really get to go back, you never really get to go back at the end of the day and see all your team members and have that support. So you just see these people who are really disadvantaged, and you see them on a one on one basis, and you go from one person to the next and then you just go home

> and then you do it again. Like, it's very isolating. ...You're not talking to other people who are going through the same thing as you. So you feel isolated because you're just doing it all on your own. So it just feels a bit heavy. (Lindy)

Experienced care and support workers keenly felt such changes as the degradation of work and care. They observed new casual employees arriving for shifts without adequate knowledge of procedures for keeping their clients and themselves safe, and without information about the needs or preferences of the people they were supporting. Workers were worried about organisations not responding when they raised concerns about clients' well-being. The lean models being adopted in their organisations meant workers providing support in people's homes found themselves unable to contact a supervisor when urgently needing advice, or when they needed to stay with an ill person at a time they were scheduled to be providing care to someone else.

> So, they're replacing (staff who have left the organisation) with casuals now. Some of them are very young. They come in with no training, half of them don't have a clue. ... It's not all their fault, mind. No-one's given them a briefing. ... (They) haven't been given the client files to read. ... So this new girl, how was she supposed to know the client needed this routine? It could have been a real mess. (Claire)

> They used to have team meetings where you could talk about what's going on (with clients) and people would have ideas. Everyone would be in the loop. ... (if there were any problems) you could run things past people. We worked together and we would be a team that could work things out. There's not really a team now. There's a team leader but we don't have any team meetings, none at all. Apparently its not in the funding package to have meetings. ... It doesn't feel the same now... there's no feedback and you can't do that brainstorming. (Julia)

> Yeah, so it's easier to not even waste your time hanging on the phone hoping (my supervisor's) going to answer. I figure it's better to just sort it out myself. It's not my job but what am I supposed to do? I need to find another worker to fill in, so I start ringing round. I'm not paid for that and anyway I'm supposed to be driving over to the next person who's waiting for her dinner. ... That's not a once-off thing, its regular now. (Tanya)

Workers often expressed gratitude and appreciation for the 'hard work' of their managers and staff in their organisations who were responsible for rostering. However, they also spoke of being pressured to take on extra shifts, being contacted repeatedly on their days off, being 'punished' or made to feel guilty for declining extra shifts at short notice or on their single day off in a fortnight. Employees experienced a disconnect between, on the one hand, the increased demands on them to be available, endlessly flexible and responsible for providing good quality support and, on the other hand, diminished respect and support for them as employees, as skilled workers and as people whose own well-being mattered.

> So we don't go into the office any more, hardly ever. There used to be training meetings, not like formal training but where we'd get updated on new things, new procedures and stuff. Like catch up meetings, maybe every six weeks. ... Now the main time I talk to anyone in the office is when I get 'please, please can you do this extra shift?'... It'll be on my day off when I've told them I've got my granddaughter. I've told them a hundred times, but they take no notice, they'll ring anyway. (Neo)

Distancing Work and Degrading Support

Consistent with survey findings about changes in organisational practices under the NDIS (IPSOS Public Affairs 2018; Cortis and van Toorn 2020), workers commonly reported lack of organisational support in their work. They felt this translated into lack of care for the people receiving support. For example, Wendy had worked in the sector for many years and was shocked that she could be sent to a private home to provide support to a person with complex health issues, but be given 'no information about the person or guidance' and for no-one in her organisation to be available for her to contact if she needed either. Asked what sort of guidance she might need, Wendy said:

> Whether to call an ambulance or not. Whether this is something that's occurred before. Whether with a client that I've been working with, her estranged husband comes to the door, and she has no idea what's going on, I've never met him before. Is there protocol? Is there any systems in place? What's the procedure if this happens? Give me some guidance. ... Where I've worked previously ... we've always had team meetings, at least every fortnight. It'd be like a big debriefing. Anybody got any problems

> with work? Anybody need any support or advice, or assistance in other areas? And you could go to a supervisor, they would make themselves available. ... And you had contact with other support workers. (Wendy)

Another experienced support worker, Elsa, had been excited to start work with a newly-established service provider, but was discovering that the organisation was not what she had expected, prompting her to plan to leave this job:

> People aren't being supervised properly and they're working with really...with people with high needs. How does that seem appropriate? You know, how, it's just so unjust. ... I've heard that some workplaces, supervisors will actually go out and see the clients.... But I don't think that's going to really happen much. At least, I'm witnessing that it's not at [this organisation]. (Elsa)

Competition and funding pressures may be leading to service provider organisations taking less care for the safety of people with disability and workers under the NDIS, including through reducing their oversight and coordination of supports. In general, much more attention has been paid in Australia to the risks to people with disability in large institutionalised settings, than to risks in home and community-based support. There has been very little focus on the risks to workers' safety in these settings (Charlesworth et al. 2020), with a few important exceptions (Bohle et al. 2009; Evesson and Oxenbridge 2017; Quinlan et al. 2015).

In early 2020, the risks of support and care provided without organisational or regulatory oversight were made horribly apparent when a woman reliant on NDIS support died in her home, having been neglected by her sole support worker over a long period. The support worker was employed by an NDIS-registered service provider that had taken over Anne-Marie Smith's care after the South Australian Government privatised their public disability service in 2018 (Bassano 2020). This tragic case puts a spotlight on the shortcomings of a hands-off complaints-based approach to social care regulation; it serves to illustrate the vulnerability of people who have to rely on others for assistance with the tasks of day-to-day living. The case also directs attention to how vulnerability and marginalisation in themselves can be barriers to the effective use of individualised funding supports (Needham 2013; Warr et al. 2017).

Individualising Responsibility for Consumer Choice and Control

On the one hand, workers experienced increased isolation and reduced time and resources as downgrading care and support. On the other hand, many workers felt their employers had raised expectations that workers be individually responsible for the quality of care and support people the organisation provided.

The idea that empowering people with disability through the NDIS individualised funding requires a shifting of power *away from* frontline support workers *to* people with disability was expressed by some service providers and some family carers in focus groups. However, in addition to being described in terms of power over supports, this was also expressed as needing to get a better balance between workers' rights and the rights of people with disability, referred to as a 'zero-sum game' (Baines et al. 2020). As outlined in Chapter 3, the rights and power of frontline care and support workers in individualised support relationships have not actually been closely interrogated. While personalisation or self-directed support is understood to demand a shift in power away from professional social workers and others who have had control over supports, no real focus has been put on the place of frontline care and support workers in this situation. Nevertheless, in the NDIS, the idea that workers' rights must be balanced against—or traded off for—the rights of people with disability does play out in the workplace. This occurs through employers' treatment of workers that suggests to workers they should take individual responsibility for making consumer choice and control possible, regardless of whether the organisation provides adequate support and resources or paid time for them to do so.

One common way in which workers were held responsible for ensuring clients' choice and control was through employers increasing or establishing new expectations for workers to be available to change shift times at very short notice. As in the example provided in Chapter 7 of Heather, who said her manager told her 'it is what the client has requested and he is your client, he's on your roster', workers reported feeling that they were being treated as if, in Zoe's words, 'it's entirely down to us now if people are happy'. Another common example was of organisations refusing to support workers who wanted to assert their rights to privacy. One example, previously reported (Macdonald 2020), is of a worker whose employer would not support her refusal to become a Facebook friend with the person she supported, despite that she only ever used

Facebook as a means to network within her own family. Other workers described feeling pressured by employers to give their personal mobile numbers to clients so they could be contacted directly. Thea was new to her job and felt she had little choice but to agree to this. She was contacted regularly by a person she supported. She said:

> It's starting to do my head in, he texts at all times of the day and night, it's about nothing most of the time. I don't think he's got many friends. … I complained to (my supervisor) and so, she tells me to just turn (my mobile phone) off. But I need it (on) for personal reasons … I really do need it. Since my nanna had a heart attack it's always on. I can't afford to miss a call. … I don't know why (my supervisor) can't just tell him to stop spamming me … (Thea)

Younger and more inexperienced workers in service provider organisations were more vulnerable to these types of problems than other workers. More generally, social and economic vulnerability of workers contributes to increased risks to the well-being and safety of people requiring support as well as risks to workers themselves. This is discussed later in the next section that examines risks for workers employed outside of organisations, in direct employment and contracting arrangements.

Isolation and Individualisation in Solo Care and Support Work

> Direct employment of staff may give you the ultimate control over the people who work with you, the hours they work and the tasks that they perform. (NDIA 2019)

In personal and/or home-based (privatised) support relations, where there may be no active oversight by a regulator, service provider, employer or other third party, the risks for workers associated with isolation and individualisation are heightened and multiplied. While various third parties, such as labour hire firms and digital platforms, are involved in some direct employment and self-employed contracting care relationships, their presence appears to provide little or no assistance to many workers who are navigating the complexities and uncertainties of these arrangements. Workers may have little support or guidance at all. As direct employees or self-employed contractors, inexperienced workers readily accept that their jobs are, as described in Chapter 7, 'whatever they are required to do'. However, workers also saw themselves as having considerable individual responsibility for ensuring consumer choice, involving managing support relationships and making difficult decisions in the interests of their employer's or client's independence and control.

Some workers have very close and rewarding relationships with their employers and clients. However, as described in Chapter 7, blurring of boundaries in relationships and crossing of boundaries lead to risks of emotionalised relationships and risks of intimacy. These risks are complicated and sometimes heightened by their co-existence and interaction with other risks of isolation and individualisation, including the risks arising from the devolution to workers of responsibility for enabling choice and control, as discussed above. One young worker's experience is helpful as an illustration of how this can entail risks to the isolated worker.

Georgie's client had repeatedly sexually harassed her over some months, with this becoming more serious over time. Georgie felt she had unsatisfactorily dealt with this problem by avoiding shifts that required her and her male client to be physically close in private and only taking on shifts supporting him at his workplace. She worried her client might be harassing other young women in his support team. She couldn't speak to any of the other workers as she had never met them. Georgie thought she should report the behaviour to the company that brokered her engagement with the client. However, she didn't want to do this as she thought it might cause the man to lose his access to other support workers, or even lose his access to self-managing his supports altogether. Georgie said she felt responsible for resolving this issue in a way that would not jeopardise the man's 'right to have independent support'. She felt increasingly stressed at work but didn't know who she could talk to to get support. Eventually, she sought advice from her family doctor.

Other young workers also struggled without support or training to deal with complex issues, while sharing with Georgie the belief that they should be able to make things work for the people they supported because 'making it work' was the aim of direct employment arrangements. Shelley had been looking for information on how she might work with her employer, whose behaviour was increasingly aggressive towards her. She said:

> Most of the time I just end up feeling really drained 'cause like you feel like you have to monitor your own emotional state for an hour, two hours while you're dealing with someone who's doing just, yeah, like little micro-aggressions all along the way and then she sometimes she just goes berserk at you over really small things. It becomes difficult when you don't have any training, I guess, and you don't really know where things are coming from, where the boundaries are, like, what someone's disability is and what's, what behaviours are caused by that disability and what behaviours aren't.. *Interviewer*: So how do you work any of that out? *Shelley:* Well I like, Google, ask Google. I guess I think I should be able to manage. … You just, yeah, you end up just kind of like, I talk to, yeah, like my good friend (who has some relevant family experience) but then, yeah, but then sometimes you just think, is this just a person with really bad behaviours that have been accepted for a very long time? I just don't know. (Shelley)

Other workers spoke of tolerating unreasonable treatment as they understood the behaviour to be a manifestation of a person's disability, pain or discomfort. Like Shelley, they often had little information on which to base their understanding but saw their responsibility as being to put up with the situation. If they sought advice, it was usually from family and friends.

Negotiating boundary setting with the people they support in informalised support relationships can be complicated and sometimes impossible for workers who tried to manage this alone. Inexperienced workers often didn't manage this very well at all, as illustrated here. James tried to include his client, Ben, into his own social world and organised activities with his own friends that would include Ben. A disagreement arose between the two when Ben appeared to change his mind about an excursion James thought had been agreed. This led to Ben saying he no longer wanted James to support him. Emily's situation was very complicated as, by the time she was in her late 20s and after fours years of being the main support worker for Maddy, she was deeply embedded in Maddy's family. Emily said she had no-one outside Maddy's family and support network from whom she could seek advice. She loved her full-time job and couldn't imagine not supporting Maddy, who had become her closest friend, or not being part of Maddy's family. Emily felt she had become indispensable and Maddy might not cope without her. However, Emily also wondered how she might make a life and family of her own. She could not see how this could be possible. She had not spoken about these worries to anyone and even talking about the issues felt like a 'betrayal' of Maddy and her family.

Workers relayed many instances of taking individual responsibility for decisions without guidance in situations that involved immediate risks to their safety and the safety of their employers or clients. Younger and inexperienced workers in particular found it difficult to balance what they saw as their duty to support their employers to have control over their lives with their own responsibility for the quality and safety of care and support. They often felt very uncertain and alone. For some workers, supporting people in a family situation meant they had some guidance, while this could also complicate matters as workers got caught in the middle of family disagreements about support.

All workers providing social care services funded by the NDIS must comply with the NDIS Code of Conduct. Awareness of this Code was not high among workers, although some interviews with workers were conducted not long after the Code was established, so this may not reflect a more generalised or ongoing problem. However, there was common experience of labour hire agencies and other third parties that brokered services taking a box-ticking approach to employment and care agreements and associated regulatory requirements including insurance and safety. For example, Jasmine was engaged as a self-employed contractor by a person with disability through a third party 'care agency', although Jasmine described the agency as 'employer. She had a pile of papers with her at the time of her interview for this research and, when asked if she had a written contract, Jasmine looked through her papers and explained:

> Well, so I have some very long emails about that. So, let's see, code of conduct, crim check, induction checklist. So the lady who I just signed up with, she just filled out the form that says...the actual filled out one is here somewhere. You know, this person has been taught how to use hoists. This person has been taught how to use blah, blah, blah, blah, blah, administer medications. *Interviewer*: Did you fill all this out with her? *Jasmine*: No, she filled it out for me, but I've never done any of this. So she just filled it out and asked me to sign it. Which is pretty sus(pect), I know. *Interviewer:* Do they cover you for insurance? *Jasmine:* I have no idea. It has been bizarre. Like I have never filled out this much paperwork for any job before. ... The interaction I've had with (the organisation) is just through that email address, it's just getting more paperwork to fill out. That's the only thing. I haven't gotten training or anything like that or any

> information about the organisation at all. I do get a position description. (Jasmine)

Younger workers' lack of knowledge of the nature of contracting and their rights, obligations and risks contributes to their vulnerability, as does their inexperience as support workers. There were many examples of workers discovering, when they sought help from the third parties brokering their employment and care relationships, that these organisations did not provide support or advice to workers.

Aged 30, Van was unemployed for almost two years before undertaking a certificate course and commencing work as a disability support worker. He worked as a self-employed contractor, engaged directly by the people he supported through two digital platforms. He referred to the platforms as his 'employers' and seemed a bit puzzled by their apparent lack of interest in and care for him. As a fairly inexperienced support worker, Van keenly felt the absence of any mentoring, supervision and peer support working through the platforms. He recently had an experience when he felt both he and the person he was supporting were unsafe. After the event, Van was concerned about the potential for ongoing risks to the safety of the person and to other support workers in future. He felt conflicted and uncertain, on the one hand wanting to respect the person's right to make their own decisions, and on the other hand, thinking he should take control of the situation to keep his client and others safe. Van wrote a report detailing his concerns and emailed it to the platform company. However, the response he received led him to think that:

> I'm not their client, it's the person looking for support workers that's their client. They were pretty clear about that,... keeping (their clients) matters more than me. They aren't obligated to look after support workers. We have to look after ourselves. (Van)

Van wanted a high star rating on this platform to get more work, and he would 'need to be careful' about pursuing issues in future. Platforms present worker ratings as systems of quality assurance for people seeking supports (Industrial Relations Victoria 2016, p. 89). Ratings are critical for workers in competitive labour markets, as a good rating means a worker's profile will be seen by potential clients. Conversely, a bad rating could lead to reputational damage with long-term consequences (Flanagan 2019; McDonald et al. 2019). This is a very one-sided process, workers being unable to rate clients and with little evidence on platform sites of any mechanisms for workers to challenge ratings. Nor do the platforms offer dispute resolution.

The final sections of the chapter concern the *risks of fragmenting work, working time and work-life*. These risks associated with the temporal aspects of care and support work intersect and overlap with risks identified above and in Chapter 6.

Risks of Fragmenting Work, Working Time & Life

Fragmenting work, working time and life are perhaps the most conspicuous of the individualised risks for workers. Individualised funding transforms care and support into a market-based hourly-priced commodity for purchase by individual consumers in small pieces as needed. Gaps in employment regulation provide the spaces for incidences of care work to be de-linked from the labouring worker and their working day and life, as they are treated as units of service.

Fragmentation of work occurs through Taylorisation processes that separate face-to-face care and support for a person from all other tasks and people required for good quality supports; it overlaps with the atomisation of work discussed above. *Fragmentation of working time* occurs at multiple levels as work times become multiple short periods that may be constantly changing in unpredictable ways, and often are dispersed throughout long hours over entire days and across all the days of the week. Work bleeds into unpaid time as tasks that are now excluded from the funded unit of paid time for face-to-face support remain the worker's responsibility. In addition, for some workers, the tasks of finding and managing work and getting paid are ongoing and substantial. *The fragmentation of life* occurs over multiple timescales. It occurs over periods of hours and days as the fragmentation of work time leads to periods of non-work time that are not actually available to the worker to spend on life activities. This establishes the conditions for fragmentation of opportunity and of pathways to better jobs and pay over the working lifetime.

All these risks arise for NDIS care and support workers. Consequences include insecurity of income and insecure work-life arrangements, including psychological stress and material hardship. Workers find it difficult to plan, and their participation in other life activities can be severely disrupted. Insecurity of employment and income underpin people's tolerance of fragmented working time arrangements due to their concerns about losing hours in future, or not having a job at all. This was the case for interviewed workers regardless of whether they were employed for a few or many hours a week. Fragmentation of work and working time were also strongly linked to reduced quality of careand support, especially in the eyes of experienced workers—as already described in this chapter, and in Chapter 7.

Self-employed and directly employed workers who are on the boundaries of or outside labour law's protections are highly vulnerable to risks of fragmentation. They are in the kind of jobs that are presented in policy and in the market as providing NDIS fundholders with the maximum flexibility and control over their supports. Under individualised funding, risks of fragmented work, working time and life are also greatly heightened for many employees of registered service providers. Employment regulation fails to provide effective protection from having work degraded. The risks for workers in service provider employment are explored below followed by risks for workers outside organisational employment.

Organisational Employment: Minimisation of Paid Time in the Flexible Workforce

Within service provider organisations, the minimisation of unfunded time, along with increased variability and diversity of support times and locations, has led to increased demand for a flexible workforce. The use of casual employment arrangements achieves this and also shifts many of the business risks of increased variability and unpredictability of support provision to employees. It may also shift risks to service users as it impacts negatively on service quality and continuity, as has been found in survey research (Cortis et al. 2017; Cortis and van Toorn 2020; IPSOS Public Affairs 2018).

Over the NDIS implementation period, disability support jobs with registered service providers appear to have become more insecure. Data from service provider surveys shows a growth in the share of casual employment among disability support workers (National Disability Services 2018). These jobs are constructed as insecure jobs, with employees having no guarantee of regular or ongoing work. Permanent part-time employees also experience very fragmented working time, due to the strategies used by some employers to maximise flexibility. This is despite ostensibly having much better protection from treatment as 'on-demand' workers than casuals (Campbell et al. 2019). Although part-time employees do have some rights to regular hours, protection against job loss and access to paid leave, significant deficiencies remain in working time minimum standards in the industrial award as explained in Chapter 5. Employers can exploit these and treat permanent part-time employees as on-demand workers. This appears to be a strategy adopted by some employers to gain maximum flexibility in the wake of the NDIS changes (Macdonald et al. 2018).

The idea that part-time disability support jobs offer employees some control over their working time pervades recruitment advertisements for this work. Flexible working time is presented as family-friendly and as supporting work-life balance. However, employees' experiences suggest that, in some workplaces, flexible working time arrangements are the opposite to this portrayal; they are arrangements that undermine predictability of work and increase insecurity. With employers reducing paid work time to the minimum in line with the individualised funding model, and to manage increased uncertainty, the labour of care and support is atomised into some tasks that are given the status of legitimate paid work, and other tasks that are excluded from paid time. Workers—and the people they support—often bear the costs.

The experiences of one worker, Jo, illustrates some of the problems. Jo's typical week usually involved working over six days, although she only had about 20 hours of paid work time a week. Jo worked for a not-for-profit provider of disability support and home care services. She had worked with the same employer for the past three years as a permanent part-time employee, and in a similar role for over 15 years before that. As required under the minimum industrial award standards for permanent part-time employees, Jo had a schedule of regular work hours. However, like many of her colleagues, this schedule was for many fewer hours than she actually wanted to work, and it was also for many fewer hours than her employer regularly asked her to work. Every week, in addition to her regular part-time roster of 10 hours, Jo usually worked an additional 10 hours or so. The additional shifts varied every week, many were very short shifts involving considerable travel, and her employer's requests to work these shifts were often made with very little notice. Jo's workdays were often very long even though she had only a few paid hours work in the day.[1]

[1] Jo's working week is the topic of a short animation published online at https://cpow.org.au/dayinthelife/.

Jo, and other workers interviewed, spoke of previously having their work scheduled in big blocks of time during which they would travel (in paid work time) between different locations providing support and care to different people in their homes. Under the NDIS funding arrangements, individual support and care visits were organised by their employers as separate smaller work shifts or broken shifts with unpaid time between them. Travel time between clients became non-work time. Workers often finished their working days eight or 10 h after they started, but had only performed five hours paid work, made up of several separate visits to people's homes to provide care and support. Much of the time in between paid work was spent on work-related activities.

Workers travelled multiple times between home and work in the day and spent other time on unpaid work such as required administration, communicating with family members, staying with people longer to provide necessary care and support or organising appointments for clients. Workers were expected to arrive early, complete tasks for which they had inadequate paid time and stay with clients when another worker, family member or carer was late arriving. They often spent a lot of other time waiting between shifts, in the car, at home or in cafes as fragments of time were often not long enough or predictable enough to allow people to do anything else. To illustrate, this is an account of one worker's day:

> I can start at quarter to eight in the morning and I can finish at four o'clock at night, and I only have done five hours. That's the worst part – any carer will tell you that's the worst part of this job – that you can go and do two (visits), and then you've got an hour and a half off. Fortunately I live here, so I can run home and put the washing on or prepare dinner or something, and then you go back out for an hour and a half, and then you come home, and two hours later you go out and do the evening. It's just a pain... I'm sounding a bit bitter, aren't I! I'm just over it. (Liz)

With work increasingly organised in very short shifts, underemployment is a problems for many workers—one resolved unsatisfactorily by multiple job-holding. Melanie had previously been employed by the local government authority, that had ceased providing services under the NDIS. She now held multiple jobs to get the number of hours of work she used to get in one job.

> (Now) I've got to work more hours for less money (than when the local government authority ran the service prior to the NDIS). And not that I'm in this for money. I really do love my job. But because it, when it was all under one umbrella, we were working for the one company doing all this different work, you could plan your life better. But now you're working for three different companies, you've got to sort of, I've got to run by diary, so I know what to do. And sometimes they might ask you to do more work and you've got to make sure that you're in line with this employer. And it's just made life really difficult. (Melanie)

For disability support workers employed in permanent and casual jobs with service providers, the unpaid tasks performed might each only take a small amount of time, but these tasks were frequent and regular and if paid would provide workers with a substantial amount of extra money. For example, time diaries kept over three days by workers providing home-based care and support showed unpaid time spent on essential work tasks was as much as an additional 20% over the time for which workers were paid (Macdonald et al. 2018). This would have made a difference of about $60 a week for some workers.

Almost all workers in one group of 22 home and community-based care and support workers interviewed for this research said their ideal would be to work five days a week during the day, and to have weekends off—in other words, the so-called 'standard' working week. For most, the downsides of their flexible working time far outweighed the positives. However, in their current jobs, workers generally welcomed weekend shifts because of the higher pay rates for weekend work, with several noting that they couldn't afford to live on their wages if they didn't get some weekend shifts.

Flexible Supports and Transforming Relations of Care and Support

The treatment of workers as flexible services results in fragmentation of work, working time and work-life for workers in self-employed contracting, or direct employment arrangements with NDIS self-managing clients. Workers are on-demand, and the work itself can be whatever it needs to be. These ideas, embedded in the NDIS individualised funding model, are further advanced by digital care platforms that present disability support (and support workers) as off-the-shelf services, available for as short or as long a time as a consumer wants, and eminently interchangeable.

Alongside this emerging treatment of disability support work as odd-jobs or service, many support workers are in long-term and often intensive and interdependent work and care relationships with clients and employers. The fragmentation problems in these types of roles arise from these ongoing dependencies and from obligations developed in informal family-like support relationships. As illustrated in workers' accounts in this and the previous chapter, fragmentation risks arise where clients and employers expect workers to be available on-call and to be always open to change. Workers find they are unable to have time for their own lives, and some take on responsibility for managing individuals' supports, as illustrated in Sheena's case:

> It does make life a bit tricky because basically I'm on call 24/7, yeah. I have tried over the years to compartmentalise my hours. It doesn't work. So particularly, because (the person with disability's) mum can't help. A lot of that sort of, well all of the responsibility has fallen on me, so I'm being called and texted and whatever across seven days of the week. (Sheena)

One of the main reasons that people choose to directly employ or engage their support workers is to gain flexibility of their support time (Purcal et al. 2016). While working time regulation applies to work in direct employment—but not self-employed contracting—situations, workers' accounts suggest it is far from effective. Arrangements are made in the context of informal relations—relations in which neither party may have any familiarity with the regulation, or even consider that it applies to them (this view was put forward by a number of family members of NDIS participants in a focus group). The self-management option is promoted as the means for gaining maximum control, as explained in Chapter 4. Workers may not be intentionally exploited by their employers, whose changing demands may reflect changing health or other needs. Nevertheless, working time insecurity remains a considerable risk in direct employment, as illustrated in this example:

> So, she said to pick her up at 11 (pm), but I get there and she doesn't come out until after 12 … I text her at 11.30 but I don't know, maybe she just ignored it. … I did say something on the way home … She said the reason she wanted to employ her own workers was so she could have

> that flexibility. She said if she wants to come home at midnight that's her choice ... But I only get the flat rate for driving her, I don't get paid for sitting in the car for an hour. (Jade)

In individualised supports, where a team of workers are involved, the collective effort can provide workers with a means to gain some control over working time, as illustrated by the example of Gemma below. However, as Gemma's case also illustrates, where the idea that the work is inherently or naturally flexible is built into the NDIS—and strengthened in the market through market actors' strategies—it can be extremely difficult for workers to assert the right to some control over their working time.

Gemma's employer engaged three workers who supported their client on weekdays. As one of these three, Gemma, set up an arrangement, so the three workers could use an app to organise the shift rosters between them. Their employer said he was happy with this. However, Gemma said, since she had set the roster up and the workers had better control over their time, a trade-off seemed to arise in that 'somehow now we are kind of expected (by our employer) to take responsibility for everything'. The app was now regularly used by their employer to contact the workers whenever he needed support, often at short notice. Gemma explained her employer now 'expects one of us to come at any time, regardless of the time of day or night, or on the weekends, or whether its urgent or not, or even if its something his family could do'.

Workers often complained about clients and employers cutting their shifts short once they were at work. Shelley was looking for another job as her employer regularly 'just kicks me out after an hour and half, it's supposed to be a three hour shift'. She said: 'I think she rosters me just in case she needs something, you know, to make sure I have time'. Jasmine had a similar problem where she had committed to a regular four hour shift, but her client would often 'send me home after two hours'. She had taken the job because it offered a four hour shift, even though it was not very convenient to her home, involving almost an hour's travel each way. She said: '(the client) didn't say anything about it being a "maybe four hours sometimes" job so it was pretty annoying'. Jasmine did raise the issue with her client and asked him if he could set a three hour minimum as he required her to be available for a four hour shift; he agreed to do this. She said: 'he's, like, he is a very, very kind, like, pretty chill person so I just said to him, like if you set a shift for 4 hours, is it okay if I have a 3 hours minimum pay, and he's like, "that's fine"'. While it annoyed Jasmine that her client continued to cut her four hour shifts short on a regular basis, she said 'at least I know how much money is coming in now, so at least I know how much I'm going to have at the end of the week'.

Another self-employed contractor support worker, Finn, also had a client who frequently cut short his agreed shift. Taking his mother's advice, Finn told his employer he wanted to establish a 50% cancellation fee for shifts that were cancelled or cut short on the same day due to a change of mind. His employer agreed with this, but soon after said he was cutting Finn's pay to about 80% of the agreed rate, on a take it or leave it basis.

The fragmentation of working life that arises from the insecurity of working time in flexible disability support jobs is multiplied when workers are reliant on patching together multiple jobs to make a living. While digital platforms depicted the short hours and occasional on-demand work they offered as being undertaken by workers as extra jobs for non-essential income (Industrial Relations Victoria 2020), the experiences of the workers interviewed challenges this representation, suggesting many people may be just managing with multiple small jobs.

As an illustrative example, Amrutha has four 'jobs', three as a disability support worker and the fourth as a receptionist. One of her support jobs is as a casual employee, with occasional shifts in a community residential setting with a not-for-profit services provider. Her other two support worker 'jobs' are actually multiple support engagements—some one-off gigs and others ongoing—that she gains through two digital platforms. In a typical week, Amrutha usually gets about 20 to 25 hours' work in all jobs combined, with her work usually spread over six to seven days. On a 'big week', she can get up to 40 hours' work. On these weeks, she earns enough to put some money away for expenses on leaner weeks.

Amrutha said she needs full-time work to cover her living expenses. Her ideal working arrangement would be to work day shifts in her receptionist role—her 'most reliable' job—and to do occasional evening or weekend shifts as a support worker in the community residential setting, because she likes 'spending time' with the residents there. In contrast to her support jobs, in her employment as a receptionist she is given her shift roster a month in advance, does not have her shifts cancelled without notice and is not expected to be 'always' available to take on extra shifts at very short notice. She says the platform jobs 'are the worst' as people often cancel or change things at the last minute. She said:

> So, people texting me at the last minute saying 'come half an hour later' when I'm already on my way there. They never stop to think I might be doing something else (at the time they want me to stay later). One guy, we agreed 6.00 to 8.00 (o'clock). He lived at (the end of the train line). He was always putting me off 'can you come later, come later' ... So I'm left stuck in the dark at (the isolated train station) at 9.30 at night and the trains don't run much at that time so I can be stuck there for half an hour. ... That's not a good place to be at that time of night ... I might not get home until after 10.30. (Amrutha)

Disability support work through digital platforms is promoted as offering workers almost absolute control over their working time as well as over what work they do and for whom. For example, one platform entices workers with this offer: 'Choose your hours, choose who you work with and choose the work you want to do. It's that flexible!' (Like Family 2020) while another offers workers the ability to: 'Set your own rates' as well as choosing the jobs and hours they want (Careseekers 2020).

While a few workers were able to use platforms to pick up work that suited them well, most workers had to deal with highly fragmented working time. As noted in Chapter 6, support workers are now represented on some platforms as one-off support services that people can purchase on the same day they need them (Mable 2020).

Conclusion

This chapter has explored how the NDIS creates risks of isolating and individualising workers, and risks of fragmenting work, working time and working lives. It has shown how in the intersections of the individualised care scheme and employment regulation, market actors' strategies shape work and employment to create these risks. Risks for care and support workers are shaped by NDIS mechanisms such as pricing, and by the ways employers and others respond to provide support and reduce costs and/or make profit. Risks of business, care provision and employment are devolved to workers and to service users.

The chapter has also shown how the ideas embedded in the individualised scheme and translated by organisations in the market that were outlined in earlier chapters are taken up by individual service users, and by workers themselves, to generate new norms: individual workers and people with disability engage in practices that undermine regulated wages and further de-link disability support work from the broader system of regulated working conditions, benefits and protections.

The impacts of risks on workers are multiple. Many of the workers interviewed spoke of care and support work as a short-term employment option only. Experienced workers most often cited their concerns that quality of care and support was declining under individualisation and that they and/or their organisations were unable to provide good care and support, a cause of great distress to some workers. The other most commonly cited reasons for intentions to leave the occupation concerned working time and pay. Even workers who 'loved' their jobs—and many did—often did not it feasible for them to continue in this work in the longer-term.

References

ARTD Consultants. (2015). *National disability insurance scheme quality and safeguarding framework consultation report*. Canberra: Commonwealth of Australia. https://engage.dss.gov.au/wp-content/uploads/2015/11/consultation_report_ndis_quality_safeguarding_framework.pdf. Accessed 16 December 2019.

Baines, D., Macdonald, F., & Stanford, J. (2020). Zero-sum social policy: Going gig and the Australian national disability insurance scheme. *Studies in Political Economy, 101*(1), 17–34. https://doi.org/10.1080/07078552.2020.1738778.

Bassano. (2020, 27 May). Single carer for Ann Marie Smith should have raised 'huge red flags'. *In Daily*. https://indaily.co/311260. Accessed 24 September 2020.

Bohle, P., Finn, J., Quinlan, M., & Rawlings-Way, O. (2009). *The occupational health and safety of home care contract workers in Adelaide and the Barossa region, a report prepared for the office of employee Ombudsman*. Adelaide: Office of Employee Ombudsman, South Australia. https://core.ac.uk/download/pdf/17196008.pdf. Accessed 20 Feb 2020.

Campbell, I., Macdonald, F., & Charlesworth, S. (2019). On-demand work in Australia. In M. O'Sullivan, J. Lavelle, J. McMahon, L. Ryan, C. Murphy, T. Turner, et al. (Eds.), *Zero-hours and on-call work in anglo-saxon countries* (pp. 67–90). Singapore: Springer Press.

Careseekers. (2020). Why join Careseekers. *Careseekers*. https://www.careseekers.com.au/carer. Accessed 4 October 2020.

Charlesworth, S., Macdonald, F., & Clarke, J. (2020). *Nature and extent of gender-based violence in individualised disability support & aged care services in Victoria*. Scoping study report for WorkSafe Victoria. Melbourne: Centre for People, Organisation and Work, RMIT University. https://cpow.org.au/unacceptable-forms-of-work-gender-based-violence/. Accessed 19 October 2020.

Christensen, K., & Manthorpe, J. (2016). Personalised risk: New risk encounters facing migrant care workers. *Health, Risk & Society, 18*(3–4), 137–152. https://doi.org/10.1080/13698575.2016.1182628.

Cortis, N., & van Toorn, G. (2020). *Working in new disability markets: A survey of Australia's disability workforce*. Sydney: Social Policy Research Centre, University of New South Wales. https://www.arts.unsw.edu.au/sprc/our-projects/NDIS-workforce. Accessed 22 May 2020.

Cortis, N., Macdonald, F., Davidson, B., & Bentham, E. (2017). *Reasonable, necessary and valued: Pricing disability services for quality support and decent jobs*. Sydney: Social Policy Research Centre, University of New South Wales. https://www.arts.unsw.edu.au/sites/default/files/documents/NDIS_Pricing_Report.pdf. Accessed 17 September 2020.

Evesson, J., & Oxenbridge, S. (2017). *The psychosocial health and safety of Australian home care workers: Risks and solutions*. Sydney: Centre for Applied Disability Research. https://www.nds.org.au/resources/centre-for-applied-disability-research-cadr. Accessed 8 August 2019.

Flanagan, F. (2019). Theorising the gig economy and home-based service work. *Journal of Industrial Relations, 61*(1), 57–78. https://doi.org/10.1177/0022185618800518.

Hampson, I., & Junor, A. 2010. Putting the process back in: Rethinking service sector skill. *Work, Employment and Society, 24*(3), 526–545. https://doi.org/10.1177/0950017010371664.

Industrial Relations Victoria. (2016). *Victorian inquiry into the labour hire industry and insecure work*, final report. Melbourne: Industrial Relations Victoria. https://engage.vic.gov.au/inquiry-labour-hire-industry-and-insecure-work. Accessed 12 November 2020.

Industrial Relations Victoria. (2020). *Report of the inquiry into the Victorian on-demand workforce* (Industrial Relations Victoria, Ed.). Melbourne: Victorian Government.

Ipsos Public Affairs. (2018). *Understanding the workforce experience of the NDIS*. Longitudinal Research Project—Year One. Melbourne: Department of Premier and Cabinet (Victoria). https://www.vic.gov.au/sites/default/files/2019-03/NDIS-Longitudinal-Workforce-Research-Study-Report-2018.PDF. Accessed 21 November 2019.

Like Family. (2020). Why work with Like Family? *Like Family*. https://likefamily.com.au/social-carers/onboardings/new. Accessed 12 October 2020.

Mable. (2020). *The fastest way to find support on Mable*. Mable. https://mable.com.au/last-minute-jobs/. Accessed 18 October 2020.

Macdonald, F. (2020). 'Personalised risk' in paid care work and the impacts of 'gig economy' care platforms and other market-based organisations. *International Journal of Care and Caring,* Online first, pp. 1–17. https://doi.org/10.1332/239788220X15966470624270.

Macdonald, F., Bentham, E., & Malone, J. (2018). Wage theft, underpayment and unpaid work in marketised social care. *The Economic and Labour Relations Review, 29*(1), 80–96. https://doi.org/10.1177/1035304618758252.

McDonald, P., Williams, P., Stewart, A., Mayes, R., & Oliver, D. (2019). *Digital platform work in Australia. Prevalence, nature and impact*. Queensland University of Technology. https://eprints.qut.edu.au/203119/. Accessed 22 August 2020.

McKinsey and Company. (2018). Independent pricing review. National Disability Insurance Agency. *NDIA*. https://www.ndis.gov.au/providers/price-guides-and-pricing/independent-pricing-review. Accessed 20 January 2019.

National Disability Insurance Agency (NDIA). (2019). *Directly engaging your own staff*. NDIA. https://www.ndis.gov.au/participants/using-your-plan/self-management. Accessed 1 October 2020.

National Disability Services (NDS). (2017). *Australian disability workforce report July 2017*. Sydney: NDS. https://www.nds.org.au/news/australian-disability-workforce-report-first-edition-released. Accessed 9 April 2020.

National Disability Services. (2018). *Australian disability workforce report February 2018*. Sydney: NDS. https://www.nds.org.au/images/workforce/ADWR_Third_Edition_July_2018.pdf. Accessed 17 December 2019.

Needham, C. (2013). *The boundaries of budgets: Why should individuals make spending choices about their health and social care?* Centre for Health and the Public Impact. https://chpi.org.uk/wp-content/uploads/2013/07/Boundaries-of-Budgets-Catherine-Needham-July-31.pdf. Accessed 19 October 2020.

Prassl, J. (2018). *Humans as service: The promise and perils of work in the gig economy*. Oxford: Oxford University Press.

Purcal, C., Zmudzki, F., & Fisher, K. R. (2016). *Direct funding trial: Final evaluation report*. Sydney: Social Policy Research Centre, University of New South Wales. https://www.sprc.unsw.edu.au/media/SPRCFile/Direct_Funding_Trial.pdf. Accessed 3 September 2020.

Quinlan, M., Bohle, P., & Rawlings-Way, O. (2015). Health and safety of homecare workers engaged by temporary employment agencies. *Journal of Industrial Relations, 57*(1), 94–114. https://doi.org/10.1177/0022185614541179.

Warr, D., Dickinson, H., Olney, S., Arstein-Kerslake, A., Wilson, E., Hargrave, J., et al. (2017). *Choice, control and the NDIS: Service users' perspectives on having choice and control in the new National Disability Insurance Scheme.*

University of Melbourne. https://socialequity.unimelb.edu.au/__data/assets/pdf_file/0010/2364499/Choice-Control-and-the-NDIS-Report-Melbourne-Social-Equity-Institute.pdf. Accessed 19 October 2020.

CHAPTER 9

Changing Course Towards Decent Work

Introduction

Social care policy and *employment regulation* establish the conditions for businesses' participation in publicly-funded care and the potential for social care employment to provide decent work to frontline social care workers. Employers' low-road employment strategies and other market actors' re-organisation of social care work as self-employed contracting are critical drivers of individualised risk and precarious employment in Australia's new cash-for-care system for support for people with disability, the National Disability Insurance Scheme (NDIS). However, as in other publicly-funded social care systems, public authorities retain significant control over how care is provided, who can provide it and under what conditions. They have control over who benefits from the public funding of care. The government also establishes the legal protections and standards for employment and the circumstances and ease with which workers can organise and bargain collectively. In short, the state bears a great deal of the responsibility for the impacts on workers of state-funded and managed social care markets as well as for impacts on social care users.

If the NDIS is at all successful as a person-centred care system, then many people's lives will be improved. However, as a key element of a nation's social welfare infrastructure, a publicly-funded social care system should provide benefits equitably and should not exacerbate and create disadvantage, vulnerability and inequality to achieve benefits. Through a

F. Macdonald, *Individualising Risk*,
https://doi.org/10.1007/978-981-33-6366-3_9

case study of Australia's NDIS, the research reported here has demonstrated how highly marketised, individualised social care systems can *contribute* to significant disadvantage, vulnerability and gender inequality. Furthermore, it has shown how care system design can facilitate the adoption of business models and employment strategies that place workers on the margins, or beyond the effective reach, of protective employment regulation. Some businesses in the NDIS care market appeared to rely on doing so to make profit from their involvement in publicly-funded social care. It is imperative for governments to ensure that social care systems reduce, rather than create, vulnerability and disadvantage.

In this study, I explored the ways that disadvantage and vulnerability arise for frontline social care workers in cash-for-care systems using the idea of ***individualised risks***. Individualised risks include risks of reinforcing gendered undervaluation; risks of isolating and individualising workers; and risks of fragmenting work, working time and work-life. These risks entail negative impacts on individual workers and on prospects for workforce sustainability and decent work for care workers in future. They have implications for care and support quality and for the well-being and safety of people with disability. To prevent, manage and/or mitigate these risks, governments, with others, need to better value care and care work; build opportunity for collective effort, responsibility and voice; and re-fashion care jobs as sustainable and secure work. In this chapter, I suggest some possible strategies in each of these areas. First, I consider some of the bases for political action to drive change.

Markets, Care and Coalitions

While primary responsibility for the types of changes needed to prevent the creation of disadvantage lies with governments, the impetus for change may require the efforts of broad coalitions. Arguably, Australia's cash-for-care system has proceeded on an assumption that conflict necessarily exists between workers' rights and the rights of people with disability. This is evident in the absence of space for consideration of workers' rights and working conditions in the design and operations of the individualised care system. The same assumption is present in individualised care systems elsewhere, as outlined in Chapter 3 concerning adult social care in England. Nevertheless, there are expanding grounds on which social care workers, people with disability, family carers and others might build coalitions for action for better care and better care jobs.

Experiences of some people with disability during the transformation to Australia's new cash-for-care disability services market have shown that markets do not provide equitable access or support equitable outcomes for marginalised groups and people with complex needs and, in fact, may increase social and economic inequalities (Brotherhood of St. Laurence 2019; Carey et al. 2020; Malbon et al. 2019; Warr et al. 2017). Among the problems are inadequate supports, unskilled and inexperienced workers and inconsistency of support and care, all problems that are linked to the declining quality of social care jobs. Individualised pricing and inadequate funding make it difficult for employers to attract, support and retain skilled workers, while employers adopt strategies that casualise the frontline care and support workforce (Cortis et al. 2017; Macdonald et al. 2018). The present study has also shown how the degradation of care and support accompanies the degradation of social care jobs, as described in Chapters 7 and 8.

Internationally, there is an emerging body of evidence concerning person-centred care that introduces a greater diversity of perspectives and experience than those that dominate the earlier personalisation literature from the UK (discussed in Chapter 3) that shaped ideas about individualised funding and direct employment of care workers by care users. Recent research has begun to unpack what underlies care and support outcomes to develop a better understanding of the factors contributing to good person-centred care and support. In this process, researchers are separating out what makes a good support relationship from the assumption that it is necessarily an individual employer-employee or client/contractor relationship (Topping et al. 2019). This research points to many areas of common interest between care and support workers and people requiring care and support.

So, there are both normative and pragmatic reasons for people with disability to support decent working conditions and pay for disability support workers (Bagenstos 2017; Cranford 2020). Strong coalitions of care users and care workers can achieve changes; in the USA, these coalitions have been critical to the success of community-based organising of marginalised care workers (Cranford 2020). In Australia, community and worker coalitions played a role in a successful equal pay campaign for social care workers. In the context of the introduction of individualised care funding, new campaigns for a better deal for *unpaid carers* have developed (The Caring Fairly Coalition 2018). The gendered undervaluation of care is a key concern for unpaid carers and is a common concern on which paid care workers and unpaid carers could find opportunity for joint political action to challenge the valuing of care in marketised system.

Valuing Care and Care Work

In Chapter 1, I argued that how we value social care workers is critical for gender equality, for decent work and for the quality of care. This study has shown that in a highly marketised cash-for-care system social care workers are not valued. It has shown how gender equality, decent work and quality care are all undermined as market-based individualised funding drives shifts to work in more informalised, lower-skilled, insecure employment where workers have little access to training and development or career opportunities.

In the Australian system, as in other many other social care systems, increased public funding for social care is necessary for revaluing care and care work to address gendered undervaluation, but it is not enough. Identification of workforce capabilities by social care quality and safeguarding bodies must be accompanied by the establishment of system requirements and mechanisms for workers to be skilled and trained, and by investment to achieve this. Quality and safeguarding requirements should apply to all organisations and workers in the care system. Where an unregulated sector exists within a social care market, such as in the NDIS, some organisations avoid the costs of meeting quality and safeguarding requirements and then compete on price. Regulated employers that maintain quality care and support, skill workers and provide career development opportunities are less competitive and less viable.

Social care systems need highly skilled and experienced workers, including disability support, where many people with complex needs require intensive care and support. Worker retention and opportunities for skills development and advancement require care funding that provides for worker progression. Skills-based pathways must be recognised in wage-setting and through skills-based classifications. In the Australian industrial relations system, the mechanisms for establishing recognition and pathways already exist, including in the industrial award that applies to social care workers.

Care systems should include mechanisms for sharing responsibility for training and development. Industry-wide schemes could establish system accountability for workers' training, guaranteeing provision for individual worker training while reducing or removing reliance on investment by individual workers and their employers. Ryan and Stanford (2018) have proposed an industry-wide portable training entitlement for care and support workers in the NDIS, underpinned by an industry capacity-building fund and by support worker registration. Under the proposal, social care workers would accrue entitlements to training linked to the number of hours they have delivered NDIS-funded supports. The entitlement would be transferable across providers and earn workers' credit towards qualifications.

It should not be possible for social care workers to be engaged outside formal employment arrangements where their remuneration may be less than regulated minimum wages and employment standards and protections are not applied. Worker's experiences documented in this study add to the international body of research on home-based care work that shows how workers' poorer access to basic employment protections undermines the goal of decent work, including gender equality. Creating better social care jobs means creating better jobs for workers employed in other people's homes. Internationally, the adoption by the International Labour Organization (ILO) of *Convention 189 on Decent Work for Domestic Workers 2011 (ILO Convention 189)* establishes a basis for equal treatment of care workers who perform their work in households. However, the work may still be undervalued in local employment standards, as it is in Australia, and it is often beyond the effective reach of labour regulation (Charlesworth and Malone 2017). This study has shown how individualised care funding reinforces the informality and, associated with this, the undervaluation of care and support work that is located within the private realms of the personal and domestic spheres and can create unacceptable risks for workers and for care users. While strong advocates of direct employment arrangements argue people with disability have a right to decide what risks they wish to take, as do all people, this does not negate workers' rights to safe work nor their responsibility to provide safe care and support.

Equal recognition and protection for care workers under labour laws and other regulation when work is in private households are vital to addressing many of the unacceptable risks of home-based work. However, as the experiences of workers in this study show, along with the international research on domestic and home care work, the effective reach of regulation into home-based employment is likely to be a problem where a private individual/householder is the employer. There is a good case for organisational oversight and management of home-based care and support in a publicly-funded care system, including that employment arrangements should not be left up to individuals and to informal work relationships.

Individual rights are not likely to be sufficient to remedy many of the problems faced by social care workers, as Hayes (2017) has pointed out in the UK context. Support for collective organisation, including access to sectoral bargaining, is an important counter to the individualisation of care workers and has led to some key protections for care workers internationally. For example, in mid-2020, a sector-wide collective agreement negotiated by the FNV trade union in the Netherlands for care workers of people with disability won the right for workers not to be contactable during their time off (New Economics Foundation 2020, p. 8). In Australia, as in many other countries, governments play a key role in determining worker pay and conditions as they are system architects, managers and funders, making sectoral bargaining an imperative.

Building Opportunity for Collective Effort, Responsibility and Voice

Some of the main ways in which cash-for-care contributes to poor outcomes for frontline workers are through the atomisation of care and loss of collective and holistic approaches; these can also degrade the quality of care and support. Increasing opportunity for collective effort and responsibility in individualised care systems could increase equity and access, empower service users and strengthen system capacity to meet needs, as well as providing the basis for better jobs and fewer risks for social care workers.

Early enthusiasm for Australia's cash-for-care system was based on the perceived potential for genuine partnerships, co-production and empowerment through participation. In hindsight, this enthusiasm seems somewhat misplaced as these goals are overshadowed by a system ambition for a much more narrowly-conceived consumer choice and control ideal. The original conception of Australia's NDIS, like personalisation in England and self-directed support more generally, involved building collective and community capacity for the provision of care and support, including through increasing the inclusiveness of all services. Australia's individualised system was to include collective and advocacy components but these were largely lost in implementation. The Productivity Commission (2011) envisaged the NDIS Local Area Coordinators (LACs) as community development bodies that would connect people with disability to their communities. Instead, the not-for-profit community services organisations that were contracted to be LACs were charged with assessing need and establishing individuals' support plans on behalf of the system manager (NDIA 2020). Currently, the cash-for-care system does not provide adequate structural capacity, incentive or resourcing to meet broader expectations for all or even for most people who depend on it.

System-wide support and assistance for collective commissioning of care and support could be an important element of a broader response to the problems of atomised care and support in cash-for-care systems. For example, local area commissioning and commissioning by groups of people with similar support needs could help to build the collective capacity and holistic approach required to offer meaningful choice and control. Currently, the managers of Australia's social care system only contemplate these types of options as exceptional responses in clear cases of market failure. These approaches could provide the basis for collectivising risks for frontline workers and provide good person-centred care and support. They offer the potential for job security and worker organisation and access to collective representation and bargaining, as well as for providing day-to-day organisational oversight and quality assurance, supervisor and peer support and the means to ensure safe work.

Within the long-standing not-for-profit sector, there is considerable expertise that could be harnessed for the development of person-centred support and care that empowers and builds on collective effort and partnerships. There are community and worker-led initiatives in individualised social care systems in Australia and elsewhere that demonstrate good *organisation-based* models of person-centred support that also support decent work for frontline workers. In the NDIS, not-for-profit service providers have led various such initiatives (NDS 2018). However, the government only supports these types of innovations through short-term funding of limited pilot projects. The design and funding of a public social care system that is inclusive and equitable should accommodate a variety of approaches to achieving person-centred care and support and should not be built on the degradation of social care workers' working conditions and pay. The successful development of innovative business and service models in Australia requires a genuine willingness on the part of all groups with interests in the marketised system to engage in open discussion about what is not working well and for whom.

Some worker and consumer-led approaches to improving support and care quality and care jobs in individualised social care systems have attracted growing attention internationally. The adoption of cooperative business models is worth considering briefly as it is an approach that some governments have been keen to promote (Andrews 2014; McFee 2018; Needham 2011). International case study evidence suggests there are some benefits of worker-controlled and joint worker/service user-controlled cooperatives for care workers' wages and conditions, with reinvestment of profits sometimes leading to higher wages, health insurance, guaranteed hours and retirement plans, many of which are not available more widely, including in individualised care systems in the UK and Australia (Matthew 2017). Greater job satisfaction can arise through worker empowerment; however, a risk for workers is an often heavy reliance on unpaid work. Cooperatives can formalise otherwise informal employment, provide access to training and facilitate safer working conditions.

Ultimately, the ability of cooperatives to provide higher wages and benefits, and better and safer working conditions for frontline workers depends on their being free of the financial constraints of inadequate social care funding (Matthew 2017). It also depends on their engaging workers in forms of employment that provide adequate protections and benefits, like the benefits and protections that accompany employment in organisation-based ongoing employment relationships. The international evidence suggests this is not the model adopted by many care cooperatives.

For instance, home care cooperatives have operated in the USA for some time. While they support inclusion and collectivise risks, some of the main benefits they offer are in providing workers with protections that most other workers in that country already have as rights under labour laws (Berry and Bell 2018; Boris and Klein 2012). This same issue applies to the emerging social care 'platform cooperatives' that are appearing in Europe and elsewhere as responses to the growth of Uber-style for-profit care platforms (Borkin 2019; Scholz 2016; Trojansky 2020). Models vary, but it appears care platform cooperatives are mostly collectives for self-employed care workers, rather than organisations that take on the role of employer of care worker employees. So, it appears that cooperatives take on some risks and provide some opportunity for worker collective representation but have not been able to challenge the exclusion of workers from employment protections, as workers remain engaged by individual clients as self-employed contractors.

Re-Fashioning Care Jobs as Sustainable and Secure Work

While many of the critical changes to address the problems of cash-for-care identified in this study lie in the design and regulation of the care system, the rejuvenation of employment regulation is also critical for ensuring decent work for care and support workers. Priorities include addressing regulatory gaps to prevent workers being placed on the margins or outside the boundaries of the protections offered by labour laws, where business and employment risks are devolved to them. There are good reasons why individualised direct employment and self-employed contracting arrangements do not need to be—and should not be—the foundation of person-centred care and support. Organisation-based employment relationships for frontline support and care workers can collectivise the responsibilities and risks of care provision and facilitate the creation of decent work while providing for individual empowerment and control. Nevertheless, addressing the lack of protections and benefits for self-employed contractors is important for addressing some of the worst problems currently faced by care and support workers in individualised care systems. Doing so could make this form of employment less attractive as a cheaper alternative to secure jobs in employment relationships.

There is a strong public interest case for addressing the problems of self-employed contracting and gig work in publicly-funded care systems, indicated by the growing public attention to this issue during the current COVID-19 pandemic (Hardaker 2020; Visontay 2020). Given this attention and as public authorities regulate and control quasi-markets, the care sectors could provide testing grounds for addressing the problems faced by self-employed contractors and gig workers in other industries.

In the NDIS, under Australia's labour laws, it appears to be easy to legally characterise a care and support worker as a self-employed contractor, if only on the basis that the worker provides services to multiple unrelated individual clients—one aspect of tests of self-employment in law (Stewart et al. 2016, p. 195). Workers may be considered to have multiple 'clients', but they often understand themselves to be multiple job holders or to be 'working for' platforms or other brokers. As shown in Chapters 7 and 8, workers' employment arrangements are often determined according to the preference of individual clients and/or a third party's business model, rather than reflecting any choice on the part of workers to be independent self-employed workers running their own businesses. As shown in those chapters, the risks accompanying self-employed contracting are significant, including that inexperienced and underemployed social care workers are highly vulnerable to accepting the market as the sole arbiter of their pay and conditions.

Exclusion of self-employed workers from the protection of labour laws—especially the exclusion of workers who are vulnerable or in a weak position in the labour market—is counter to most international labour conventions concerned with fundamental labour rights; these ILO conventions apply to *all workers* (Fenwick et al. 2007). For at least the past 20 years, internationally, legal scholars have called for the extension of the scope of labour laws beyond their application to employees in traditional employment relationships (Freedland and Kountouris 2011; Fudge and Owens 2006; Fudge et al. 2002; McCrystal 2006; Supiot 2001). The recent emergence of digital platforms in all types of consumer service markets has brought new attention to this problem, and it is now the subject much work by industrial relations academics and labour lawyers globally to address the issues (De Stefano 2015; Fredman and Fudge 2013; Stewart and Stanford 2017). Solutions have been proposed that are very relevant to the situation of social care workers in cash-for-care schemes.

Broadening the scope of labour law to include workers currently excluded from protections because they are not in dependent employment relationships is one way to begin to address this problem. Another way is to make *all* parties that substantially determine a worker's terms of engagement and employment accountable (Countouris and De Stefano 2019).

Drawing on earlier work of Freedland and Kountouris (2011), a recent proposal is for the adoption of a concept of 'personal work relation' that can be used to define the scope of application of labour law as being 'to any person engaged by another to provide labour, unless that person is genuinely operating a business on her or his own account' (Countouris and De Stefano 2019, p. 65). So, rather than the fact that a worker is providing work under the direction of a specific person or is economically dependent on a main employer, Countouris and De Stefano propose the personal work relation as the basis for worker protections under labour laws. Underpinning this proposal is the argument that:

> the fact of earning a living mainly off their personal labour, as opposed to living mainly off other people's labour and through the organisation of capital assets, is a better indicator of somebody's relative strength in the labour market. (Countouris and De Stefano 2019, p. 66)

Some European countries have enacted laws that go some way towards models consistent with this concept. For example, in France, the fact that a worker provides services to multiple clients does not necessarily exclude them from being treated as an employee. Domestic and care workers are among those identified in the French Labour Code as workers who provide personal work and services (Countouris and De Stefano 2019, p. 35). In line with the idea of adopting a model approach in the social care sector, laws could be enacted that deem social care workers to be employees. In Australia, deeming provisions have been in place for some workers in the past (Briggs and Buchanan 2005, p. 183). French law also provides self-employed persons the right to form and join trade unions and this applies to platform workers (Countouris and De Stefano 2019, pp. 31–32).

Finding ways to protect workers in arrangements involving multiple parties is also challenging because labour laws are built on the idea of a single employer. In Australia, the idea of joint employment was canvassed in a recent inquiry into labour hire practices but was considered to be too big a change to make, including because of the economic costs to labour hire users (Industrial Relations Victoria 2016, pp. 115–116). In the UK, there has been a much broader proposal for the adoption of human rights due diligence legislation that would introduce requirements 'for companies to prevent or respond to adverse human rights impacts of their operations or those of their subsidiaries, subcontractors and suppliers' (Ewing et al. 2019, p. 57). Accompanying the proposal is a suggestion that it be trialled in sectors where there are protective gaps, including social care. The proposal includes the adoption of public procurement requirements on public bodies to act on due diligence in their own supply chains. This type of arrangement could provide an effective solution to many of the problems occurring in the Australian cash-for-care market.

Conclusion

This study of the new Australian cash-for-care system contributes to our understanding of the organisation and dynamics of paid work in cash-for-care social care systems. Its relevance to the future of social care work is broad. It contributes to a better understanding of how risks are created for often vulnerable social care workers in the intersections of social care policy and employment regulation. It is one of the first detailed examinations of digital platform-mediated care work, a phenomenon that has emerged only in the period in which this research was conducted. The study has demonstrated how platforms and other businesses actors can exploit gaps in employment regulation, leading to the devaluation and informalisation of essential social care work in a publicly-funded and managed system.

Employers and other market actors are responsible for the business models and employment strategies they adopt. Nevertheless, the government's design, funding and regulation of the social care system provide incentives and set constraints, strongly influencing the options available to them. The highly marketised and largely unregulated publicly-funded Australian cash-for-care system encourages and rewards businesses that avoid the costs and responsibilities of frontline social care workers' employment. In the context of limited social care funding, there are strong pressures on employers to take low-road employment approaches, or to exit the market altogether, as has occurred in Britain (Cunningham et al. 2019).

The findings detailed in this book point, firstly, to the need for governments to act. They also suggest it will be important to build on common interests and establish goals for social care that include, from the outset, consideration of gender equality and decent work. Without this, there is a risk that the situation becomes one in which decent work for care workers is seen as having to be at the expense of service users (Bottery 2020). Rather, building a better future for social care workers can lay the foundations for a more sustainable and high-quality care and support system. Achieving this requires the development of alliances of responsibility and a focus on the broader goals of social policy and employment regulation laws—to improve lives and address disadvantage and to protect vulnerable workers, uphold workers' rights and ensure prospects for decent work.

References

Andrews, K. (2014, September 12). *Address to the BCCM 'make it mutual workshop'*. Parliament of Australia. http://kevinandrews.dss.gov.au/speeches/64. Accessed 25 October 2020.

Bagenstos, S. R. (2017). *Disability rights and labor: Is this conflict really necessary?* University of Michigan Law School Scholarship Repository, University of Michigan. https://repository.law.umich.edu/articles/1852/. Accessed 5 October 2020.

Berry, D., & Bell, M. P. (2018). Worker cooperatives: Alternative governance for caring and precarious work. *Equality, Diversity and Inclusion: An International Journal, 37*(4), 376–391. https://doi.org/10.1108/edi-02-2017-0027.

Boris, E., & Klein, J. (2012). *Caring for America. Home health workers in the shadow of the welfare state*. New York: Oxford University Press.

Borkin, S. (2019). *Platform co-operatives—Solving the capital conundrum*. Nesta and Co-operatives UK. https://media.nesta.org.uk/documents/Nesta_Platform_Report_FINAL-WEB_b1qZGj7.pdf Accessed: 18 August 2020.

Bottery, S. (2020, February 27) Social care can't cope alone with the cost of the living wage. *The King's Fund Newsletter*. https://www.kingsfund.org.uk/blog/2020/02/social-care-cost-living-wage. Accessed 1 October 2020.

Briggs, C., & Buchanan, J. (2005). Work, commerce and the law: A new Australian model? *The Australian Economic Review, 38*(2), 182–191.

Brotherhood of St. Laurence. (2019). *Submission to the NDIS Thin Markets project consultation*, Department of Social Services. Fitzroy, Vic: Brotherhood of St Laurence. http://library.bsl.org.au/jspui/bitstream/1/11392/1/BSL_subm_DSS_NDIS_Thin_Markets_Consultation_Jul2019.pdf. Accessed 22 December 2019.

Carey, G., Weier, Malbon, E., Dickinson, H., & Duff, G. (2020). *How is the disability sector faring? A report from National Disability Services' annual market survey*. Sydney: Centre for Social Impact, University of New South Wales. https://www.unsw.adfa.edu.au/public-service-research-group/reports. Accessed 13 August 2020.

Charlesworth, S., & Malone, J. (2017). Re-imagining decent work for home care workers in Australia. *Labour & Industry: A Journal of the Social and Economic Relations of Work, 27*(4), 284–301. https://doi.org/10.1080/10301763.2017.1400420.

Cortis, N., Macdonald, F., Davidson, B., & Bentham, E. (2017). *Reasonable, necessary and val-ued: Pricing disability services for quality support and decent jobs*. Sydney: Social Policy Research Centre, University of New South Wales. https://www.arts.unsw.edu.au/sites/default/files/documents/NDIS_Pricing_Report.pdf. Accessed 17 September 2020.

Countouris, N., & De Stefano, V. (2019). *New trade union strategies for new forms of employment*. Brussels: European Trade Union Council. Brussels. https://www.etuc.org/en/publication/trade-unions-protecting-self-employed-workers. Accessed 21 September 2020.

Cranford, C. (2020). *Home care fault lines: Understanding tensions and creating alliances*. Ithaca, NY: Cornell University Press.

Cunningham, I., Baluch, A., James, P., Jendro, E., & Young, D. (2019). *Handing back contracts: Exploring the rising trend in third sector provider withdrawal from the social care market*. Glasgow: Coalition of Care and Support Providers Scotland. http://www.ccpscotland.org/wp-content/uploads/2019/05/Handing_Back_report_CCPS.pdf. Accessed 20 November 2019.

De Stefano, V. (2015). The rise of the just-in-time workforce: On-demand work, crowdwork, and labor protection in the gig-economy. *Comparative Labor Law and Policy Journal*, *37*(3), 471–504. https://cllpj.law.illinois.edu/archive/vol_37/.

Ewing, K. D., Hendy, J., & Jones, C. (2019). *Rolling out the manifesto for labour law*. Liverpool: Institute of Employment Rights. Available at: https://www.ier.org.uk/product/rolling-out-manifesto-labour-law/. Accessed 28 October 2020.

Fenwick, C., Howe, J., Marshall, S., & Lau, I. (2007). *Labour and labour-related laws in micro and small enterprises: Innovative regulatory approaches SEED Working Paper No. 81.* Geneva: International Labour Office.

Fredman, S., & Fudge, J. (2013). The legal construction of personal work relations and gender. *Jerusalem Review of Legal Studies, 7*(1), 112–122.

Freedland, M., & Kountouris, N. (2011). *The legal construction of personal work relations*. Oxford: Oxford University Press.

Fudge, J., & Owens, R. (2006). Precarious work, women and the new economy: The challenge to legal norms. In J. Fudge & R. Owens (Eds.), *Precarious work, women and the new economy* (pp. 3–27). Oxford, Portland and Oregon: Hart Publishing.

Fudge, J., Tucker, E., & Vosko, L. (2002). *The legal concept of employment: Marginalizing workers*. Ottawa: Law Commission of Canada. http://www.justlabour.yorku.ca/volume3/pdfs/fudge.pdf. Accessed 22 September 2020.

Hardaker, D. (2020). Revealed: The liberal, murdoch networks making millions delivering 'Uber for aged care'. *Crikey.Com*. Retrieved from https://www.crikey.com.au/2020/09/21/aged-care-mable-liberal-news-corp-connection/. Accessed 22 September 2020.

Hayes, L. J. B. (2017). *Eight good reasons why adult social care needs sectoral collective bargaining*. Liverpool: Institute of Employment Rights. https://www.ier.org.uk/product/8-good-reasons-why-adult-social-care-needs-sectoral-collective-bargaining/. Accessed 22 June 2020.

Industrial Relations Victoria. (2016). *Victorian inquiry into the labour hire industry and insecure work, final report*. Melbourne: Industrial Relations Victoria. https://engage.vic.gov.au/inquiry-labour-hire-industry-and-insecure-work. Accessed 12 November 2020.

Macdonald, F., Bentham, E., & Malone, J. (2018). Wage theft, underpayment and unpaid work in marketised social care. *The Economic and Labour Relations Review, 29*(1), 80–96. https://doi.org/10.1177/1035304618758252.

Malbon, E., Carey, G., & Meltzer, A. (2019). Personalisation schemes in social care: Are they growing social and health inequalities? *BMC Public Health, 19*(1), 805. https://doi.org/10.1186/s12889-019-7168-4.

Matthew, L. (2017). *Providing care through cooperatives 2: Literature review and case studies*. Geneva: International Labour Office.

McCrystal, S. (2006). Regulating collective rights in bargaining: Employees, self-employed persons and small businesses. In C. Arup, P. Gahan, J. Howe, R. Johnstone, R. Mitchell, & A. O'Donnell (Eds.), *Labour law and labour market regulation* (pp. 597–616). Sydney: The Federation Press.

McFee, G. A. (2018). A cooperative-led NDIS? The potential of member-run organisations. *Power to Persuade Blog*. http://www.powertopersuade.org.au/blog. Accessed 16 June 2019.

National Disability Insurance Agency (NDIA). (2020). *Partners in the community*. NDIA. https://www.ndis.gov.au/understanding/what-ndis/whos-rolling-out-ndis/lac-partners-community. Accessed 21 September 2020.

National Disability Services (NDS). (2018). *Innovative workforce fund*. NDS. https://workforce.nds.org.au/. Accessed 22 July 2020.

Needham, C. (2011). *Personalising public services: Understanding the personalisation narrative*. Bristol: Bristol University Press.

New Economics Foundation. (2020). Achieving a shorter working week across Europe. *Newsletter of the European network for the fair sharing of work*. May, Issue 5. https://neweconomics.org/uploads/files/workingtime-newsletter5.pdf. Accessed 1 November 2020.

Productivity Commission. (2011). *Disability care and support. Productivity Commission report no. 54* Canberra: Productivity Commission.

Ryan, R., & Stanford, J. (2018). *A portable training entitlement system for the disability support services sector*. Canberra: Centre for Future Work. https://www.tai.org.au/sites/default/files/ASU_Training_Report_Formatted.pdf. Accessed 2 February 2021.

Scholz, T. (2016). *Platform cooperativism: Challenging the corporate sharing economy*. New York: Rosa Luxemburg Foundation. http://www.rosalux-nyc.org/platform-cooperativism-2/. Accessed 14 July 2020.

Stewart, A., Forsyth, A., Irving, M., Johnstone, M., & McCrystal, S. (Eds.). (2016). *Creighton and Stewart's labour law*. Sydney: Federation Press.

Stewart, A., & Stanford, J. (2017). Regulating work in the gig economy: What are the options? *The Economic and Labour Relations Review, 28*(3), 420–437. https://doi.org/10.1177/1035304617722461.

Supiot, A. (2001). *Beyond employment: Changes in work and the future of labour law in Europe*. Oxford; New York: Oxford University Press.

The Caring Fairly Coalition. (2018). *The caring fairly coalition*. http://www.caringfairly.org.au/caring-fairly-coalition. Accessed 2 February 2021.

Topping, M., Douglas, J., & Winkler, D. (2019). Understanding the factors that influence the quality of paid disability support for adults with acquired neurological disability and complex needs: A scoping review protocol. *British Medical Journal Open, 9*(12), https://doi.org/10.1136/bmjopen-2019-034654.

Trojansky, A. (2020). *Towards the 'Uberisation' of care? Platform work in the sector of long-term home care and its implications for workers' rights*. Brussels: European Economic and Social Committee. https://www.eesc.europa.eu/en/our-work/publications-other-work/publications/towards-uber-isation-care#downloads. Accessed 10 October 2020.

Visontay, E. (2020, 24 August 2020). Newmarch house: Confusion over who was in charge during Covid-19 outbreak worsened outcome. *The Guardian*. https://www.theguardian.com/australia-news/2020/aug/24/newmarch-house-confusion-over-who-was-in-charge-during-covid-19-outbreak-worsened-outcome.

Warr, D., Dickinson, H., Olney, S., Arstein-Kerslake, A., Wilson, E., Hargrave, J., et al. (2017). *Choice, control and the NDIS: Service users' perspectives on having choice and control in the new National Disability Insurance Scheme*. Melbourne: University of Melbourne. https://socialequity.unimelb.edu.au/__data/assets/pdf_file/0010/2364499/Choice-Control-and-the-NDIS-Report-Melbourne-Social-Equity-Institute.pdf. Accessed 13 October 2020.

Index

F. Macdonald, *Individualising Risk*,
https://doi.org/10.1007/978-981-33-6366-3

The manufacturer's authorised representative in the EU is Springer Nature Customer Service Centre GmbH, Europaplatz 3, 69115 Heidelberg, Germany. If you have any concerns regarding our products, please contact ProductSafety@springernature.com

Printed and bound by CPI Group (UK) Ltd, Croydon, CR0 4YY
30/09/2026
02225457-0005